THE POLITICAL PHILOSOPHY OF REFUGE

How to assess and deal with the claims of millions of displaced people to find refuge and asylum in safe and prosperous countries is one of the most pressing issues of modern political philosophy. In this timely volume, fresh insights are offered into the political and moral implications of refugee crises and the treatment of asylum seekers. The contributions illustrate the widening of the debate over what is owed to refugees, and why it is assumed that national state actors and the international community owe special consideration and protection. Among the specific issues discussed are refugees' rights and duties, refugee selection, whether repatriation can be encouraged or required, and the ethics of sanctuary policies.

DAVID MILLER is Professor of Political Theory at the University of Oxford.

CHRISTINE STRAEHLE is Professor for Practical Philosophy at the University of Hamburg.

THE POLITICAL PHILOSOPHY OF REFUGE

EDITED BY

DAVID MILLER

University of Oxford

CHRISTINE STRAEHLE

University of Hamburg

CAMBRIDGE
UNIVERSITY PRESS

University Printing House, Cambridge CB2 8BS, United Kingdom

One Liberty Plaza, 20th Floor, New York, NY 10006, USA

477 Williamstown Road, Port Melbourne, VIC 3207, Australia

314–321, 3rd Floor, Plot 3, Splendor Forum, Jasola District Centre, New Delhi – 110025, India

103 Penang Road, #05–06/07, Visioncrest Commercial, Singapore 238467

Cambridge University Press is part of the University of Cambridge.

It furthers the University's mission by disseminating knowledge in the pursuit of education, learning, and research at the highest international levels of excellence.

www.cambridge.org
Information on this title: www.cambridge.org/9781108472159
DOI: 10.1017/9781108666466

© Cambridge University Press 2020

This publication is in copyright. Subject to statutory exception and to the provisions of relevant collective licensing agreements, no reproduction of any part may take place without the written permission of Cambridge University Press.

First published 2020

A catalogue record for this publication is available from the British Library.

ISBN 978-1-108-47215-9 Hardback

Cambridge University Press has no responsibility for the persistence or accuracy of URLs for external or third-party internet websites referred to in this publication and does not guarantee that any content on such websites is, or will remain, accurate or appropriate.

Contents

Contributors

MICHAEL BLAKE is Professor of Philosophy, Public Policy, and Governance at the University of Washington.

MEGAN BRADLEY is Associate Professor of Political Science and International Development Studies at McGill University.

RICHARD EKINS is Associate Professor at the University of Oxford and Tutorial Fellow in Law at St John's College, Oxford.

LUARA FERRACIOLI is Lecturer in Political Philosophy at the University of Sydney.

MATTHEW J. GIBNEY is Professor of Politics and Forced Migration at the University of Oxford and Official Fellow of Linacre College, Oxford.

ADAM OMAR HOSEIN is Associate Professor of Philosophy at Northeastern University.

PATTI TAMARA LENARD is Associate Professor of Ethics in the Graduate School of Public and International Affairs, University of Ottawa.

MATTHEW LISTER is Senior Lecturer at Deakin University Law School in Melbourne, Australia.

DAVID MILLER is Professor of Political Theory at the University of Oxford and Visiting Professor of Law and Philosophy at Queen's University, Ontario.

KIERAN OBERMAN is Senior Lecturer in Political Theory at the University of Edinburgh.

DAVID OWEN is Professor of Social and Political Philosophy at the University of Southampton.

CHRISTINE STRAEHLE is Professor for Practical Philosophy at the University of Hamburg and at the University of Ottawa.

Introduction

David Miller and Christine Straehle[1]

Of the cast of characters who populate the contemporary world, none is more familiar than the figure of the refugee. He or she is visible to us mainly as a person on the move, the victim of war or ethnic cleansing. We see her sitting surrounded by her life's possessions in a battered truck crossing the wasteland; we see him strapped into an orange lifejacket and crammed precariously on an inflatable raft; we see her waiting sorrowfully in front of a border fence hoping that a guard will one day let her cross. But our remotely acquired visual impressions can mislead. Refugees who are actively in flight make up only a small fraction of the number who qualify for that designation at any moment. The vast majority – some 25 million – are more or less stationary, living largely out of our sight in the global South, in encampments that are purpose-built or home-made, or on the margins of cities like Beirut or Peshawar. They exist in a kind of limbo, often unwelcome visitors in the countries that have little choice but to house them, but unable to return to their homelands while conditions there remain hostile or unsafe. Many would prefer to be resettled in rich, developed countries – typically more than half a million apply to do so each year. But the number who succeed is only a fraction of this, since the governments of these countries set quotas for accepting refugees and go to considerable lengths to enforce them. The events of 2015, when more than a million migrants, including many refugees, entered Europe directly and found sanctuary there, were unprecedented in the recent past, and are unlikely to be repeated. Yet, for citizens in Europe and North America, it is the minority who attempt to settle in the global North who capture most of their attention, and philosophical reflection on the moral and political claims of the refugee, of the kind that occupies this book, has also focussed mainly on those who seek admission to rich developed countries.

---

[1] We would like to thank Clare Cai for her invaluable help in preparing the Bibliography and Index for this book.

What responses do the figure of the refugee evoke in us? The first, and perhaps the strongest, is one of pity and compassion. What could be worse than to be driven from your home by persecution or violence with no certainty at all as to what will happen once you cross the border and throw yourself on the mercy of strangers? Those of us who are more fortunate must surely owe a great deal to fellow human beings who through no fault of their own find themselves in such desperate straits. However, today's world order is built around states, and its fundamental principle is that each state is responsible for looking after the welfare of its own members. So the very existence of refugees poses a moral challenge. The responsibility to provide aid unavoidably falls on states other than those that have turned their own citizens into asylum-seekers.

But what form does this responsibility take? How are refugees to be aided? Should the aim be to help them wherever they are now living, to offer them resettlement in a developed society, or to encourage and support them to return to their homelands when they are able to do so? Or is the right answer to ask the refugees themselves which solution they prefer? Since it respects their autonomy, allowing refugees to choose where to live may seem the best option from a liberal perspective. However, this could lead to large concentrations of refugees moving into a handful of rich countries in the global North, raising questions about the social impact, for any society, of taking in large numbers of refugees in a short space of time. How are they to be housed, fed, educated, cared for medically and so forth? And mightn't they may prove politically troublesome? They are, after all, exiles as well as refugees, and they may want to continue engaging in homeland politics from a distance.

Faced with these dilemmas about what is owed to refugees, we need philosophical reflection to guide us. Among the many questions that arise in moral and political philosophy are these: What are the outer limits of the duty of rescue? What is the responsibility of states to protect the human rights of those outside their borders? When is granting asylum to someone who requests it obligatory? Does residence in a society entitle a person to citizenship? Is it ever permissible to require someone to repatriate against their will? In contrast to the quantity of philosophical attention that migration issues generally have received recently, philosophers have not so far written much at length about refugees specifically.[2] To remedy this, our book draws on a range of perspectives, some taking a more

---

[2] There are some honourable exceptions, including M. Dummett, *On Immigration and Refugees* (London: Routledge, 2001); M. J. Gibney, *The Ethics and Politics of Asylum: Liberal Democracy*

expansive and some a more restrictive view of the claims that refugees can make and our obligations toward them. In this introductory chapter we lay the groundwork for the more detailed discussions that follow by asking some basic questions: First, who should count as a refugee? Second, what is the source of our obligation to those who qualify for that status? And third, what more concretely do we owe to them?

1 Who Is a Refugee?

In English the term 'refugee' was first used to describe the Protestant Huguenots who fled persecution in Catholic France following the revocation of the Edict of Nantes in 1685.[3] Its core meaning was established at that time: a person who crosses a national border in search of sanctuary to escape religious or political oppression. Yet it was used only sporadically until the turn of the twentieth century, when states began to exert greater control over who crossed their borders, and therefore became more alert to the reasons they had for moving. It was applied first to the mass movements of people displaced by the redrawing of national boundaries following World War I, and later to the Jews and others who were attempting to escape persecution in the Third Reich. But it was only in the aftermath of World War II, and especially through the signing of the *Convention Relating to the Status of Refugees* at Geneva in 1951, that refugee status became well defined in international law. Since that time international refugee law has grown exponentially, to the point where the latest edition of a standard text – *The Refugee in International Law* – now runs to 786 pages.[4] Yet this has not ended political disagreement about who should be counted as a refugee. On the contrary, we find in the relevant literature a spectrum of definitions, running from the narrowest to the widest.

1. The most restrictive definition is the one adopted in the Geneva Convention, and which formally speaking remains the definition used in international law. On this view, a refugee is a person who owing to a

---

and the Response to Refugees (Cambridge: Cambridge University Press, 2004); M. E. Price, *Rethinking Asylum: History, Purpose, and Limits* (Cambridge: Cambridge University Press, 2009); M. Bradley, *Refugee Repatriation: Justice, Responsibility and Redress* (Cambridge: Cambridge University Press, 2013); and S. Parekh, *Refugees and the Ethics of Forced Displacement* (New York: Routledge, 2017). This is in contrast to the large body of writing on immigration in general.
[3] The evolution of the concept of refugee is discussed more fully by David Owen in Chapter 1.
[4] G. Goodwin-Gill and J. McAdam, *The Refugee in International Law*, 3rd ed. (Oxford: Oxford University Press, 2007).

well-founded fear of being persecuted for reasons of race, religion, nationality, membership of a particular social group or political opinion, is outside the country of his nationality and is unable or, owing to such fear, is unwilling to avail himself of the protection of that country.[5]

As will be seen, this ties refugee status to the experience of persecution, actual or expected, and therefore omits other causes that might force someone to flee from their home country. Much depends, therefore, on how 'persecution' is understood. Over time the tendency on the part of international lawyers and others has been to broaden the concept of persecution in two ways: first, by including persecution that is not directly instigated by the government of the refugee's home state, but is carried out by gangs, local militias or rogue police officers that the state is unable or unwilling to control; second, by stretching persecution to cover such things as discriminatory employment practices aimed at one of the categories of people referred to in the Convention. So for some, denying a person their social and economic rights can count as persecution in the same way as denying them their civil and political rights.

2. Even with this broadening, however, definition 1 may be found unduly restrictive. Think, for example, of the person who is caught up in a civil war such as the one that has been raging in Syria. She may be a bystander whom neither side is targeting directly, so she does not count as a victim of persecution; nevertheless, her life may be in danger so long as she remains where she is. To capture such cases, the United Nations High Commissioner for Refugees (UNHCR) – the body set up under the Geneva Convention to help manage refugee flows – has adopted a wider definition: alongside those who have fled their country out of fear of persecution are those 'who are unable to return there owing to serious and indiscriminate threats to life, physical integrity or freedom resulting from generalised violence or events seriously disturbing public order'.[6] Definition 2, then, identifies a refugee as someone whose human rights to life, bodily security or freedom are under threat, regardless of whether this is a result of deliberate persecution or of social and political breakdown such as is likely to occur during civil wars.

---

[5] Cited in J. C. Hathaway, *The Rights of Refugees under International Law* (Cambridge: Cambridge University Press, 2005), pp. 96–97. A further clause extends refugee status to people in a similar situation who have no nationality.
[6] UNHCR, *UNHCR Resettlement Handbook* (Geneva: UNHCR, 2011), p. 19. This is also the definition underlying the UN Global Compact for Refugees, adopted in 2016 and on its way to be signed by member states. See www.unhcr.org/gcr/GCR_English.pdf.

Widening the definition of 'refugee' in this way has not gone unchallenged. Those who oppose it argue that someone who is being persecuted, either directly by the state or with its connivance, bears a special burden – the loss of membership in a political community. This gives them a special claim to be admitted to a new home where their political agency can be restored and their human rights will be protected. Matthew Price has added to this the argument that when a state grants asylum to a refugee, it is not only helping the refugee but implicitly sending a message of condemnation to the state that has made her into one.[7] But this depends on restricting the label to those who are escaping state-sponsored persecution.

3. Some philosophers have argued, however, that definition 2 is still too narrow. It picks out certain grounds on which people might be forced to quit their home countries, but leaves out others that might be just as compelling. Consider someone suffering from severe poverty or environmental degradation who as a result cannot satisfy their basic material needs. If they cross a border in search of a minimally decent life, should they not also count as refugees? Thus Andrew Shacknove has proposed an influential definition of refugees as:

> persons whose basic needs are unprotected by their country of origin, who have no remaining recourse other than to seek international restitution of their needs, and who are so situated that international assistance is possible.[8]

Shacknove distinguishes three reasons why people might be unable to meet their basic needs – persecution, natural calamities, and failures to provide minimal subsistence – and argues that there is no relevant difference that would justify restricting the term 'refugee' to those facing persecution. The key point is that the home state cannot provide for people's needs, while other states or international agencies can.

As Shacknove notes, accepting his definition would greatly expand the number of people worldwide entitled to refugee status, including all those suffering from severe poverty. But it also severs the link between refugeehood and flight, since many of those who qualify under it could be provided with assistance in their home countries. People suffering food shortages can be given famine relief in the short term and development aid in the longer term. Those who are the victims of natural disasters like

---

[7] Price, *Rethinking Asylum*, ch. 2.   [8] A. Shacknove, 'Who Is a Refugee?', *Ethics*, 95 (1985), 277.

earthquakes may need to move to find temporary shelter, but they will usually be able to return home once a relief effort is under way. The local state may require help to provide these remedies, but the bond between it and the person in need of aid has not been shattered as it has in the cases covered by definitions 1 and 2. Such a person can continue to exercise political agency, and use it to protect her human rights, while remaining within her home state.

Shacknove's version of definition 3 may therefore appear to be too wide. But it can be modified by including the condition that a person's basic needs can be met only by being granted admission to another state. In this light, Matthew Gibney defines refugees as:

> Those people in need of a new state of residence, either temporarily or permanently, because if forced to return home or remain where they are they would – as a result of either the brutality or inadequacy of their state – be persecuted *or* seriously jeopardise their physical security or vital subsistence needs.[9]

Even in this modified form, definition 3 has been criticised, especially by international lawyers, on the grounds that whereas it should be relatively easy for a court or a government agency to establish whether a person has suffered persecution, it is much harder to judge whether it is strictly necessary for someone to migrate in order to meet their basic needs. This suggests that the three definitions so far considered may be appropriate for different purposes: the first for determining the legal obligations of states, the second for guiding the behaviour of international organisations like the UNHCR who are tasked specifically with managing refugee flows, and the third for assessing the *moral* responsibilities of states to those outside their borders. If that is so, we should not expect everyone to converge on a single definition; the important point is to understand how 'refugee' is being used in any particular legal or moral argument over what is owed to them.

4. We have finally to consider the widest possible definition of 'refugee'. This is arrived at by turning things around and asking, Who has a strong claim to be admitted to our society? On this view, anyone who has such a claim should be considered as a refugee regardless of the particular reason they have for moving. Defenders of this definition argue that there is only a difference of degree, not one of kind, between refugees and economic migrants. Everyone has some claim to be admitted to the society they want to join, but so long as selection is unavoidable, those whose claims rise

---

[9] Gibney, *Ethics and Politics of Asylum*, p. 7.

above a threshold level of moral urgency should count as refugees and be given priority. Moreover, one way for a migrant to show that she has such a claim is through her willingness to expose herself to risk in the course of migration. So people who use definition 4 are likely to regard all those who undertake dangerous journeys by land or sea in order to reach the borders of the countries they wish to enter as refugees. From this perspective, the issue is not 'how in general can we best tackle poverty or environmental degradation?' but rather 'what do we owe to the particular person who has asked on such grounds to be admitted to our society?'[10] So any sufficiently strong reason for migrating, measured by the needs and interests of the migrant, qualifies him as a refugee. If he is moving from a desperately poor country in search of a better life, the fact that he *could* be given better prospects while remaining in situ is on this view irrelevant.

Definition 4 also faces some challenges. First, it stretches the concept of 'refugee' far beyond the Convention definition used in international law, so states will have legal obligations only to a small fraction of those whom definition 4 counts as refugees. It also becomes unclear why, from a moral point of view, states should pay any particular attention to those who have chosen to move, as opposed to those who face similar hardships but decide to remain in their home countries. Since it usually costs far less to attend to the needs of people living in the global South than to receive and integrate them into a Western state, any state with a finite aid budget will want to deter most definition 4 refugees from setting out in the first place. In this way, the special moral force that the term 'refugee' evokes is in danger of being lost. In contrast, each of the previous three definitions singles out refugees as people who not only have strong reasons to cross borders, but who are obliged to do so since it is impossible for their basic rights to be protected while they remain in their home state.

2   What Is the Source of Our Obligations to Refugees?

The legal obligations that states bear toward people who approach them and ask for asylum are well established, but also relatively narrow. They must first ascertain whether the person in question qualifies as a refugee, which as we have seen under international law means applying definition 1: the person must prove that she is liable to persecution if returned to her

---

[10] For this argument, see J. Carens, *The Ethics of Immigration* (New York: Oxford University Press, 2013), pp. 201–3.

home state. In the meantime, the state must protect the asylum-seeker's human rights. During the process, and after the asylum claim is validated, the principle of *non-refoulement* comes into effect. This prohibits the state from returning the refugee to her home country or to any other country where she would be at risk of persecution. The state must then admit the refugee, if not on a permanent basis, at least until she no longer faces a threat of persecution at home; or if it wishes to transfer her to a third country, it must ensure that the country in question can guarantee her safety.

Notice several respects in which this legal obligation to admit refugees is limited. First, it applies only to refugees who qualify under the most restrictive of our four definitions above, definition 1. Second, there is no obligation to make it easy for refugees to claim asylum. In most cases, it is left to the refugee to make his way to a border crossing where he can lodge the claim, and states have adopted a range of measures known as policies of *non-entrée*[11] that are designed to make it more difficult to do that, such as requiring airlines to check that passengers have already obtained entry visas before allowing them on to planes. Third, states have no legal responsibility to ensure the safety of refugees in transit, for example, by providing ships to rescue those who get into trouble crossing the high seas.

Yet many think that citizens of states with the capacity to assist have *moral* obligations to refugees that go far beyond these narrow legal responsibilities. But what, more concretely, do these obligations amount to – what exactly are we required to do to aid refugees? And how does it come about that governments and citizens have responsibilities to people who are not yet under their jurisdiction? These two questions are connected. We will take them in reverse order and start by reviewing three possible accounts of how obligations arise to people who have been turned into refugees by the malice or incompetence of their states.

The first, and probably most obvious, answer is simple humanitarianism. Refugees are people in dire need, and it would not overstretch our resources to meet their needs, either by admitting them or by supporting them in third countries. Here an analogy is often drawn with the individual duty of rescue. Just as each of us has a moral obligation to pull a drowning stranger out of the sea when the cost of doing so is small, so human beings collectively have an obligation to save refugees from the

[11] See T. Gammeltoft-Hansen and J. Hathaway, '*Non-refoulement* in a World of Cooperative Deterrence', *Law and Economics Working Papers*, Paper 106 (2004), available at http://repository .law.umich.edu/law_econ_current/106.

harm that will befall them if they stay living where they are. Since their own state will not take care of them, other states must do so.

This humanitarian answer may seem compelling at first glance, but it faces both philosophical and practical problems. Humanitarian obligations are usually thought of as imperfect, meaning that we have discretion over when and how we carry them out. The duty of rescue is an exception to the rule – we have a perfect obligation to rescue the drowning stranger – but this is acceptable because the likelihood of anyone being called on to carry out a rescue is, thankfully, very low, so imposing the strict duty is not onerous.[12] In contrast, given the number of refugees in the world today, responding to all of their claims might become very demanding. A possible solution is for states to co-operate to establish an international system to assign responsibility for looking after particular groups of refugees, so that no state is asked to do too much. But this proposal does not consort well with the humanitarian approach, which portrays us as having an open-ended but indeterminate obligation to help human beings in need. Moreover, that approach does not single out refugees in particular as deserving of our aid, nor does it tell us how to direct our moral efforts. Since we can choose how to exercise our benevolence, we might do more good overall by investing more resources in developing countries or buying only fair-trade products in the supermarket in order to help the global poor in general.

A very different way of understanding obligations to refugees is to look at them through the lens of the entire system of states in its current form. A refugee, we have seen, is someone with an urgent reason for moving out of the state she currently inhabits: she is being persecuted or denied her basic rights in some other way. But where is she to move to? States now claim jurisdiction over the entire habitable surface of the earth, so she can escape from her own state only by entering another. What, then, gives any state the right to exclude her? On this view, since all the earth is divided into state territories, states have an obligation to admit those who are in need of refuge and have no other recourse, simply because there is no *terra nullius*.

This approach portrays obligations to refugees as remedial in nature. Taken together, states have grabbed all the available land and fenced it in, so human beings can no longer exercise their natural right to wander freely over the earth's surface. The cost imposed by territorial rights becomes

---

[12] Where we can anticipate that rescues are likely to be needed more often, we appoint people such as lifeguards and mountain rescue teams whose task it is to carry them out whenever necessary.

acute in the case of refugees, who have nowhere to escape to unless another state is willing to provide refuge. So, the argument concludes, states must compensate refugees for their loss of freedom by granting them rights of entry.

This argument has some force, but it relies on a contestable thesis about political legitimacy. It assumes that any state claiming territorial jurisdiction must be able to justify its claim to every individual outside its borders.[13] Critics will say that this premise is too strong, however. Why is it not sufficient, to justify a territorial claim, to show that those who are excluded had adequate opportunities to establish their own rights-protecting states? The fact that they have not succeeded in doing so – that they are now living under despotic rule or in failed states – does not impugn the achievement of those who have created a rights-respecting political order. There might be circumstances in which refugees can justifiably advance remedial claims – against states whose foreign interventions have helped create the situations in which their human rights are imperilled – but these will be special cases, and do not show that refugees have a universal right of entry.

A third way to understand our obligations to refugees is to see them as one component of the wider responsibility that all states have to protect human rights. This responsibility is primarily discharged by each state fulfilling the human rights of its own citizens. But in the international order that has grown up in the last fifty or so years, states also increasingly acknowledge a reciprocal responsibility to protect the human rights of outsiders when their own states either cannot or will not do so. In the extreme case this may justify armed intervention to protect people from ethnic cleansing or genocide; but in less severe cases it obliges states to protect the human rights of those who qualify as refugees, either by directly granting them asylum or by supporting them in third countries.

Because this approach begins from human rights protection as a reciprocity-based practice that all states are nominally committed to, it encourages us to see refugee protection as a collective responsibility shared by all those states with the capacity to respond when a refugee crisis erupts. So it points naturally toward a burden-sharing scheme whereby each state agrees to support or resettle a certain number of refugees – a solution that as we saw was harder to justify from a humanitarian perspective. It relies,

[13] See D. Owen, 'In Loco Civitatis: On the Normative Basis of the Institution of Refugeehood and Responsibilities for Refugees', in S. Fine and L. Ypi (eds.), *Migration in Political Theory: The Ethics of Movement and Membership* (Oxford: Oxford University Press, 2016).

however, on the assumption that states have not only agreed to refrain from violating the human rights of outsiders, but acknowledged a positive obligation to help protect them, even in cases where the fault lies elsewhere. This has certainly been the hope of human rights advocates, reaching back at least as far as the UN Declaration of 1948, but it would be a brave person who asserted that states everywhere now accept such an obligation. So the human rights approach relies on a challengeable assumption about inter-state reciprocity. Why, a critic might ask, are we bound to protect the human rights of refugees coming from states that would never do the same for our own citizens?

To sum up, we have examined three ways in which we might attempt to ground a duty to refugees: as a form of humanitarian assistance, as a remedial obligation in a world where states have monopolised all of the available land, and as one component of an international practice of human rights protection. Each has its strengths and weaknesses. Moreover, they have somewhat different implications for the exact *content* of the duty owed to refugees by capable states, to which we now turn.

3 What Do We Owe to Refugees?

Whichever of the definitions of 'refugee' outlined above you favour, refugees are people in urgent need of help. Their human rights are under either direct or indirect threat. But the help they need could be provided in different forms and by different agencies. So how should responsibilities be defined and allocated?

Consider the trajectory of a typical refugee. The mass flows of 2015 aside, she is unlikely to move directly to the borders of a wealthy democratic state. Normally, she will cross directly from one country in the global South to another – from Syria to Jordan, say, or from Myanmar to Bangladesh. Her immediate need is for food, shelter and safety from violence. These basic necessities can likely be provided through an encampment, in the best case one supervised by an international body such as the UNHCR. So the first obligation that citizens of rich states have toward refugees is to contribute their due share financially to the support of these camps – an obligation that is very often flouted in the world today.

But living in a camp is only a short-term solution to the refugee's plight. There is much variation between camps, but a common theme in the literature is that even basic rights are not fully secure – there is often low-level violence generally, and sexual violence specifically, for example – while refugees are typically denied opportunities to work or be educated while they remain there.[14] So although, de facto, refugees often remain confined in camps for many years, few people would see this as an adequate way of discharging our responsibilities to them. There are then three main alternatives to which refugees might be given access: resettlement in an opportunity-rich democracy such as Canada or Sweden, local integration in the society to which they have already moved (often to a camp), and repatriation to their home country (assuming that return is now safe). Is it sufficient that at least one of these options is available to them, or are refugees entitled to choose the solution that they prefer?

It is worth exploring briefly the arguments for and against each option, both from the side of the refugee and from the side of the state that would need to implement it. Take resettlement first, possibly the preferred option for many refugees. Since they may be unsure when, if ever, they will be able to return home safely, resettlement provides the chance to make a fresh start in a country that provides stability, safety and much greater opportunities than either their homeland or the place they are now living. However, refugees may overestimate their chances of quick integration and economic success if they are admitted. As new arrivals they will have to compete for jobs and other benefits with people who have already been through the country's education and training system and who therefore appear better qualified; they may also face straightforward discrimination. These hindrances can be offset to some extent by good integration programmes, and countries such as Sweden and Canada have gone to considerable lengths to integrate refugees into their social fabric. However, better resettlement policies are often tied to fairly low annual intake quotas for refugees – in Canada's case, currently 25,000 per year for a population of 33 million.[15]

Is there a moral obligation to take in more? This of course depends on how good or bad the alternatives to resettlement are. But provisionally we can assume that the refugees with the strongest claim to resettle are those for whom successful repatriation is very unlikely – these will mainly be refugees falling under definition 1, people who would face ongoing persecution were they to try to return home. So states collectively are morally obliged to ensure that at least enough resettlement places are made

[14] For recent analysis, see A. Betts and P. Collier, *Refuge: Transforming a Broken Refugee System* (London: Allen Lane, 2017), esp. chs. 2 and 5; O. Bakewell, 'Encampment and Self-Settlement', in E. Fiddian-Qasmiyeh et al. (eds.), *The Oxford Handbook of Refugee and Forced Migration Studies* (Oxford: Oxford University Press, 2014), pp. 127–38; S. Parekh, *Refugees and the Ethics of Forced Displacement* (New York: Routledge, 2017), ch. 1.
[15] This figure does not include privately sponsored refugees.

available to accommodate those for whom the other options are inadequate. This suggests establishing a burden-sharing scheme whereby each country is allocated a quota of refugees to admit – a scheme of the kind that the EU attempted, unsuccessfully, to implement in the course of 2015.

Consider next local or regional integration. This means allowing refugees to become absorbed either into the societies to which they had originally moved or elsewhere in the South. They must be given the opportunity to live and work either in cities or on areas of land made available to allow them to provide for themselves and their families over time This of course depends on the willingness of the host countries to grant them the necessary rights, which they may be reluctant to do, fearing that it will create pressure on local jobs, housing and so forth. This is especially the case in countries that have historically received high numbers of refugees, such as Jordan, where local resources are stretched already.[16] So the role of outsiders is to try to ensure that integrating refugees locally becomes a two-way benefit, for example by means of investing in enterprise zones to provide employment.[17]

What advantages does this solution provide for refugees? It places them in a society that is likely to be considerably poorer than the societies in which they might otherwise be resettled, but whose culture (and perhaps language) may be closer to their own; given the skill set they already possess, work may be easier to find; and by remaining physically close to their homeland, they are in a better position to stay in contact with friends and relatives, and to be informed about their prospects for a safe return. On the other hand, they will probably not have many rights, especially political rights, so they will remain outsiders whose presence is likely to be tolerated by their hosts rather than actively welcomed. Full integration may come only with the next generation.

Finally, there is repatriation. Where it can be achieved with the consent of the refugees themselves, this might seem to be the most desirable solution. Repatriation holds out the promise of fully restoring refugees to social membership, and also to the homes and neighbourhoods they were driven from. There is evidence that forced displacement is experienced as an evil in its own right, quite apart from the material loss that usually accompanies it, so repatriation provides a remedy. But of course this makes some assumptions about the conditions to which the refugee is returning.

---

[16] Other countries in this category include Turkey, Pakistan Lebanon, Iran and Ethiopia.
[17] For a range of proposals along these lines, see Betts and Collier, *Refuge*.

Will she be welcomed back, or will she still be subject to (non-violent) hostility and discrimination on the part of those who have remained? Is her house still standing? Can the business she left behind be rebuilt? Is the society she returns to still recognisably the one she enjoyed living in before?

For outside states, the obligation that repatriation most clearly imposes is the obligation to help provide the material aid that makes successful return possible – rebuilding at the conclusion of a civil war, for example. The more difficult question is whether there is also an obligation to ensure that repatriation is fully voluntary. This issue arises when states have offered temporary protection to refugees rather than the right to settle permanently, and it now appears that the conditions for safe return have been met. Must the refugee be persuaded that it is now in his interests to repatriate, or can repatriation be enforced in these circumstances? Legally, it can be – this would not count as *refoulement* – but there may be a moral obligation to consider the wishes of the refugee, who may meanwhile have become socially integrated in the society that offered him sanctuary.[18]

These are just some of the issues that arise when we ask what is owed to refugees – issues that the chapters that follow examine in much greater depth than we have attempted in this Introduction.

4   Outline of the Book

The volume begins with a set of chapters that discuss the philosophy of refuge, broadly understood. In Chapter 1, 'Differentiating Refugees: Asylum, Sanctuary and Refuge', David Owen provides a historical overview to distinguish three different types of refugee status – asylum, sanctuary and refuge – and maps these onto two distinct pictures of refugeehood, namely, the humanitarian and political, which we have discussed earlier. According to Owen, a successful reorganisation of the international refugee system, including a fair distribution of duties toward refugees, will require elements of both a humanitarian and a political understanding of the source of our obligations toward refugees. Separating the three different types of refugee-hood will allow for three different responses to the plight of refugees, and can help frame the obligations toward them.

In contrast, Richard Ekins in Chapter 2 questions the basic assumption of all three ways of modelling obligations toward refugees, namely, that the duty to provide asylum overrides other considerations an asylum state may

---

[18] Bradley, *Refugee Repatriation*, ch. 8, discusses tours arranged by UNHCR and other organisations to entice refugees to repatriate.

invoke when defining its obligations. According to Ekins, a careful analysis of the Geneva Convention suggests that the state's freedom to deny entry is protected and the state's national sovereignty in deciding who should benefit from entry onto the territory remains intact. This does not imply that states have no obligations toward those fleeing persecution, but states are justified to restrict entry in order to protect public goods, peace and the conditions of self-government.

Ekins's sobering comments about possible detrimental side effects to granting asylum provide an important complement to what Michael Blake in Chapter 3 refers to as 'normative sociology': the assumption that one good thing, providing asylum, will provide for other good outcomes. While Ekins challenges this assumption within the context of the asylum state, Blake raises important concerns about the effects of granting asylum on the state of origin. He argues that the expressive component of the political model of understanding moral obligations toward refugees, namely, the criticism of the malicious or incompetent state of origin, may have negative effects for those remaining behind. In contrast to his moral model, which maps onto what we have described as the humanitarian approach, and the political model, Blake argues that asylum thus needs to be understood as fundamentally tragic: even though motivated by the best intentions, states granting asylum may not avoid doing wrong.

Kieran Oberman focusses on a different kind of tragedy: the fact that every year, thousands of refugees and other migrants die trying to cross borders. If Blake's aim is to encourage us to accept the inevitability of tragedy in refugee policy, Oberman's aim is something like the opposite: to shake people into recognising that what might appear to be an unavoidable misfortune is in fact a preventable injustice. According to Oberman, the deaths of migrants in the Mediterranean Sea, the Sonoran Desert and elsewhere are no natural phenomena, but the result of state policy. States impose migration restrictions that compel refugees and other forced migrants to resort to dangerous migration routes. States are thus causally responsible for endangering migrants. Indeed, in Oberman's view, states are also morally responsible since they violate duties to admit migrants safely. In consequence, they have a special duty to engage in search and rescue missions at their own borders and elsewhere.

Oberman's chapter pushes us to accept greater moral restrictions on the range of state policies. David Miller's chapter, by contrast, defends making room for state choice. Addressing the question of refugee selection, Miller makes a similar distinction to Owen between those asylum-seekers who need temporary protection from persecution, and who ought to be given sanctuary, and those whose need for protection is longer term and who therefore need permanent resettlement. The obligations toward those requiring sanctuary are determined by the vulnerability and need that the individual faces. In contrast, those in need of resettlement can be chosen partly based on their anticipated potential for social integration in the asylum state. Miller echoes here Ekins's concern for the public good that societies achieve in their midst, and which may be jeopardised if states have no say in the selection of refugees.

In a similar vein, and against strong defenders of the humanitarian approach to asylum, Adam Hosein in Chapter 6 argues that states can legitimately use deportation to remove those migrants whose asylum claim has been rejected. Prima facie, Hosein thus follows Ekins and Miller in endorsing the importance of national self-determination for asylum policy. However, in a second step, he cautions that there may be good reasons to grant the right to remain even to those whose claim has been rejected. Rather than invoking the human rights approach Miller employs to support his argument for sanctuary, or the social membership model that Lenard discusses in her chapter on sanctuary policies, Hosein proposes an alternative 'autonomy approach' to justify the right to remain. Accordingly, if a person has spent a significant amount of time in the asylum state, having formed preferences and life plans there, she should be allowed to remain.

Shifting the focus from the moral obligations of states toward those who flee from human rights abuse, in Chapter 7 Matthew Gibney raises the important and novel question of the possible duties of refugees, most notably the 'duty to fight' human rights abuses, the 'duty to wait' for the assessment of their claim, and the 'duty to return' to their country of origin when protection is no longer required. Examining claims made by some critics of asylum in host states, Gibney finds imposing a 'duty to fight' unduly burdensome if it involves asking individuals to put their lives at risk. The 'duty to return' is harder to assess, however. In line with Hosein's argument, Gibney considers this first as a duty toward the country of asylum. Assessing it, however, depends on how the moral basis of asylum itself is understood. If granting asylum is regarded as an act of hospitality by the receiving state, there might be a duty to leave once it is safe to do so. However, if asylum is understood as an entitlement that refugees have along the lines of the political model of asylum proposed by Price, then it is not clear that there is such a duty to return. Finally, Gibney suggests that a 'duty to return' as a duty owed to erstwhile compatriots seems hard to justify since 'the bonds of connection between an individual and the state are no longer strong enough to issue in duties'.

The nature of these bonds is also subject of the next two chapters on the right to return. Both Megan Bradley (Chapter 8) and Christine Straehle (Chapter 9) examine the moral value of return. Bradley distinguishes four possible reasons why the right of return may be valuable. It may first serve as a means of reconstituting and upholding housing, land and property rights of individual refugees, as we mentioned earlier. Return may also reestablish the boundaries of membership and reconstitute a citizenry that persecution has dispersed across other lands. Importantly, return can serve to critique and oppose ethnic cleansing – akin to the critique of abusive states that providing asylum can signal in the political model of asylum discussed above. Finally, return can be an important form of redress for individual refugees.

This last function of the right to return is at the heart of Straehle's chapter, which examines the right of return as an important tool to provide individual refugees with access to the means of individual autonomy. Straehle argues that one of the promises of asylum is to protect basic interests of individuals. One such interest is that of leading autonomous lives. In this account, one of the conditions of autonomy is access to the social and political relationships that come with belonging to a territorially bound community. And while for some, the relevant community may become that of the asylum state, for others the relevant community may remain that of the state of origin. In Straehle's view, the moral obligations of asylum thus extend beyond the humanitarian interpretation of providing protection in the state of asylum, to include the human rights perspective when enabling the right to return.

One of the possible criticisms of the right to return as part of the obligations of asylum that Straehle discusses is that expanding the promise of asylum in this way may overburden asylum states. Luara Ferracioli takes up this concern in Chapter 10, discussing the possible tension between obligations of asylum states and the right of refugees to partly determine the content of these duties. She illustrates the tension between burdens falling on the state and the rights of refugees by examining whether refugees have a right to choose where they wish to be resettled. Ferracioli's analysis of the relationship between victim and duty-bearer in cases of assistance yields the conclusion that refugees lack the right to determine their place of resettlement within the asylum state if this would make provision of assistance more burdensome.

In Chapter 11, Matthew Lister also examines the grounds for an expanded set of duties of asylum states, namely, those toward individuals outside their country of citizenship who are in need of aid but who fall outside the definition of the Geneva Convention. Lister argues for what he calls complementary protection of needy individuals. This latter category may include those who suffer economic or environmental hardship while being outside their own state. According to Lister, the motivation to provide complementary protection is simply to address need. Thus, it allows for shorter periods of engagement by protective states. It also does not serve the political objective of rebuking offending states that granting asylum often does. Yet in response to Lister, critics could also object that the argument for complementary protection seems to push the burdens onto asylum states beyond justifiable limits.

A similar criticism could be levelled at the kinds of duties of sanctuary that Patti Lenard discusses in Chapter 12 and which we have already referenced in the context of Hosein's chapter. According to Lenard, sanctuary policies are an important way for states, and often sub-state units, to offer refuge even to those individuals among them whose immigration status is irregular. Sanctuary policies aim to provide access to services such as education and emergency health care without which individuals would possibly be exposed to human rights abuses. Besides being criticised for potential overburdening of asylum states, sanctuary policies also raise the spectre of democratic illegitimacy: if individuals remain in the asylum state without, however, having been officially accepted legally there, the question of national self-determination and the protection of the public good in society is raised anew. One could argue that national governments have only one way to assert national self-determination, which is at the border, thus making sanctuary policies problematic. However, Lenard argues that only relatively few so-called sanctuary policies are directly, or even indirectly, related to the state's ability to regulate entry. Moreover, from the perspective of democratic legitimacy, especially those migrants who have resided in the country and have established the ties of social membership should be granted the right to remain.

The recently tabled UN Global Compact for Refugees indicates that issues such as the definition of a refugee, the function of asylum in international politics, and the source of moral obligations toward people fleeing human rights violations in their states of origin will remain among the most pressing of our time. Our hope is that the contributions in this volume will provide some guidance in these debates, and will promote further philosophical discussion of what is owed to refugees.

CHAPTER I

Differentiating Refugees
Asylum, Sanctuary and Refuge

David Owen[1]

Debates concerning who is entitled to refugee status and what is owed to persons with that status have proliferated in recent years. Since Andrew Shacknove's radical challenge to the 1951 Refugee Convention specification of refugeehood, posed against the background of the regional agreements expressed in the Organization of African Unity's 1969 *Convention Governing the Specific Aspects of Refugee Problems in Africa* and the 1984 *Cartagena Declaration on Refugees* in Latin America, a range of accounts have been offered that, variously, defend, amend and extend the grounds and scope of the 1951 specification and identify distinct ranges of obligations owed to the figures they specify.[2] In Section 1 of this chapter, I argue that the main axis of distinction within this debate is that between 'humanitarian' and 'political' pictures of refugeehood. That this is the case should not, I will argue, surprise us given the two pivots around which the modern refugee regime turns: the 1951 Refugee Convention and the UNHCR. Rather than attempting to decide between these accounts, my strategy in this chapter will be to propose a practice-based normative

---

[1] I am grateful to Matt Gibney for his characteristically acute and constructive comments on an earlier draft of this chapter. Christine Straehle and David Miller provided judicious editorial feedback, particularly picking up moments where the argument needed to be made clearer – and I thank them for their careful attention to the text.
[2] A. E. Shacknove, 'Who Is a Refugee?', *Ethics*, 95 (1985), 274–84; M. J. Gibney, *The Ethics and Politics of Asylum: Liberal Democracy and the Response to Refugees* (Cambridge: Cambridge University Press, 2004); M. E. Price, *Rethinking Asylum: History, Purpose, and Limits* (Cambridge: Cambridge University Press, 2009); J. Carens, *The Ethics of Immigration* (New York: Oxford University Press, 2013); M. Lister, 'Who Are Refugees?', *Law and Philosophy*, 32 (2013), 645–71; D. Owen, 'In Loco Civitatis: On the Normative Basis of the Institution of Refugeehood and Responsibilities for Refugees', in S. Fine and L. Ypi (eds.), *Migration in Political Theory: The Ethics of Movement and Membership* (Oxford: Oxford University Press, 2016), pp. 269–90; D. Miller, *Strangers in Our Midst: The Political Philosophy of Immigration* (Cambridge, MA: Harvard University Press, 2016); M. Cherem, 'Refugee Rights: Against Expanding the Definition of a "Refugee" and Unilateral Protection Elsewhere', *Journal of Political Philosophy*, 24 (2016), 183–205.

account of refugeehood.[3] Thus, in Section 2, I sketch the historical development of the practice of refugee protection and the formation and development of the modern refugee regime. Attending to this history allows us, I will claim, to reframe the debate on 'who is a refugee?' in terms of the functional role of the refugee regime within an international order of states. In Section 3, drawing on previous work that identifies the functional role of the refugee regime as a *legitimacy repair mechanism* for global political society organized as an international order of states and which addresses refugees as persons for whom this order must stand *in loco civitatis*,[4] I argue not only that the refugee regime has the scope to distinguish between distinct types of claim to refugee status in the light of the different normative grounds of these claims, but that a well-functioning refugee regime must so distinguish. The proposal that this chapter will defend is thus that we distinguish different types of refugeehood as distinct legal statuses within the general scope of the fundamental principle of *non-refoulement* in order to reconcile the pragmatics of refugee protection with the differentiation of normative claims at stake within this general status. I differentiate three basic types of claim – asylum, sanctuary and refuge – and explore what is owed to each of these types of claimant and the implications of such differentiation for the communicative role of the refugee regime in shaping the appropriate response of the international community to the state from which refugees take flight (or to which persons are unwilling to return).[5]

1   Two Pictures of Refugeehood

We can begin by outlining two distinct pictures of the figure of the refugee. The first picture sees refugees as continuous with other subjects

---

[3] I am influenced here by C. Beitz, *The Idea of Human Rights* (Oxford: Oxford University Press, 2009), and by A. Sangiovanni, 'How Practices Matter', *Journal of Political Philosophy*, 24 (2016), 3–23.

[4] The phrase 'in loco civitatis' is proposed by analogy with the phrase 'in loco parentis' in that just as the latter phrase picks out an obligation on an agent (for example, the state) to take up the task of standing in a 'parental' relation to children whose own parents fail to stand in this relationship of love and care to them, so the former picks out an obligation on the international order of states to take up the task of standing in this civic relation to persons whose basic rights are unprotected by their state and can be effectively protected only through recourse to the international society of states (via a political agency such as another state or international organization), where it can so act without breaching the constitutive norms of the regime of global governance (most pertinently, the Janus-faced norm of sovereignty/non-intervention). See Owen, 'In Loco Civitatis', pp. 269–80.

[5] I will shorten this slightly cumbersome expression by speaking of flight in the remainder of this chapter, but it should be understood to encompass persons already outside their state who are unwilling to return.

of undeserved harm, such as famine or environmental disaster, and hence as subjects to whom we owe moral solidarity in the form of humanitarian aid. This 'humanitarian' picture of refugees identifies them as subjects within the general domain of an ethics of rescue. By contrast, the second picture views refugees as importantly distinct from subjects of undeserved harm in virtue of the specificity of the wrong to which they are subject, namely, the denial of their political standing as members of a state. This 'political' picture of refugees identifies them as subjects to whom the international community owes a duty to reassert their entitlement to political standing in global political society by way of membership of a state – and hence as falling within the general domain of an ethics of membership. In this section, I will focus on sketching the distinct logics of these pictures, before turning in the next section to contextualise this debate within the historical emergence and development of refugee protection practices.

The first humanitarian picture of refugees and our relationship to them 'pervades the public imagination and academic literature':

> The term 'refugee' connotes people fleeing war, famine, and failed states. They are portrayed as victims waiting in camps until they can return or be resettled. These are the 'neediest' of the needy such that 'a refugee's plight appears morally tantamount to that of a baby who has been left on one's doorstep in the dead of winter.'[6]

Such a picture is widespread in NGOs, international institutions and in the self-understanding of the UNHCR as a humanitarian organisation. Those holding this humanitarian view are immediately drawn toward the claim that the current 1951 Convention specification of the figure of the refugee is too restrictive. As Andrew Shacknove's classic article noted, this specification of the figure of the refugee takes *persecution* and *alienage* as individually necessary and jointly sufficient conditions of refugeehood. From a humanitarian standpoint, however, neither of these elements appears necessary: persecution appears as only one manifestation of the absence of state protection of citizens' basic needs and alienage as a subset of the physical access of the international community to the unprotected person.[7] Such considerations lead Shacknove to propose an alternative and considerably broader account of who is entitled to refugee status. Others within this orientation may not go so far as Shacknove's recasting of

---

[6] Cherem, 'Refugee Rights', 185.   [7] Shacknove, 'Who Is a Refugee?', 277.

refugeehood (indeed, the UNHCR does not), but they endorse the logic of need as driving the question of definition. As Cherem notes:

> Despite holding opposed views on immigration, Chandran Kukathas and David Miller agree here. Kukathas warns the Convention 'adopts a very narrow definition of a refugee ... people fleeing war, natural disaster or famine are, on this definition, not refugees'. Miller concurs, 'there is clearly a good case for broadening the definition to include people who are being deprived of rights to subsistence, basic healthcare, etc.'[8]

Notice, however, that this humanitarian picture of the refugee not only reframes who is entitled to refugee status to encompass a wide range of need-based harms, it also shapes what obligations are owed to refugees which, in turn, has significant implications for how such obligations should be shared and the nature of the grant of refugee status as an expressive act. The obligation is to provide a refuge within which basic needs can be secured and protected and the extent of the obligation is to do so as long as costs are not unreasonably burdensome. If this is the responsibility owed by the international community to refugees, then it should be noted that it can generally be satisfied by a division of responsibility between those who host and those who pay. More precisely, we may say that for *humanitarian refuge* where the key considerations are physical access (typically a function of geographic proximity in mass refugee events), security from refoulement, and basic needs protection, a division of responsibility to protect can be reasonably constructed in terms of the duty of the states to which refugees immediately flee to provide a *place* of refuge and the duty of states generally to provide, according to their abilities (and acknowledging any hosting contribution they have made), the resources needed to secure the basic needs of those who have fled. The act of granting refuge and of providing resources for refugees is a communicative act that expresses a general commitment to the moral standing of human beings as entitled to, in Miller's terms,[9] the conditions of a minimally decent life.

The contrasting 'political' picture of refugeehood typically endorses the existing 1951 Convention specification of the refugee. This orientation focuses on the distinctiveness of the wrong to which refugees are subject. For example, Michael Walzer distinguishes 'necessitous strangers' from 'refugees':

---

[8] Cherem, 'Refugee Rights', 190.
[9] D. Miller, *National Responsibility and Global Justice* (Oxford: Oxford University Press, 2007), pp. 163–200.

Both are distinct from immigrants. Necessitous strangers are 'destitute and hungry' people fleeing generalized catastrophes. Their needs can be met 'by yielding territory' or 'exporting wealth' while withholding membership. Yet refugees are ''victims of ... persecution' whose 'need is for membership itself, a non-exportable good'.[10]

More recently, Matthew Price's adopts Rawls's distinction between burdened societies and outlaw states to point to the normative salience of the distinction between cases in which a state lacks the capacity to secure basic rights for its members and cases where a state is not disposed to secure these rights for some (or all) of its members: 'Citizens of burdened societies lack protection of their basic rights, but they retain their standing as members. The appropriate stance of outsiders to burdened societies is to lend assistance, not to condemn their failings.'[11] By contrast, this view claims that asylum in another state is the appropriate response for dealing with those of its citizens targeted by outlaw states which flout 'the requirements of international legitimacy by violating basic human rights' since it provides these persecuted citizens whose very standing as members is being denied with protection 'in a manner that also expresses the condemnation that is deserved'.[12] Relatedly, Max Cherem argues that

> Refugees are special because persecution is a special harm. Refugees 'are targeted for harm in a manner that repudiates their claim to political membership'; their 'rights go unprotected because they are unrecognized' rather than for other reasons.... Refugees are persecuted and, for this reason, cannot be helped at home.... Refugees are distinctive because their country of origin has effectively repudiated their membership and the protection it affords. The status on which almost all their other rights hinge is gone.[13]

In identifying refugeehood in terms of its link to membership, this picture construes responsibility to refugees in terms of *asylum as 'surrogate membership'* (in Price's apposite phrase) where the key concerns are those of refugee inclusion and pathways to civic integration. Whereas the humanitarian picture can be aligned with a division of shared responsibility between those who host and those who pay, the political picture does not fit easily with a separation between proximate 'hosts' and distant 'funders'. Rather, it entails acknowledging both the ongoing responsibilities of the states to whom application of asylum is made and

---

[10] M. Walzer, *Spheres of Justice: A Defense of Pluralism and Justice* (New York: Basic Books, 1983), pp. 44–45, cited in Cherem, 'Refugee Rights', 191.
[11] Price, *Rethinking Asylum*, p. 73.   [12] Ibid.   [13] Cherem, 'Refugee Rights', 191.

that providing refugees with membership conditions calls for a different division of responsibility.[14]

The distinction between these two pictures appears stark, and the contrast between their respective practical implications is normatively consequential for how we conceive the grounds, nature and scope of refugee protection as well as for the fair division of international responsibility for that task. My aim in this chapter is to propose a practice-based account of refugeehood that enables us to move beyond the opposition between these two pictures.

2 Contextualising the Debate: The Emergence and Development of the Modern Refugee Regime

The emergence of the modern refugee regime in the aftermath of the Second World War can be traced back to at least three prior lines of descent that coalesce in its formation, and I will begin by briefly reviewing these before addressing the construction of the modern refugee regime and its subsequent development.

Lines of Descent

The first, which provides the word *refugee*, is the flight of the Huguenots from France in 1685 following the revocation of the Edict of Nantes. The fact that Louis XIV forbade the Huguenot flight and that this forbidding breached the terms of religious liberty articulated as *jus emigrandi* in the Peace of Westphalia[15] created a dilemma for the states to which the Huguenots fled who needed both to be able to register their condemnation of this violation and to try to avoid conflict with France.[16] They resolved this dilemma by creating a distinct category of migrants: 'ones who, because they could no longer count on the protection of their own state, should be allowed to leave that state and receive protection elsewhere'.[17] This response to religious refugees was extended to political refugees in the context of persons fleeing the American and French Revolutions, before being further adapted and refined in the context of debates about asylum and non-extradition in the nineteenth century[18] such that 'States in the nineteenth century held a consistent view of refugees as people fleeing

---

[14] See D. Owen, 'Refugees and Responsibilities of Justice', *Global Justice*, 11 (2018), 26–36.
[15] P. Orchard, *A Right to Flee: Refugees, States, and the Construction of International Cooperation* (Cambridge: Cambridge University Press, 2014), p. 45.
[16] Orchard, *Right to Flee*, p. 1.   [17] Ibid.   [18] Ibid., pp. 71–104.

political and religious persecution who should be allowed to leave their own states, who should be offered protection in domestic law, and who should not be returned.'[19] Moreover, whereas prior practice (such as the response to Huguenots) was in significant part based on the religious interests and economic advantages that their admission served for receiving states, the practice that emerged in the nineteenth century identified admission and protection as normative requirements of hospitality and humanitarian duty even where there were prudential reasons not to do so.[20]

A second line of descent emerges with the mass flight of ethnic minorities, particularly from the multinational Ottoman and Russian empires in the late nineteenth and early twentieth century. This put significant pressure on the norms developed in nineteenth century in the context of relatively small numbers of religious and political refugees in part because it also put pressure on the public political perception of who counted as a refugee through the emergence of numerous targeted humanitarian relief organisations such as the International Committee for the Relief of Turkish Refugees.[21] The third line of descent is the shattering of the Austro-Hungarian and Ottoman empires in the course and aftermath of the First World War in combination with the Russian Revolution and Civil War. The former gave rise to a range of post-imperial successor states immediately characterised by national minority problems to which flight by ethnic minorities was one response: 'Ethnic Hungarians who feared for their future in Romania, Czechoslovakia or Yugoslavia fled to the truncated state of Hungary, a defeated country in which most of them had never set foot.'[22] The latter saw (now stateless) Russians scattered across the globe, and, following an approach to the League of Nations by the International Committee of the Red Cross, in September 1921 the explorer Fridtjof Nansen was appointed as League of Nations High Commissioner for Refugees (LNHCR), being granted 'a temporary mandate to assist 'any person of Russian origin who does not enjoy or who no longer enjoys the protection of the Government of the USSR, and who has not acquired another nationality'.[23] Notably, it was the case that the ICRC 'in particular emphasized that this assistance should be understood as politically neutral humanitarianism',[24] an understanding that was supported by the central role of charitable relief organisations in supporting Nansen's efforts (and that would be repeated in relation to the foundation

[19] Ibid., p. 102.   [20] Ibid.
[21] P. Gatrell, *The Making of the Modern Refugee* (Oxford: Oxford University Press, 2013), p. 24.
[22] Ibid., p. 53.   [23] Ibid., p. 55.   [24] Ibid.

of the UNHCR). Nansen's mandate was soon extended beyond the case of stateless Russians to address new refugee flows, for each of which a new *Arrangement* had to be negotiated.[25]

Following Nansen's death, there was an attempt to move to a multilateral approach with the weakly endorsed 1933 *Convention Relating to the International Status of Refugees* which, in generalising from the previous *Arrangements* system, took a group-based approach to refugees.[26] This was followed by the 1938 *Convention Concerning the Status of Refugees Coming from Germany* which shifted to an individualised specification and introduced the principle that 'refugees who have been authorised to reside therein may not be subjected by the authorities to measures of expulsion or recondition unless such measures are dictated by reasons of national security or public order'.[27] This agreement, like Roosevelt's formation of the *Inter-Governmental Committee for Refugees* (IGCR) in the same year, came too late and was made effectively redundant by the outbreak of the Second World War.[28] Indeed, the mass denationalisations of the 1930s and the increasing reluctance of states to admit refugees as domestic concerns about sovereignty and immigration trumped (what were seen as) humanitarian policies, even as states acknowledged the need for a multilateral international response, overwhelmed the nascent multilateral refugee regime with the tragic consequences which provoked Arendt's reflections on the impotence of human rights in the absence of effective national citizenship.[29]

These three lines of descent combine to provide a conception of refugees as persons whose claim is predicated on lacking the protection of their own state and who are outside that state, a principle of *non-refoulement*, the use of both individualised and group-based determination procedures, and the central role of humanitarian organisations in both advocacy and assistance roles. In other words, they provide much of the conceptual and practical basis for the formation of the modern refugee regime.

Constructing the Modern Regime

Significant as they were, the population displacements of the interwar years were dwarfed by those during and that resulted from the Second World

[25] Orchard, *Right to Flee*, pp. 114–16.   [26] Ibid., pp. 116–17.

[27] League of Nations, *Convention Concerning the Status of Refugees Coming from Germany* (1938), League of Nations Treaty Series, Vol. CXCII, No. 4461, p. 59, available at www .refworld.org/docid/3dd8d12a4.html (accessed 12 August 2018).

[28] Orchard, *Right to Flee*, p. 117.

[29] H. Arendt, *The Origins of Totalitarianism*, 2nd ed. (New York: Meridian Books, 1958).

War. This gave new impetus to the political issue of refugees and to the organisational politics of refugee protection. For our current purposes, however, the key development is the establishment and gradual empowerment of the Office of the United Nations High Commissioner for Refugees which, although intended as a temporary humanitarian organisation that 'should be a "non-operational" body dependent on voluntary organisations to assist refugees',[30] has become the central international organisation for contemporary refugee protection.[31] Alongside the UNHCR, the other pivot on which the contemporary refugee regime turns is the 1951 Refugee Convention (following the lifting of its original geographic and temporal restrictions through the 1967 Protocol).

The importance of highlighting both the 1951 Convention and the UNHCR is that while the former was clearly political in the sense of its focus on the persecution/membership nexus, the role, focus and self-understanding of the latter was primarily humanitarian – and as the UNHCR developed from its limited beginnings, this became increasingly important for the practice of refugee protection. The UNHCR established itself as the central agency of refugee protection through its role in a series of refugee crises which did not easily or directly fall under the scope of the 1951 Convention. While its leadership in response to the refugee crisis following the 1956 Hungarian Revolution was central to establishing it as the most important IO for refugee protection, this case also indicated a degree of flexibility in relation to restrictions of the 1951 Convention[32] that would be further developed through the emergence of the 'good offices' extension of its role into Asia[33] and Africa.[34]

The 'good offices' extension allowed the UNHCR to expand its remit beyond refugees that it was mandated to address under the 1951 Convention. Initially the 'good offices' extension took a case-by-case form, but, echoing the earlier pattern with regard to 'Arrangements' in the interwar period, this was dropped and in 1961 the UN adopted a resolution that gave the UNHCR authority 'to assist both "refugees within his mandate and those for whom he extends his good offices", effectively removing the

---

[30] Gatrell, *Making of the Modern Refugee*, p. 109.
[31] There were two exceptions to scope of UNHCR relating to Palestine and Korea. The remaining exception is that of Palestinian refugees who fall under the remit of the United Nations Works and Relief Agency for Palestinian Refugees in the Near East (UNWRA) established in 1949 following their dispossession in the violent conflicts that marked the creation of the State of Israel.
[32] G. Loescher, *The UNHCR and World Politics: A Perilous Path* (Oxford: Oxford University Press, 2001), pp. 82–87.
[33] Ibid., pp. 92–95.   [34] Ibid., pp. 105–34.

legal and institutional barriers to future UNHCR action for non-mandate refugees'.[35] Importantly for our concerns: 'The good offices basis for action contained no assumption of persecution and avoided most of the limitation for action in the international refugee legal instruments.'[36] In 1965, the distinction between 'mandate' and 'good offices' refugees was abandoned, with the UN General Assembly requesting that the UNHCR provide protection and permanent solutions to all groups within its competence.[37] Awareness that the legal specification of refugees in the 1951 Convention had been developed for the post-war context in Europe and did not fit well with the pragmatics of forced migration in the developing world led the UNHCR both to push for removal of the temporal and geographic restrictions of the 1951 Convention through the 1967 Protocol and to work with the Organisation of African Unity (OAU) to develop a regional refugee convention – the 1969 OAU *Convention Governing the Specific Aspects of Refugee Problems in Africa* – that was rooted in the newly universalised 1951 Convention but extended the scope of refugeehood to respond to the pragmatics of the African postcolonial context. These two developments set the stage for the global expansion of the work of the UNHCR over the following decades during which it would further adapt its practices in response to new refugee crises, political and budgetary constraints, and ongoing debates about how best to fulfil its role.

For the purposes of this chapter, however, the key points are already apparent. The first, and most important, is that the history of the modern refugee regime in practice is one in which both political and humanitarian orientations toward refugeehood are manifest in the dialectic between the interpretation of 1951 Convention and the work of UNHCR, perhaps most clearly illustrated in the regional refugee instruments adopted in Africa and Latin America as well as in the expansion of legal instruments of complementary protection in Europe, America and elsewhere for 'refugees' who do not fall under (state interpretations of) the Convention definition.[38] From this perspective, Shacknove's article can be seen as an attempt to provide a coherent intellectual underpinning to the pragmatics of refugee assistance and protection undertaken by the UNHCR, even if the UNHCR has adopted a less expansive view than Shacknove proposes,

---

[35] Ibid., pp. 112–13.   [36] Ibid., p. 113.   [37] Ibid.

[38] It is an important issue that the scope of the 1951 Convention specification of refugeehood is determined by the state to which a claim of asylum is made, a feature that can give rise to very varied admission criteria and rates. This is not, however, an issue that I can properly address in this chapter.

while the ripostes by authors such as Price and Cherem in defence of the 1951 Convention can be seen as motivated by the concern that Shacknove's argument flattens out the salient normative difference between the claims of those fleeing persecution relative to those fleeing, for example, the general breakdown of public order or famine. What is needed is an account that reconciles acknowledgement of the historical practice of refugeehood with the differential normative claims at stake in this general status.

3 The Refugee Regime, Legitimacy Repair and International Order

How should we understand the functional role of the modern refugee regime? In earlier work,[39] I have proposed that the combination of an international order of states and a universal human rights regime establishes a general division of responsibility between states and a set of legitimacy conditions for the international order of states. The division of responsibility is articulated in terms of the norm that states are primary responsibility-holders for respecting, protecting and fulfilling the human rights of their citizens. The legitimacy conditions for the international order of states hold that states are collectively responsible for securing conditions under which individual states are generally capable of, and disposed to, compliance with the norm of respecting, protecting and fulfilling the human rights of their citizens. In proposing this view, my point is to draw attention to the fact that states are the primary agents through which the normative ordering of global political society is reproduced as an international order in which agents recognised as having the distinct normative status of statehood are characterised by wide-ranging rights of dominion with respect to a given territorial jurisdiction and population as well as duties of non-intervention with respect to other territorial jurisdictions. Against this background, the failure of particular states to conform to the responsibility norm represents a legitimacy problem not only for those states but also for the international order of states as a dispersed structure of global political rule. It is this that generates the need for legitimacy-repair mechanisms on the part of this structure of rule, that is, institutional practices that act effectively to ensure that the basic security, liberty, and welfare of those subject to a non-conforming state are protected to the greatest degree possible without breaching the constitutive

---

[39] Owen, 'In Loco Civitatis', pp. 269–90.

norms of the regime. The international refugee regime is, I propose, one such mechanism in that the institution of refugeehood provides a route by which a specific class of those who are subject to non-conforming states can be provided with protection in a way that is compatible with the *grundnorm* of state sovereignty/non-intervention. The scope of this institution can be understood as one in which refugees are understood as persons whose basic rights are unprotected by their state and can be protected only through recourse to the international order of states (via a political agency such as another state or international organization) acting *in loco civitatis*, where it can so act without breaching the constitutive norms of the regime of governance. Importantly for the purpose of this chapter, however, this view is not only compatible with, but requires, distinguishing different types of claim to refugeehood if the institution of refugeehood is to play its functional role.

Consider, for example, the difference marked in the contrast between Price's normative reconstruction of the institution of asylum and Gibney's defence of the UNHCR's practice of refugee protection. Gibney advances the claim that in cases of environmental disaster, famine or civil war, the capabilities and/or disposition of international society may be such that it is both rational and reasonable for those situated such that they can secure their basic rights only by crossing borders to do so, and it is certainly right that they be granted at least short-term refuge if 'there is no reasonable prospect of that person finding protection any other way'.[40] It is true that they may well not need asylum in the sense reconstructed by the surrogate membership view, but they do require refuge, even if it is temporary in duration. The principle of *non-refoulement* is an instrument by means of which the international order of states can effectively bind itself (via a duty on each of its members) to try to ensure that such refuge is provided. Price's objection to the kind of position that Gibney defends is that it undermines the expressive act of condemnation that a grant of asylum performs. This 'communicative' objection derives its force from the presumption that refugeehood is a single undifferentiated category to which asylum is the sole response. However, the historical practice of refugee protection offers a more complex picture than this objection admits – and the problem seems rather to be that the complexities of practice are not readily signalled by distinct legal statuses that differentiate types of refugees in terms of the diverse relationships that standing *in loco civitatis* may involve. What justifies treating the different cases encompassed by

[40] Gibney, *Ethics and Politics of Asylum*, p. 8.

UNHCR practice under the institution of refugeehood is that, in all of these cases, the persons or groups concerned have compelling grounds not to be willing to avail themselves of the protection of their home state, and, hence (with one minor complication that we will address shortly), the principle of *non-refoulement* serves as a basic normative requirement of the relevant forms of legitimacy repair on the part of the international community. In this section, I want to try to develop this case by distinguishing three distinct normative statuses – asylum, sanctuary and refuge – that, I argue, should be differentiated under the general institution of refugeehood and what is owed to each of these types of refugee.[41]

Asylum

Being persecuted (or left wilfully unprotected from persecution) by one's state for one's religious or political beliefs, or because one is a member of a social group, is both a distinctive wrong and a serious harm. The wrong consists in the denial of one's standing as a member of the political community of the state that is performed when the agent who has primary responsibility for respecting, protecting and fulfilling one's human rights is the agent who is breaching one's human rights or disposed to allow others to violate them and, hence, the denial in an international order of states of one's standing as a member of global political society. The harm consists in the fact that in being thus rendered de facto stateless, one is made acutely vulnerable both to contingencies of circumstance and to the dominating agency of others. In this respect, I am in general agreement with Price's view that a grant of asylum can be seen as expressing condemnation of the persecuting state (or the state not disposed to protect from persecution)[42] as well as the view expressed by Price and Cherem that central to asylum is the granting of a claim to membership. Asylum refugees are people who

> not only face a threat to their bodily integrity or liberty; they are also effectively expelled from their political communities. They are not only victims, but also exiles. Asylum responds not only to victims' need for protection, but also to their need for political standing, by extending membership in a new political community.[43]

---

[41] I am grateful to Matthew Gibney in commenting on a draft of this chapter for drawing my attention to an article by J.-F. Durieux, 'Three Asylum Paradigms', *International Journal on Minority and Group Rights*, 20 (2013), 147–77.

[42] The case of a refugee from a state that is incapable of protection is, I think, better conceived under the category of sanctuary than that of asylum.

[43] Price, *Rethinking Asylum*, p. 248.

In response to this political argument, David Miller contends that 'it seems wrong to single out those who are escaping persecution and grant them permanent residence immediately on the grounds that having arrived they will all choose to identify politically with the society that takes them in'.[44] Miller's response betrays the humanitarian picture that informs his own account in missing the point of the argument that Price and Cherem are advancing. This argument does not swing on whether the person entitled to asylum will immediately politically identify with state of new membership nor on whether they may later choose to return to their state of original nationality under transformed conditions but on the obligation to assert, through the granting of new membership, the entitlement to political standing of the person whose political standing has been denied by their home state. In a world in which effective state membership is a practical condition of political standing, it is a duty of the international order of states to ensure that all persons enjoy such standing – and when it is denied through persecution to provide protection in a way that reaffirms the right to such standing – and this is what the legal status of asylum as a distinctive type of refugee status should be conceived as providing. Hence, a person who reaches a border and advances a claim to asylum is asserting a claim against that state (as a member of the international order of states) that not only entitles them to a fair process of determination but, supposing their claim is validated, makes that state responsible for ensuring that they are not returned to their home state and that they are granted new membership in a state (which may or may not be the state of asylum determination) where there are good reasons to be confident that their security, liberty and welfare will be protected.

Sanctuary

Whereas asylum is an appropriate response to persons who are (or have good reason to believe that they will be) *targeted* for persecution by their state of nationality or *identified* by the state as persons it is not disposed to protect from persecution by private agents (each of which denies the standing of such persons as members), it does not align well with the claims of those persons who are fleeing the generalized violence and breakdown of public order who are not targets but would fall into the condition of being, as it were, collateral damage nor the claims of those that the state is simply incapable of protecting from persecution by private

---

[44] Miller, *Strangers in Our Midst*, pp. 135–36, see also p. 133.

agents. The extension of the 1951 Convention definition in the 1969 OAU Convention is an acknowledgement of the claim of such persons to protection which, given the norm of non-intervention, will generally require that they have crossed an international border. I say 'generally' since on the '*in loco civitatis*' account that I defend, it may be the case that where the government of a state has broken down so completely that there is no agent that can reasonably claim to serve as the political agent of representation of the state (examples from recent history would include governmental collapse in Somalia and the break-up of the former Yugoslavia) that agents of the international community can legitimately enter and establish 'safe havens' as de facto international territory within the territory of this nominal state. In such circumstances, and here we address the 'slight complication' signalled earlier, the norm of *non-refoulement* still applies but has the specific and special sense of not returning persons from safe havens to territory within the state outside such de facto international territorial zones of protection.[45]

The claim advanced against the states to which such persons flee is a claim to *sanctuary* conceived as a space where one is protected against the threats to one's basic security, liberty and welfare posed by generalized violence and the breakdown of public order in one's home state (or, absent such generalised conditions, by the incapacity of the state to protect one from private agents) without fear of being returned to that state insofar as the relevant conditions persist. Notice that, in contrast to the claim to asylum, the relationship to membership in this case is rather different. While in both cases we may say that membership has become ineffective or inoperative in the sense that it does not play the protective or enabling roles which define its normal functioning, in the case of the claim to asylum, this harm is the product of a specific wrong (the targeted denial of one's political standing) that demands redress, whereas this is not the case with regard to claims to sanctuary. In this context, the primary responsibility of the state that adjudicates the status of sanctuary-seekers is to ensure that, if their claims are valid, they are subject to the norm of *non-refoulement* and have access to the basic security, liberty and welfare that the protective and enabling functions of citizenship would normally provide. This does not *require* rapid admission to new membership nor

---

[45] Whether establishing such 'safe havens' is a prudent move is a distinct question that would depend very heavily on contextual factors, the salient point here is simply to register a conceptual difference between the 'alienage' and '*in loco civitatis*' accounts in that the latter does not rule out the institution of refugeehood applying to persons in such safe havens.

does it rule out non-voluntary repatriation in the way that asylum should be understood as entailing. Rather, the relationship to membership (and, hence, to voluntary or non-voluntary repatriation) is an altogether more complex issue in contexts of sanctuary where at least three considerations are in play. The first describes the general situation of forced migrants, where such a person

> is not simply to be an individual who has lost the protection of her basic rights; it is to be someone deprived of her social world. It is to be someone who has been displaced from the communities, associations, relationships and cultural context that have shaped one's identity and around which one's life plan has hitherto been organised.[46]

The second is that it is a pervasive feature of refugee crises that their time horizon is liable to be indeterminate – and the consequent positioning of refugees as persons who are 'situated in a condition of social and civic limbo, unable to commit to building a new life because they may be returned to the old, unable to commit to the old life because they may never be able to take it up once more'.[47] To be a person requiring sanctuary is, to a very significant degree, to lack an ability that is taken for granted by citizens who conduct their lives against the background of a right to secure residence of a state, namely, the ability to plan their futures, to make choices about the medium-term or long-term direction of their lives. The point here is that the kinds of choices and, hence, plans available to an agent are significantly dependent on the institutions, practices and relationships that compose the social context that they inhabit. Everyday social contexts shape the horizon within which persons coherently conceive of, and act to realize, their future selves – and to inhabit a condition in which the social conditions of one's agency are constitutively open to being ruptured through non-voluntary repatriation is to lack a secure horizon in terms of which to engage in the activity of planning and shaping one's future. The third consideration pertains to the states that offer sanctuary and their citizens for whom providing the basic security, liberty and welfare that the protective and enabling functions of citizenship would normally offer and providing citizenship are distinct commitments. The question raised by these considerations concerns whether and when states of sanctuary acquire a duty to enable persons of sanctuary to acquire

[46] M. J. Gibney, 'Refugees and Justice Between States', *European Journal of Political Theory*, 14 (2015), 459.
[47] D. Owen, 'Citizenship and the Marginalities of Migrants', *Critical Review of International Social and Political Philosophy*, 16 (2013), 334.

membership of the state (and, hence, become immune from non-voluntary repatriation). Drawing on any of 'subjection', 'social membership' or 'stakeholder' accounts of citizenship, it may be supposed that they should, at the very least, enjoy the same conditions of access to membership as those owed to lawfully resident migrants in general (absent any requirements to surrender their existing nationality) and, given the distinctive challenges of their circumstances, that there are reasonable grounds to suppose that more rapid access to membership would be justified. That persons of sanctuary are not a matter of 'voluntary admissions' on the part of the state does not undermine this claim; rather, it highlights the point that considerations of fairness to states of sanctuary matter in terms of the division of international responsibility-sharing for such persons precisely because granting sanctuary entails duties to admit to membership after a reasonable period of residence. Providing asylum to individuals will change the membership of the state and providing sanctuary may (and typically does) change the membership of the state. Precisely because these are *unchosen* changes to state membership, the fair division of responsibility for asylum and sanctuary refugees between states needs to acknowledge this consequence – and that speaks against any simple division between states who host and states who pay. It should further be noted that this does not rule out states of sanctuary providing support, encouragement or incentives for persons of sanctuary who have become members of the state to engage in voluntary repatriation when circumstances in the original state of nationality allow, where the risks of such returns would be mitigated by the possession of the nationality of the state of sanctuary.

Refuge

The distinctiveness of the case of refuge is that it applies in the context of discrete and specific events such as a famine or natural disaster[48] where a person is so situated that they can only or best secure themselves from the threat to their basic rights posed by the event in question by seeking immediate shelter across an international border. Grants of refuge thus act as to acknowledge and express a commitment to the basic rights and welfare of persons in the face of circumstances beyond the immediate control of their home state, and repatriation as soon as reasonably possible is the appropriate response. Refuge here serves the same basic function as

---

[48] In this respect, it does not cover non-discrete events such as climate change, although it may certainly cover specific discrete events that are effects of climate change.

international humanitarian assistance to persons displaced by the relevant events within the state and is essentially part of the same emergency humanitarian response policy tool-kit. It generates no basis to claims of membership in the state of refuge nor, typically, to social integration in that state, but rather to immediate humanitarian relief. The role of *non-refoulement* in relation to the status of refuge is to secure persons from being returned to circumstances where, through no fault of their home state, their basic rights and welfare cannot be protected.

Distinguishing these three types of claim to refugee status as the distinct legal statuses of asylum, sanctuary and refuge is not only appropriately responsive to the distinct reasons for forced flight of the relevant persons (and hence discloses the distinct relations to persons that standing *in loco civitatis* can require) but is also essential to the proper functioning of the institution of refugeehood within global political society in its communicative role. Each type of status signals a distinct requirement to the international community in terms of action not only toward refugees but also toward the state from which refugees flee (or to which persons are unwilling to return).

Under the former aspect, each status picks out distinct criteria that are appropriate in terms of the international division of responsibility for refugee protection. The status of *asylum* makes civic standing and integration central in ways that make salient both secure human rights fulfilment and refugee choices concerning the state of asylum as key criteria for dividing responsibility. This is not to argue that asylum refugees are entitled to determine in which state they enjoy asylum (since this is liable to be incompatible with a fair division of responsibility between states) but that well-grounded reasons for having certain preferences should be given significant weight.[49] The status of *sanctuary* makes social integration central and may be taken as identifying support for refugee self-reliance through educational, employment and welfare provision and support for cultural community as key elements for fair division of responsibility. The status of *refuge* identifies access to immediate humanitarian assistance as the key criterion.

Under the latter aspect, each status communicates judgements concerning the appropriate mode of response on the part of the international community to the state from which refugees flee. The status of asylum expresses condemnation of persecution (or unwillingness to protect from persecution) on the part of the home state and, hence, the duty of the

---

[49] See Owen, 'Refugees and Responsibilities', 36–40.

international community to act legitimately on that state in order to try to bring it into conformity with the appropriate dispositional norm. This may include sanctions of various kinds. The status of sanctuary expresses political concern at the breakdown of public order in the home state and, hence, the duty of the international community to support the reestablishment of legitimate public order. This may, for example, call for peace-building efforts. The status of refuge expresses humanitarian concern at the circumstances confronted by the home state and, hence, the duty of the international community to provide humanitarian assistance. If the international refugee regime is to be a well-functioning regime, it is important not only that it provides the appropriate support to distinct types of refugee and divides responsibility for them fairly between states but also that it communicates the appropriate form of international response to the home state in terms of the specific legitimacy issues raised by each type of flight.

Such an internal differentiation of refugeehood avoids the radical narrowing of the application of the norm of *non-refoulement* represented by the 'political' views of Price and Cherem that abstract from the practice of the modern refugee regime, but it also avoids the flattening of distinctions and failure of appropriate communicative clarity represented by, for example, the fourth conclusion of the Cartagena Declaration:

> To confirm the peaceful, non-political and exclusively humanitarian nature of grant of asylum or recognition of the status of refugee and to underline the importance of the internationally accepted principle that nothing in either shall be interpreted as an unfriendly act towards the country of origin of refugees.[50]

It thus provides a normative reconstruction of the institution of refugeehood that is capable of encompassing the modern practice of refugee protection but that better supports the legitimacy-repair work that the institution serves.

4   Conclusion

In this chapter, I have offered an argument for the differentiation of three types of refugee status against the background of a normative reconstruction of the functional role of the international refugee regime informed by

---

[50] *Cartagena Declaration on Refugees* (1984), available at www.oas.org/dil/1984_cartagena_declaration_on_refugees.pdf (accessed 19 August 2018).

the history and practice of this regime. However, while the conceptual distinctions between asylum, sanctuary and refuge – and their respective practical implications for just refugee policies and their communicative roles in global political society – are clear, it should be acknowledged that drawing these distinctions in practice can be difficult. Thus, for example, the line between misfortune and injustice with respect to, say, famine is often a fraught one in which those most exposed to the danger of starvation are politically marginalized groups. Or, again, with respect to the distinction between asylum and sanctuary, those who seem to be victims of collateral damage in a civil war may often be, in effect, those imputed to be on one side or the other politically (hence, for example, UNHCR's representation of displaced Syrians as Convention refugees).[51] This is not a direct objection to the argument that I have made but it does force an acknowledgement that differentiating refugee statuses is liable to introduce another layer of political judgement and, hence, of politics into this terrain. At the same time, however, the conceptual and practical clarification proposed provides a coherent principled basis for contesting current policies that, often simultaneously, mobilise a restrictive reading of the 1951 Convention to deny refugee status to persons reaching Western states, while utilising a much wider UNHCR conception to justify keeping refugees in the states of immediate refuge into which they initially cross by adopting a protection model focused on a distinction between hosting states and funding states. Getting clear about the different claims of distinct types of refugees does not remove us from the realm of politics but it can act to disable certain forms of politics even as it enables others. At a time when the question of a new global compact for refugees is on the international agenda, the issue of the differentiation of refugee statuses is, I think, a topic that requires serious attention.

---

[51] I am grateful to Matthew Gibney for pushing me to acknowledge this point.

CHAPTER 2

The State's Right to Exclude Asylum-Seekers and (Some) Refugees

Richard Ekins[1]

1 Introduction

The plight of those seeking refuge calls for action. The question this chapter considers is how far, if at all, that action should take the form of disabling states from excluding asylum-seekers or refugees. The argument of the chapter is that while states have wide-ranging responsibilities to vulnerable non-citizens, these responsibilities do not extinguish the state's right to prevent asylum-seekers from entering its territory or to expel (some) refugees who have entered. This freedom is carefully preserved in the Refugee Convention 1951 and is important if states are to safeguard the common good which is their paramount responsibility and to decide prudently how best to discharge their responsibilities. The chapter begins by considering the distinction between citizens and non-citizens and defending the general liability of the latter to exclusion. Refugees are a special subset of non-citizens whom the Convention protects in various ways. The chapter traces these modes of protection and argues that they rightly do not eliminate the state's freedom to deny entry to asylum-seekers or to expel some refugees. Undermining this freedom encourages refugees to become economic migrants and economic migrants to misrepresent themselves as asylum-seekers. The state's responsibility to vulnerable non-citizens will often best be discharged by supporting other states adjacent to the country of origin. The chapter concludes by considering the significance of the atrophy of the right to exclude in the context of the European migration crisis.

[1] I am grateful to David Goodhart, Tom Simpson, Grégoire Webber and the editors for helpful comments on an earlier draft; the usual disclaimer applies.

2 Citizens, Non-citizens and Common Good

The responsibilities that states owe to refugees cannot be understood without first reflecting on the point of the state and the importance of the distinction between citizen and non-citizen. The reason to form and maintain a state is to secure the common good of a people, viz. a group of persons willing and able, perhaps due to force of circumstance, to live well together, forming a community. This group may share a long history and a rich culture – it may already conceive of itself as a nation – or it may choose to come together in response to a felt need for political association, as, for example, Maori and British did in New Zealand in 1840.[2] In the latter case, the group will likely come to share a history and a culture in the course of otherwise sharing their lives. The reason for this form of association, the reason to recognise others as fellow participants in a common project, is to secure a common good, a good they share, which would otherwise not be secured.

Every human being should be a member – a citizen – of some state, for this is the form of political community in which decent social life and (democratic) self-government is possible. Statelessness is an evil to avoid and to minimise, which states rightly accept responsibilities to ameliorate.[3] In thinking about the rights and duties of states, the distinction between citizens and non-citizens is vital. The common good of the political community that constitutes the state is the primary object of the state's action – it is to secure and promote this good that this state exists and it is the particular responsibility of this state and of no other. The common good is not the aggregate of the interests of the state's members. Rather, it this group living well together, forming itself into a decent community that secures the conditions – political, social, material – that enable its members to live well. The common good thus consists in realisation of the human rights of members of the group – what each is owed, and owes others, in justice – as well as the development of public goods that make social life better. Civic friendship, solidarity and social cohesion, sharing of life with others, generalised trust, and loyalty to one another all form part of the common good for they are defining features of a decent community and make it possible for the community to act well.

The central members of the community are its citizens, but its members may also include non-citizens who have been permitted to reside. This is a

---

[2] R. Ekins, 'How to Be a Free People', *American Journal of Jurisprudence*, 58 (2013), 163–82.
[3] UNHCR, *Convention Relating to the Status of Stateless Persons* (Geneva: UNHCR, 2014).

matter of permission because the state should permit non-citizens to enter and remain only if they are at least not a threat to the common good. And it should develop the capacity to be able to control entry and thus to exclude non-citizens when need be. Living in a state other than one's own is a privilege, for one enjoys the advantage of life in a political community that others have constituted, including the protection of its authorities. This is true in a sense for citizens, including children and others lacking full capacity, insofar as the political community is the product of the action of *other* citizens, including especially earlier citizens. Each citizen owes those many others a debt of gratitude for the common home they have built. The citizen is entitled to participate in the political community as a matter of right, for it was built for him or her, and for other citizens, and in the division of the world into sovereign states, this is the state which does and should recognise him or her as its own. Non-citizens do not stand in this way to a state that is not their own, even if it permits them to enter and remain (unless, of course, they go on to become citizens as many do). Non-citizens to whom the privilege of entry is extended should be recognised as conditional subjects, enjoying the protections of property and person that citizens enjoy and being bound by a similar duty of allegiance.[4] Most non-citizens will not enjoy the same rights of political participation as citizens and, unlike citizens, may be subject to conditions imposed on entry. In particular, resident non-citizens will be subject to continuing liability to removal in the event that they pose a risk to the common good, as they may if they commit crime, or are unable to find work or to support themselves or their dependents, or if they encourage social unrest.

The liability of non-citizens to removal is a justified asymmetry with citizens, who in the modern world cannot lawfully be removed or banished.[5] Citizens are required to tolerate risks arising from the continuing presence of other citizens – this is part of what it is to share a common project of social life and government. It would be unjust for one state to expose other states to risks arising from the exclusion (banishment) of its own citizens. However, citizens are not obliged to tolerate the same risks from non-citizens, who may reasonably be excluded and thus returned to their own state or some other state that is willing to receive them. Thus, other states may rightly exclude our citizens just as we may exclude theirs.

---

[4] R. Ekins et al., 'Aiding the Enemy', *Policy Exchange* (2018), available at http://policyexchange.org .uk/publication/aiding-the-enemy/.

[5] J. Finnis, 'Nationality, Alienage and Constitutional Principle', *Law Quarterly Review*, 123 (2007), 422–23.

It is for this reason that the power to control the entry and continuing presence of non-citizens is a fundamental state prerogative.[6] Its neglect or atrophy is dangerous.

An important objection to this analysis is that the state is not just an association of persons but is *territorial*, claiming the exclusive right to some territory, with the world divided between such associations.[7] The justice of those territorial holdings is contestable, the argument runs, which means that the state's right to exclude may be compromised by the injustice of existing boundaries. Admitting non-citizens to enter one's territory may thus be a requirement of justice. I agree that it would be wrong, as Gibney puts it, to sacralise existing territorial boundaries, the justice of which is often open to question. The extent to which different states are populated may well be relevant to the admission policies that relatively under-populated states should adopt. However, admission into a state is more than admission to its territory, even when those admitted are somehow confined and quarantined, as may indeed happen temporarily with some who claim asylum or are suspected of carrying disease. Attempts to enter a state are, understandably and reasonably, attempts to enter into its social life, to live among citizens (and other lawful residents) of the state, and to enjoy the protection of their authorities and the benefit of their public goods. This is quite different from attempts to establish an isolated settlement within some otherwise unoccupied part of the state's territory. The justice of the latter move is obviously open to question, but, like voluntary cession of some area to another state, it would be a more direct response to concerns about the justice of territorial holdings than would be the state's renunciation of authority to exclude non-citizens.[8] The state might act unjustly in insisting upon its existing holdings, but this is severable from its right to exclude non-citizens from its association. In any case, even if existing boundaries are unjust, it would be rash indeed to attempt to address this injustice by unilateral or non-state action.

The clarity of the distinction between citizen and non-citizen is important in maintaining the willingness of citizens to view the state as a shared

[6] 'The power to admit, exclude and expel aliens was among the earliest and most widely recognized powers of the sovereign state.' See *R. (European Roma Rights Centre)* v. *Immigration Officer at Prague Airport* [2004] UKHL 55; [2005] 2 A.C. 1 at [11] (Lord Bingham of Cornhill).

[7] M. Gibney, *The Ethics and Politics of Asylum: Liberal Democracy and the Response to Refugees* (Cambridge: Cambridge University Press, 2004), pp. 39–41; S. Song, 'The Significance of Territorial Presence and the Rights of Immigrants', in S. Fine and L. Ypi (eds.), *Migration in Political Theory: The Ethics of Movement and Membership* (Oxford: Oxford University Press, 2016), pp. 239–46.

[8] Cf. Gibney, *Ethics and Politics of Asylum*, pp. 40–41.

project, oriented toward a common good that they have a particular responsibility to support and uphold. Citizens stand to the state in a special relationship, including as persons whom the state should strive to protect when they are outside the territory of the state and as persons who are implicated, for good or for ill, in the state's action. The assurance that the state is disposed to secure a common good they share is vital in encouraging citizens willingly to conform to its authority, which willingness makes it possible for the state in fact to secure the common good and to do so without recourse to widespread coercion. More generally, the state's capacity to secure the common good, or to act decisively for the good of others, will be radically impaired unless citizens act jointly, choosing to recognise the same authorities and being disposed to trust one another and to make sacrifices for one another in time of crisis or otherwise.

Acting jointly in this way, sharing in social life and self-government, requires a sense of common feeling and a disposition to trust other citizens. The disposition is reasonable when citizens recognise that they share a common good with one another, that their lives and futures are intertwined, and that they ought to continue to pursue that good with one another. The common feeling that makes this possible or likely will often turn on the sharing of history, culture, religion and language, although communities are able to integrate outsiders who share only some of these features if they are committed to becoming part of a people to which these commonalities are or have been central. More needs to be shared than commitment to political principle. It follows that this common feeling and disposition to trust itself forms part of the common good, which states ought to cultivate, by just means, or at a minimum ought not recklessly to neglect or undermine.

One might object that the political history of the United States, and other settler polities, shows that membership may turn simply on adherence to the principles of liberal democracy. The objection fails, for these principles are always lived in some particular historical and social context. The American experiment in government is distinguishable from the Australian or Canadian political experience, and while there is a family resemblance among them the common feeing that holds among members of each polity is deeper and more complex than this. It is difficult for a political community to be stable or well governed, and especially to be self-governing, unless it conceives of itself as a people who intend to live together. The history, language, and culture that a people share not only form part of the common good that the state may act to conserve but also are constituents of the distinctive character of the community, which forms part of the conditions that makes possible effective action to secure that common good more generally. In recognising and preserving that good and this character, the state's right, in its own law and international law, to exclude non-citizens is important.

The legal freedom that states enjoy to exclude non-citizens does not entail that states are morally free to exclude whomever they please.[9] However, the state, and thus the people it incorporates, should be free to decide for itself what entry policies ought to be imposed. That is, the state should reason about the common good for which it is responsible and should adopt intelligent means to that good, while reflecting also on the responsibilities it owes to others (non-citizens and other states) not to pursue that good by immoral or dishonourable means and to use its capacity to help others when this is possible without sacrificing or imperilling the common good. The state should consider the extent of its capacity to receive and integrate non-citizens, including the opportunities that its territory or economy might provide for them to thrive, and should reflect also on the impact its entry policies may have on other states, including countries of origin. In different conditions, it may be reasonable for states to adopt either a very generous or a very restrictive entry policy. But the state has no general obligation to renounce the authority to control entry and very often such renunciation would be a dereliction of duty. Non-citizens have no general right to enter any other political community, and even when permitted to enter they are liable to subsequent exclusion.

3   Responsibilities for Refugees

The state has responsibilities, by virtue of its capacity, to others whom it is able to help, provided that in helping them it does not unreasonably sacrifice the common good which is its first responsibility. Hence, states are subject to open-ended responsibilities to support just institutions in other countries, to defend them from aggression, to trade on fair terms and not otherwise to exploit or despoil them, and to provide relief and aid in times of crisis. The bounds of these responsibilities will vary widely among states and over time, partly on the grounds of particular associations and commitments, including historical connections, and partly by reason of the scope of the state's capacities and the press of other duties. How a particular state should best discharge its responsibilities to other states and

---

[9] Cf. ibid., pp. 32–34.

non-citizens will often turn on considerations of prudence rather than of justice.

International law imposes important but narrow duties on states in relation to refugees. Article 1 of the 1951 Convention defines "refugees" as persons who are outside their country of nationality (or country of habitual residence if they have no nationality) owing to a well-founded fear of being persecuted on the grounds of race, religion, nationality, membership of a social group, or political opinion and who are unable or, due to fear of persecution, unwilling to avail themselves of the protection of that country. Non-citizens who are outside the state's territory and who wish to enter to claim asylum may be termed asylum-seekers. The state has no legal duty to them unless and until they enter the state's territory at which point it owes them duties if they truly are refugees and may have to refrain from expelling them while it evaluates their claims to be such.

There is no general right for a non-citizen to be admitted to another state to claim asylum. The Universal Declaration of Human Rights (UDHR) affirms, in Article 14, a right to seek and to enjoy in other countries asylum from persecution. It does not follow that states are under a duty to allow persons seeking asylum to enter their territory or that states have a duty to facilitate the exit of such persons from their country of origin. Similarly, while the UDHR recognises, in Article 13, a right to leave one's own country, it does not recognise a right to be admitted to any other country. Like most rights in the UDHR, the right to seek and enjoy asylum is underspecified.

The UDHR affirms a right to seek and enjoy asylum from *persecution*. The focus of the 1951 Convention is similar, as the terms of Article 1 make clear. This focus on persecution is much criticised, with many scholars concluding that it is an arbitrary and unconscionable limitation of the responsibilities that states owe to those in desperate circumstances.[10] I disagree. There are good reasons for international law to recognise the plight of the persecuted in particular and to make provision for their protection by way of concrete legal rights and obligations.[11] The scheme set out in the 1951 Convention certainly does not exhaust the responsibilities states owe to non-citizens, but it does mark out part of those responsibilities that is apt for legal specification.

---

[10] C. Kukathas, 'Are Refugees Special?', in S. Fine and L. Ypi (eds.), *Migration in Political Theory: The Ethics of Movement and Membership* (Oxford: Oxford University Press, 2016), pp. 249–68; cf. M. Lister, 'Who Are Refugees?', *Law and Philosophy*, 32 (2013), 645–71.

[11] M. E. Price, *Rethinking Asylum: History, Purpose, and Limits* (Cambridge: Cambridge University Press, 2009).

All persons should be able to live in a state that protects them, which makes it possible for them to live well and to exercise self-government with others. The refugee in the narrow legal sense is a person who has fled his or her country because it has turned on him or her, a person who would face active hostility if he or she were to return to his or her country of origin. The point is not just that life in that country is dangerous or miserable but that the person is rejected by his or her fellows and cannot continue to live with them – and is outside his or her country of origin. The plight of the persecuted who remain in the country of origin, and who may be prevented from leaving by their persecutors, warrants concern and may justify diplomatic or even military action, but does not fall within the Convention. Thus, the Convention is concerned only with what states owe to those who have already fled and who have entered the territory of another state.

The Convention imposes duties on states only in relation to persons who have entered their territory. It does not constitute a scheme for determining whether any person should be admitted into its territory – it does not disable states from denying entry at the border to persons seeking asylum – or for distributing refugees among states, let alone a scheme for extracting from other states persons who would be entitled to claim asylum if they were outside their country of origin. These matters are obviously important, but the Convention leaves them to states to resolve by way of negotiation and agreement, including negotiation with persecuting states, which may in some circumstances be enjoined to release some of the persecuted when another state is willing to accept them. It will often be reasonable for states actively to seek the release of the persecuted and to stand ready to provide refuge for them. Protecting vulnerable persons from the hostility of some other state or community is an honourable course of action, often a fit use of the state's capacity, not only for the good it does for the person who is protected but also for the opportunity it provides to denounce the wrong of persecution. Standing ready to grant asylum is in part a reasonable exercise of the state's capacity to help others and in part a technique of foreign policy.

The right to seek asylum is not a right to migrate, to be naturalised, or to enter any other state. It is a right, when one has entered a country that is not one's own, to claim protection from persecution. Making the claim, when one has entered a state's territory, effectively obliges the state to consider whether one should be recognised as a refugee. Refugees have duties to the country in which they find themselves, viz. to obey the law and other measures for public order.[12] The Convention requires states to

---

[12] Article 2.

extend to all refugees in their territory certain rights, regardless of whether they are lawfully or unlawfully present.[13] Refugees who are lawfully present enjoy further rights.[14] Some of these are rights to the same treatment as nationals and some are rights to be treated no less favourably than other non-citizens, including non-citizens resident in the country. Signatories to the Convention jointly undertake, in Article 34, to facilitate assimilation and naturalisation of refugees, but no refugee has a right to be naturalised in the state in which he or she claims asylum or indeed in any other state. The Convention thus requires refugees in effect to be treated like other non-citizens who have been permitted to enter the state, subject to two important differences. The first is that refugees that enter the state unlawfully, in violation of the state's laws of entry, are not liable to punishment, provided that they enter the state directly from a territory where they face persecution and promptly present themselves to the authorities. The second is that the state undertakes (1) not to expel a refugee who is lawfully in its territory and (2) not to expel any refugee to the frontiers of territories where he or she would face persecution.

The protections that refugees enjoy from exclusion are subject to limits. The Convention stipulates that a person is not a refugee at all if there are serious reasons for considering that he or she has committed war crimes or crimes against humanity or has committed a serious non-political crime prior to his or her admission to the country of refuge.[15] The duty not to expel refugees lawfully in one's territory is subject to an exception on the grounds of national security and public order,[16] although this in turn has to be read with the further prohibition on returning any refugee to the frontiers of territories where he or she would face persecution (the duty of *non-refoulement*).[17] That prohibition is itself subject, however, to the proviso that it does not apply to a refugee whom there are reasonable grounds to regard as a danger to the security of the country or a refugee who, having been convicted of a particularly serious crime, constitutes a danger to that country.[18]

---

[13] Articles 12 (Personal Status), Article 13 (Movable and Immovable Property), Article 14 (Artistic Rights and Industrial Property), Article 16 (Access to Courts), Article 20 (Rationing), Article 22 (Public Education), Article 27 (Identity Papers), Article 29 (Fiscal Charges), Article 30 (Transfer of Assets).

[14] Article 15 (Right of Association), Article 17 (Wage-Earning Employment), Article 18 (Self-Employment), Article 19 (Liberal Professions), Article 21 (Housing), Article 23 (Public Relief), Article 24 (Labour Legislation and Social Security), Article 26 (Freedom of Movement), and Article 28 (Travel Documents).

[15] Article 1.   [16] Article 31.   [17] Article 32(1).   [18] Article 32(2).

The Convention preserves the state's capacity to protect its citizens from persons who are reasonably suspected of complicity in war crimes or other serious crimes. This limitation also safeguards the integrity of the asylum system itself, which will rightly fall into disrepute if exploited as a means of sanctuary for serious criminals and especially war criminals. The state's freedom to expel refugees unlawfully in its territory, provided they are not returned to the country of persecution, enables the state to secure the integrity of its borders and to maintain lawful control over admission to its territory. And even the most important duty in the Convention, the duty of *non-refoulement*, is qualified when the continuing presence of the refugee would endanger the state and its citizens. In committing itself to the Convention, the state is clearly not undertaking to accept non-citizens who endanger the community for whose good it is responsible.

The duty to grant asylum arises when the state concludes that a person who has entered its territory is a refugee within the meaning of the Convention. The state is not under a duty to permit the persecuted to enter its territory. The state has no legal obligation to open its borders to any person claiming asylum, and any person whom it does admit to this end, or who succeeds in entering unlawfully directly from a persecuting state, is entitled to claim asylum, but not necessarily to remain in the state or to be naturalised as a citizen. The state is free to expel refugees who enter unlawfully, provided that it does not expel them to the persecuting state itself. The country of refuge undertakes to treat the refugee like a conditional subject, enjoying many of the same rights as citizens and not as vulnerable as most other non-citizens to exclusion for the public good, but liable in the end to removal if his or her continuing presence endangers others.

Luara Ferracioli takes a very different view, arguing that the Convention wrongly fails to recognise that refugees have a positive right to start a new life in another country.[19] The principle of *non-refoulement* is too thin, she says, for it is consistent with placement in refugee camps or temporary protection, whereas refugees should be entitled to *settle* in a receiving country and not merely be protected from expulsion. Likewise, she objects to the exceptions on the duty not to expel refugees, reasoning that providing refuge creates (or should create) a bond equal to citizenship, which forbids banishment. Ferracioli is conscious that states fear being overwhelmed and therefore proposes a new Convention that recognises a

[19] L. Ferracioli, 'The Appeal and Danger of a New Refugee Convention', *Social Theory and Practice*, 40 (2014), 123–44.

universal right to migrate to secure basic human rights but also provides that no state is obliged to bear unreasonable costs in accepting such migrants.

Replacing the 1951 Convention with a right to migrate is not wise. Notwithstanding that Ferracioli proposes to prioritise resettlement over integration of persons entering a state directly, the new Convention she envisages would expose states to major risks and would undercut the willingness to provide refuge at all. States have very good reason to resist loss of control over which non-citizens, if any, are to be naturalised as citizens. Her proposal would replace participation in a scheme for protection of (some of) the persecuted with a scheme for mass migration, which would expose states to the ongoing arrival of new members, for so long as non-citizens need to migrate. No state, not even one with vast integrative capacity, could responsibly entertain this risk. Transmuting asylum-seekers into migrants, and widening the scope of who is entitled to asylum, would change the calculus for states, which would face the prospect not of providing refuge, for so long as return is impossible, but of a stream of new citizens. What refugees need, first and foremost, is protection, not new citizenship, although of course often, and over time, the latter may be appropriate.

The state has far-reaching responsibilities for persecuted persons outside its borders and for other desperate persons but how best to discharge these responsibilities is often a matter of fine judgment. A scheme that requires states to permit the persecuted and desperate to enter, settle and be naturalised would put the common good in danger and would not prove stable.

4 When and Why to Exclude Asylum-Seekers and Refugees

States should permit asylum-seekers to enter their territory only when their entry will not put the common good at risk. Individuals reasonably suspected of war crimes or other serious crimes ought to be refused entry. The same holds when by reason of numbers and origin the admission of large groups of asylum-seekers would undermine community cohesion and compromise the fellow feeling among citizens which is necessary to self-government and decent social life. That is, the state should reflect on how granting asylum to some particular group of refugees – or to refugees drawn from multiple persecuting states or failed states – will change the character of the community and will bear on its capacity and willingness to uphold public goods. The extent to which some group of asylum-seekers already shares fellow feeling with citizens, who may have a similar cultural or religious background, will be relevant, as will the anticipated numbers of refugees (and others who may join them over time) and whether there is any reasonable expectation that refuge will be temporary. Likewise, the state's capacity – fiscal and social – to receive and integrate non-citizens will be important, although again granting refuge will be much less costly and risky insofar as it is limited in duration.

Unquestionably, states should often choose to admit asylum-seekers who attempt to enter directly from a persecuting state, as well as to admit others who flee from war or environmental catastrophe. However, the freedom to control who enters, and to expel those who enter unlawfully (subject to the duty of *non-refoulement*), protects the state from 'mass influx', to use the UN's term,[20] where a mass movement of persons might threaten the state's territorial integrity or the capacity of its public services. If some of those crossing the border are combatants, perhaps those now on the losing side of a civil war, then it may be prudent for the state to deny entry, to prevent hostilities spilling over onto the state's territory or to prevent armed groups having the capacity to threaten its government and citizens. If there are reasons to think that many of those crossing the border will be hostile, perhaps lethally so, to a racial or religious group within the adjacent state, this too is a reason to deny entry.

In closing its borders, a state may redirect the flow of persons to other states or elsewhere in the country of origin. If all adjacent states were to close their borders, vulnerable persons might be trapped and at risk of genocide or other horrors. This would obviously strengthen the moral case for one or more states to admit some of those at risk – or to intervene militarily. States adjacent to war zones are usually in the developing world and often lack the capacity effectively to prevent mass movements of people. They often also, to their credit, recognise the plight of those who flee and generously allow them entry, while hoping that they will soon return home. The main problem in protecting those fleeing war is not that most states adjacent to the country of origin are disposed to deny them entry, but that the conditions under which they then live, whether in refugee camps or among the urban poor, are often socially and materially inadequate.[21] In search of better conditions, many refugees leave the relatively poor, adjacent states in which they found initial shelter, aiming to enter and settle instead in more prosperous states in the developed world.

---

[20] *Declaration on Territorial Asylum* (1967), Article 3(2).
[21] A. Betts and P. Collier, *Refuge: Transforming a Broken Refugee System* (London: Allen Lane, 2017), pp. 52–55.

When refugees leave a safe country, where they do not face persecution or war, to travel to a relatively more prosperous country in order there to claim asylum, they become economic migrants.[22] They do not enter the latter country directly from a persecuting (or war-torn) state and therefore the Convention does not immunise them from punishment for unlawful entry. More importantly, it will more often be reasonable for such distant states to deny asylum-seekers entry than will be the case for an adjacent state. The asylum-seekers who have entered into an adjacent state are already safe. True, they may not yet have found conditions in which they may live well but the urgency of escape is absent. Onward movement is thus migration rather than flight from war or persecution. More distant states should deny entry to asylum-seekers in these circumstances to discourage the unlawful movement across borders that it involves. The promise of entry tempts those who are in a place of safety to undertake dangerous journeys in which many will die, enriching people-traffickers who will exploit or endanger them and others. Those who migrate in this way will be the relatively well resourced, for people-traffickers charge considerable sums, and if successful in entering a distant state, the asylum-seeker is much less likely ever to return home than if living in an adjacent state. Failure to deny entry encourages a minority of refugees living in adjacent states to migrate – the majority who lack equivalent resources cannot move – and might in time rob their country of many resourceful and well-resourced citizens whom it will need when it becomes possible to return and rebuild.[23]

Resettlement from camps is preferable to settlement of those who enter directly. It is orderly, safe, and avoids giving unfair priority to young, strong, and relatively wealthy asylum-seekers. It avoids also the problem of fraud at the border by economic migrants, who are incentivised to misrepresent themselves as asylum-seekers in order to seek admission. But note that states cannot prioritise resettlement over direct entry unless they retain and exercise the freedom to deny entry to would-be asylum-seekers. The more persons enter directly, the less political will and integrative capacity there will be to resettle the relatively infirm and weak from camps.

It will often be reasonable for distant states to resettle refugees living in camps. However, this is hardly mandatory. There are good reasons for refugees to remain in adjacent states. These states are often culturally and economically similar to their country of origin, which makes it easier peacefully to receive incomers and minimises the risk of irreversible change

---

[22] Ibid., p. 107.   [23] Ibid., pp. 119–20.

to the character of the community. Their proximity to the country of origin makes return a realistic prospect. Further, it is much more cost-effective to provide support to refugees in adjacent states than it is in distant states.[24] Finally, differences in education mean that refugees resettled in the developed world may often struggle to find work. The inadequate conditions in which many refugees live, whether in camps or among the urban poor, may be addressed by increased economic support from abroad, support that permits and enables economic activity among refugees in adjacent states. If resettlement comes at the cost of such material support, which is a risk, it is an inefficient means to aid the vulnerable.

States should honour their commitments under the Convention and should be open to how best to aid the persecuted and other vulnerable non-citizens, which may, but need not, involve permitting them to enter or, better, resettling them from camps in adjacent states. This leaves room, of course, for some states to be selfish and to shirk their responsibilities.[25] There are good reasons for states to cooperate in protecting the persecuted or aiding other citizens of rogue or failed states. In particular, wealthy states, relatively insulated from direct entry by asylum-seekers, ought to provide financial and logistical support to the poorer states, adjacent to war zones, where most refugees live. It does not follow, however, that 'states cannot rightly turn away refugees until they have shown that they have (a) taken their fair share of refugees and (b) have done what they can toward the establishment of [an] authority' that might require states to accept their fair share. While states should work together, there is no 'fair share' of refugees which each state should accept. It will often make more sense for most refugees to remain in adjacent states, with the international community providing material support to those states. How to act in this context is a question of prudence not justice.

Introducing an international authority that would compel states to accept refugees might address the problem of selfish states but at quite some cost. It would disable states from determining themselves how best to aid those in need and would expose them to changes in the character of their community that might put their common good in peril. The likelihood of this taking place is suggested by the ease with which some scholars discount the significance of changes in national culture and assert that priority for one's common good must yield to the basic interests of

---

[24] Ibid., p. 3, 'For every $135 of public money spent on an asylum-seeker in Europe, just $1 is spent on a refugee in the developing world.'

[25] Ibid., pp. 48–49; I deny that carrier restrictions are an example of such selfishness.

non-citizens.[26] It is confirmed also by the more general recklessness of arguments that states are morally obliged to maximise the number of refugees they admit, without seriously damaging their citizens' basic needs, in circumstances when the consequences of maximal compliance are highly uncertain.[27] Stilz argues that the question is what weight self-determination should have when it conflicts with other vital interests and that the answer one should adopt is that it is wrong to 'require some people [refugees] to sacrifice their basic needs in order that others can enjoy benefits that are not morally urgent'.[28] But failing to admit asylum-seekers does not require them to sacrifice their basic needs. And the most important costs of admitting asylum-seekers are not material, although they are relevant (especially if the cost is born by other, relatively more vulnerable persons who have not travelled to our borders), but social, viz. the changed character of the community, the erosion of civil peace and fellow feeling, and the compromise of self-government. Political communities should reason carefully about their responsibilities to vulnerable non-citizens, but international law should preserve their freedom to act on the conclusion of their reasoning. An international authority that coordinated refugee flows without power to compel states to accept refugees would be less objectionable but again would presuppose a duty to accept one's fair share, when the state might instead reasonably help in other ways.

Like other non-citizens, asylum-seekers should not be permitted to enter unless the state is satisfied that their entry will not impair the common good. And once admitted, refugees, like other non-citizens, remain liable to expulsion if their continuing presence threatens the common good, save that in most cases they cannot be expelled to the frontiers of the persecuting state in question. David Owen argues that the refugee enjoys an exceptional status as a non-citizen entitled to the protection of a state that is not his or her own. There is something to this insofar as one is speaking of refugees in the strict sense – persecuted persons who have entered another state and are thereby entitled to various rights. However, Owen is wrong to take this exceptional status to involve 'an exemption from the norm that states have sovereign discretion over admissions into, and removals from, their territorial jurisdiction'.[29] In reaching

---

[26] A. Stilz, 'The Morally Excruciating Dilemma of Refugees', *European Political Science*, 17 (2018), 656–57.

[27] Gibney, *Ethics and Politics of Asylum*, p. 227.   [28] Stilz, 'Morally Excruciating Dilemma', 657.

[29] D. Owen, 'In Loco Civitatis: On the Normative Basis of the Institution of Refugeehood and Responsibilities for Refugees', in S. Fine and L. Ypi (eds.), *Migration in Political Theory: The Ethics of Movement and Membership* (Oxford: Oxford University Press, 2016), p. 271.

this conclusion, Owen wrongly presupposes that *non-refoulement* prevents states from denying entry to asylum-seekers at the frontier.

Owen argues that 'refugeehood' is a legitimacy-repair mechanism, whereby the international order of states acknowledges its responsibility for all human beings and affirms the responsibility of each state for its people by clarifying that the refugee occupies an exceptional status. The mechanism is instantiated by the duty of *non-refoulement* and the entitlement to seek asylum. Owen thus maintains that a duty to protect refugees (asylum-seekers) is held by all states, and, to the extent they are unprotected, laws governing entry into other states do not bind them or citizens who smuggle them across borders.[30] This analysis is unpersuasive. The Convention immunises refugees from liability for unlawful entry if they enter directly from a persecuting state. However, it also preserves the authority of states to refuse entry. To the extent that Owen denies the latter he misunderstands the Convention and would prevent sovereign states from protecting their peoples. Owen's claim is that states have an obligation not only to take their fair share of refugees but also to take their share of the surplus of unprotected refugees, which arises because some states shirk their responsibilities. But it seems that even a state that met this test would not, on Owen's account, have legitimate borders, for refugees would be 'justified in entering illegally into any state where they have grounds for believing this act would better ensure the protection of their basic rights – and citizens of such states would be justified in helping them do so'.[31] It is unclear how far Owen envisages this immunity from the state's right to exclude would stretch and especially whether it would encompass refugees who leave a safe country to travel to wealthier states.

The failure of one state to protect its citizens and the failure of other states to discharge their responsibilities does not require other states to renounce their authority to exclude non-citizens when this is necessary to secure the common good. That is, states should not accept that their right to exclude is illegitimate. They should deny entry to asylum-seekers when this is necessary to protect the community, which may turn on the numbers of those seeking to enter and the locations from whence they seek to enter, and they may choose to support refugees in adjacent states over resettlement. Similarly, asylum-seekers who are admitted, or who succeed in entering, and are granted refuge remain non-citizens, although many may in time be naturalised as citizens. They therefore remain liable to expulsion on the grounds specified in the Convention, and states should

[30] Ibid., p. 285.   [31] Ibid., p. 288.

exercise this power to protect citizens against risks to national security or public order, especially in those cases when refugees have been convicted of serious crimes such that they pose a continuing danger to others. It will often be difficult to expel refugees, and they should be returned to their country of origin (as the Convention expressly allows) only if no other option is open. However, in failing to exercise the power to exclude in such cases, the state would make its citizens bear the risks posed by the dangerous refugee, which would in general be unreasonable.

5 The Atrophy of the Right to Exclude

The philosophical critique of the state's right to exclude has its juridical counterpart in the jurisprudence of the European Court of Human Rights, which has undercut the right of European states to deny entry to asylum-seekers or to expel failed asylum-seekers or refugees in circumstances when the 1951 Convention permits expulsion. In a series of cases,[32] the Court has misconstrued Article 3 of the European Convention on Human Rights (ECHR), which affirms that 'No one shall be subjected to torture or to inhuman or degrading treatment or punishment', to provide that the state cannot expel non-citizens to other states where they face a risk of torture or inhuman treatment (whether from that other state or from third parties) or where they face a risk of deportation to some further state where such risks might arise. This transforms Article 3 from a prohibition on states intentionally torturing or inhumanely treating others, a prohibition which is and ought to be absolute, into a responsibility to protect persons from the risk of such treatment at the hands of others. The imposition of this responsibility exposes citizens (and other residents) of European states to risks arising from the continuing presence of non-citizens who would otherwise be expelled. The responsibility is incoherent for it asserts an absolute prohibition on causing risks of death or ill-treatment which cannot be realised without causing such risks to arise for others. The Court's jurisprudence disarms states from protecting their citizens, prioritising prevention of risks to the non-citizen over risks to citizens.

This Article 3 jurisprudence undermines the protections that the 1951 Convention preserves for states to expel refugees, let alone failed

---

[32] *Saadi* v. *Italy* (2008) 24 BHRC 123; *Chahal* v. *United Kingdom* (1996) 23 EHRR 413; see further J. Finnis, 'Judicial Law-Making and the "Living" Instrumentalisation of the ECHR', in N. W. Barber, R. Ekins and P. Yowell (eds.), *Lord Sumption and the Limits of Law* (Oxford: Hart Publishing, 2016), pp. 73–120.

asylum-seekers or other unlawful migrants, when they are plausibly thought to present a risk to the common good, especially a threat to national security or a danger confirmed by conviction for a serious crime. The Court has also undercut the state's right to deny entry to asylum-seekers at the border or even well beyond the border on the high seas. The Court has extended the reach of the ECHR beyond the territory of the member states so that it is now taken to govern the actions of the state in interdicting ships at sea and returning them to the country of origin.[33] In consequence, states that attempt to prevent non-citizens from crossing the Mediterranean and landing on their shores, or who rescue non-citizens from dangerous boats and who return them to the port of embarkation, are held thereby to have brought them within their jurisdiction and to be responsible for exposing them to dangerous conditions in, say, Libya, or in other countries to which they might later be expelled. The Court ignores the fact that many non-citizens chose to travel through Libya in order to unlawfully enter a European state. That is, while Libya is dangerous it is not a country persecuting or otherwise threatening (most of) the persons who depart from it. Yet the Court disables states from attempting to prevent boats embarking from Libya for Europe.

One should add, by way of background, that the Court has also misconstrued Article 8 of the ECHR, which guarantees respect for private and family life, in order to generate a right on the part of non-citizens unlawfully in the state to be immune from deportation and to enjoy various social and economic rights. This line of cases further disables the state's right to exclude for it means that the passage of time, and the formation of family relationships after unlawful entry, may frustrate removal. It follows that many whose claim for asylum is rejected – or whose need for refuge has passed – will remain, and, further, their families will often be able to assert a subsequent right to join them. The signifi-cance of this is obvious: admission of asylum-seekers carries with it the very real risk that the political community will be forced permanently to accept the presence of persons who are not – or are no longer – entitled to the protection of the Refugee Convention regardless of how this changes the character of the community or weakens community cohesion, and regard-less of the threat some pose to national security or the crimes they or others may commit.

This disabling of states has been by way of supra-national judicial fiat. It has not been a free, generous choice on the part of states to forbear from

---

[33] *Hirsi Jamaa* v. *Italy* (27765/09) 23 February 2012 (GC).

excluding desperate non-citizens, whether genuine asylum-seekers or economic migrants. It thus undercuts self-government and warrants condemnation on this ground if no other. But its consequences are notable too and include the encouragement of hundreds of thousands of refugees to become economic migrants, deaths of thousands at sea, the vast expansion of the people-trafficking industry, with all the horrors that entails, and the exposure of European peoples, especially in Greece and Italy, to an ongoing stream of new arrivals, few of whom will ever return home.[34] This open-ended exposure to the entry of non-citizens, from very different cultures and economies, threatens to radically change the character of frontier European states (and others in the Schengen Area), exposing citizens to real risks to public safety and community cohesion. The incapacity of citizens to limit who enters and for whose good the state should act tends to undermine the distinction between citizens and non-citizens, compromising the common feeling and disposition to trust that is foundational to decent self-government. Political communities which are subject to such pressures are not likely to long remain peaceful or prosperous. More immediately, European states are unable to assure their peoples that their common good will be protected, an incapacity that is driving the contemporary transformation of European politics. And unfortunately, the crisis is likely to make still more difficult a sober, generous taking up of responsibilities for the majority of refugees and asylum-seekers still located in non-European states, including Syrian refugees in Turkey, Lebanon, and Jordan.

6 Conclusion

The state's right to exclude asylum-seekers and (some) refugees is an important power, which protects the common good of the political community. It preserves the distinction between citizen and non-citizen on which decent social life and effective self-government depends. The commitments states undertook in the 1951 Convention were carefully framed to require refugees to be treated well, but not to expose states to open-ended liability to accept persons fleeing persecution or war, let alone poverty. The Convention preserves the state's right to deny entry to asylum-seekers and to expel some refugees. How and when the right to deny entry or to expel should be exercised varies from case to case. States adjacent to a persecuting state or a war zone have good reason to admit

---

[34] Betts and Collier, *Refuge*, pp. 108–9.

many asylum-seekers, especially when they are culturally similar and can have some hope that those admitted will one day be able to return home. More distant states may accept refugees for resettlement and/or should provide material support to adjacent states. The question of how best to discharge responsibilities to refugees is not straightforward and calls for prudence. The state's freedom to decide how best it should contribute, and to adopt one means over another, requires robust preservation of its right to exclude. The neglect or atrophy of this right exposes states – and thus peoples – to major risks to peace, self-government, and other public goods. States should not lightly tolerate the fettering of their right to exclude.

CHAPTER 3

Asylum, Speech, and Tragedy

Michael Blake

Consider the following three statements, each of which was made in justification of, or in response to, a state's decision to provide someone with asylum:

1. In 1965, President Lyndon B. Johnson signed the Cuban Adjustment Act, which provided asylum for those fleeing the rule of Fidel Castro: "I declare this afternoon to the people of Cuba that those who seek refuge here in America will find it. The dedication of America to our traditions as an asylum for the oppressed is going to be upheld.... It stamps the mark of failure on a regime when many of its citizens voluntarily choose to leave the land of their birth for a more hopeful home in America. The future holds little hope for any government where the present holds no hope for the people. And so we Americans will welcome these Cuban people."[1]

2. In 2012, the government of Ecuador granted Julian Assange asylum, while he was physically present within their embassy in London. The government issued an official justification of their decision: "[T]he judicial evidence shows clearly that, given an extradition to the United States, Mr. Assange would not have a fair trial, he could be judged by a special or military court, and it is not unlikely that he would receive a cruel and demeaning treatment and he would be condemned to a life sentence or the death penalty, which would not respect his human rights.... [A]ccording to several public statements and diplomatic communications made by officials from Great Britain, Sweden and the United States, it is deduced that those governments would not respect the international conventions and treaties and would give

---

[1] President Lyndon B. Johnson's Remarks at the Signing of the Immigration Bill, 3 October 1965. Available at www.lbjlibrary.org/lyndon-baines-johnson/timeline/lbj-on-immigration.

priority to internal laws of secondary hierarchy, contravening explicit norms of universal application."[2]

3. In 2014, finally, Denise Harvey sought asylum in Canada, after fleeing the United States. She had been convicted in Florida of having sexual contact with a sixteen-year-old boy, and was sentenced to thirty years' imprisonment. Her action would not have been a crime in Canada, which led the Canadian judicial system to provide her with "protected person" status, which entails immunity from extradition to the United States. The Minister of Citizenship and Immigration, Chris Armstrong, sought a review of the ruling: "I find it mind-boggling that individuals from the United States, which has been designated a safe country, precisely because it respects human rights and does not normally produce refugees, think it is acceptable to file asylum claims in Canada. Lucky for them, they have no understanding of what true persecution is, and what it means to be a genuine refugee."[3]

In all three of these speeches, the concern of the speaker is at least partly directed toward the *state* from which that person is seeking asylum. President Johnson states that the Cuban Adjustment Act marks the Castro regime out as a moral failure – as a regime from which one must be rescued; this speech is directed to any number of audiences, but the Castro regime is certainly foremost among them. The government of Ecuador, similarly, uses the person of Julian Assange as a tool with which to criticize the criminal justice system of the United States.[4] Chris Armstrong, in contrast, is deeply worried that the grant of "protected person" status to Denise Harvey will be viewed by the United States as a condemnatory judgment on the American legal system. His efforts to overturn the verdict here are best understood as efforts to negate the decision's implicit judgment regarding United States – and, more importantly, to preserve the relationship between Canada and the United States.

Considerations of the expressive function of asylum are rare in the literature on the ethics of migration. Matthew E. Price's 2009 book

---

[2] Statement of the Government of the Republic of Ecuador on the asylum request of Julian Assange. Available at www.cancilleria.gob.ec/statement-of-the-government-of-the-republic-of-ecuador-on-the-asylum-request-of-julian-assange/.

[3] Cited in "Florida Sex Offender Granted Asylum in Canada," *CBC News*, 14 May 2014. Available at www.cbc.ca/news/canada/saskatchewan/florida-sex-offender-granted-asylum-in-canada-1.2646061.

[4] They have since come to regret their decision, and increasingly view Assange as an expensive luxury – and a rather rude houseguest. See J. Ball, "Ecuador's Patience with Assange Has Run Out – and He Has Himself to Blame," *The Guardian*, 29 March 2018.

Rethinking Asylum: History, Purpose, and Limits is a rare exception to this rule.[5] Price differentiates two distinct models of how we might approach the ethical significance of the expressive effects of asylum in international relations. The first model – which he terms the *palliative* model – insists that the state granting asylum is obliged to look solely at the individual person seeking asylum, and should not consider the effects of that judgment on the state from which the individual is seeking refuge. The palliative model dominates in academic discussions of asylum. International bodies, moreover, have long sought to minimize the expressive power of asylum declarations. The 1967 United Nations General Assembly Resolution on Territorial Asylum asserts that the grant of asylum should not be interpreted as involving moral condemnation. The Resolution explicitly recognized that "the grant of asylum by a State to persons entitled to invoke article 14 of the Universal Declaration of Human Rights is a peaceful and humanitarian act and that, as such, it cannot be regarded as unfriendly by any other State."[6] Article 14, however, involves the right to seek asylum in the face of persecution; and, as Price notes, persecution is a morally laden concept. This vision undergirds the second model of asylum, the *political* model, on which one function of the practice of asylum is to express judgments about political morality. In particular, to grant asylum to someone fleeing persecution in their state of origin is to endorse the thought that the individual is, indeed, being persecuted – and that this persecution constitutes a form of injustice from which people generally have a right to be freed. Price notes that this expressive vision of asylum was dominant for much of the history of asylum as a practice. Grotius, for one, regards asylum as an exception to the general principle that states are to extradite those criminals to their countries of origin – and states that this exception shall be granted to those who "suffer from undeserved enmity" (*immerito odio laborant*) in their original countries. What constitutes "undeserved enmity" is, of course, open for philosophical debate. But the very fact that we are discussing this indicates the right – and necessity – of discussing what cannot be justly done by a foreign government on its own soil. Price's book argues that we ought to accept the implications of what we do, in the granting of asylum; and this argument is one with which I am in sympathy.

[5] M. E. Price, *Rethinking Asylum: History, Purpose, and Limits* (Cambridge: Cambridge University Press, 2009).

[6] A/RES/2312(XXII), 14 December 1967. Available at www.refworld.org/docid/3boofo5a2c.html.

My purpose in the present chapter, though, is neither to defend the political nor the palliative model, but to suggest some reasons for thinking both models somewhat inadequate. Price's two models, I should note, are normative accounts; they are models for what we ought to think the *point* of asylum ought to be. I want to begin, instead, with the simple fact that declarations of asylum often *will* have effects on the country from which asylum is sought. To call something *persecution* is to morally condemn that thing, and we lose track of something important when we pretend that being condemned is not an unwelcome experience. To declare that a given person merits asylum, then, is a form of speech, and it is speech that we can expect the foreign state to hear. Speech acts, moreover, can have effects on the behaviour of those who hear them. The actual effects of the speech acts are sometimes unpredictable. Oona Hathaway's analysis, for instance, finds that one effect of signing on to the Convention Against Torture is frequently an increase in the actual prevalence of torture; those countries that declared themselves to be torture-free sometimes regarded the virtue expressed in that declaration as sufficient justification to indulge in vice elsewhere.[7] But the general point that speech is related to actions in international relations seems hard to dispel. The international theory of Allen Buchanan, for instance, is premised largely on the thought that international recognition *as* a state is morally significant, and should be used to motivate better behaviour by newly created political institutions.[8] If states are motivated by speech that recognizes them as legitimately holding political power, we can expect them similarly to be dismayed by speech that declares them to be *persecutors*.

I want to examine how a state providing refuge – one that is, we might assume, just or nearly just, and wants to do right in the world – ought to understand its duties, if a declaration of asylum actually does have the effects I have ascribed to it. And to make things more complex still, I will imagine that there is a possibility that the same declaration might have different effects on different stakeholders. What is undoubtedly a benefit to the one seeking asylum might, under some circumstances, lead to worse treatment for those left behind. We might understand this, with David Schmidtz, as the distinction between type-effect and token-effect. The same act might have benefits for a particular token, who is given the right

---

[7] O. A. Hathaway, "Do Human Rights Treaties Make a Difference?," *Yale Law Journal*, 111 (2001), 1935–2042. For an alternative perspective, see K. Sikkink, *The Justice Cascade* (New York: W. W. Norton, 2011).

[8] A. Buchanan, *Justice, Legitimacy, and Self-Determination: Moral Foundations for International Law* (Oxford: Oxford University Press, 2004).

to enter into a new and (we presume) more justified form of political life; and costs for a set of people who share that token's type. Schmidtz uses these ideas to critique the demanding consequentialism of Peter Singer, by arguing that his vision of altruism might help particular recipients of aid, while leading to profoundly negative results for a wide variety of other people – including the global poor who are unable to access our altruistic donations.[9] I think something similar may sometimes hold true in cases of asylum. The decision to grant asylum to a particular token might lead to worse injustice toward the type from which that token emerges – simply because the state oppressing that type might react rather poorly to the implicit speech act present in the declaration of asylum.

I claim, here, only that this is a possibility; I do not make any claims about how common this sort of dilemma will be. I can, however, claim that versions of this structural problem sometimes seem to have arisen. Here, I will give only two examples.

1. *Fauziya Kasinga.* In April 1995, Fauziya Kasinga – a native of Togo – applied for asylum in the United States, claiming that she was facing female genital mutilation (FGM) in her home country. Kasinga's claim was initially denied. On appeal, her attorney Karen Musalo sought a declaration that FGM was a form of gender-based persecution.[10] In order to motivate the declaration, Musalo was forced to paint an image of Togo as a monolithic and patriarchal society, in which women were oppressed by traditional forms of folk belief.[11] This presentation, though, immediately led to resentment on the part of many Togolese, who viewed the argument here as functionally akin to the racist narratives of the colonial period, in which the African woman must be saved from the brutality of the African man. The circumstances were thus created under which FGM itself became a point of resistance against the perceived colonialism of the Western discourse about African bodies and African beliefs. Later, a woman calling herself Adelaide Abankwah used the materials from Kasinga's trial to seek asylum in the United States, claiming she was fleeing FGM in Ghana. Abankwah's claim was met with widespread derision

---

[9] D. Schmidtz, "Islands in a Sea of Obligation: Limits to the Duty to Rescue," *Law and Philosophy*, 19 (2000), 683–705.

[10] C. W. Dugger, "U.S. Grants Asylum to Woman Fleeing Genital Mutilation Rite," *New York Times*, 14 June 1996. In the interests of full disclosure, I was Musalo's research assistant for a period in 1994 and 1995.

[11] L. Malone and G. Wood, "In re Kasinga," *American Journal of International Law*, 91 (1997), 140–47.

and hatred in Ghana, which neither had nor has a widespread practice of FGM. Abankwah was ultimately determined to be using another woman's passport, and had no knowledge of either FGM or Ghana. Abankwah's lawyer, however, noted at the conclusion of her trial that the sheer amount of publicity given to her case in Ghana meant that, were she to be sent to Ghana, she would undoubtedly be placed at the mercy of "people in Ghana who feel angry about her being found to have slandered Ghana."[12]

2. *The Jackson–Vanik Amendment.* After the Second World War, many Jewish citizens of the Soviet Union sought to emigrate to the newly founded state of Israel. A great many of these citizens were refused the right to emigrate; the fact that they wanted to emigrate, though, marked them out as traitors to the Soviet cause. Thus, many of those who sought to emigrate found themselves stripped of credentials needed for their work – and, thereafter, subjected to persecution and harassment as social "parasites." Those refused permission to emigrate – the *refuseniks* – worked with international organizations to bring attention to their plight. When they were successful, the response from the Soviet Union was generally to take the international agitation on behalf of Jewish citizens as evidence that these citizens were not loyal to the Soviet cause. Indeed, the American Jewish Conference on Soviet Jewry noted that the Soviet response to this activism echoed the long-standing anti-Semitic canard of an "international Jewish conspiracy" – which, paradoxically, reflected the very anti-Semitism the *refuseniks* were trying to escape. In response to these issues, the United States Congress passed the Jackson–Vanik Amendment, which limited the president's ability to extend Most Favored Nation status to those countries which did not allow their citizens to emigrate. The response by the Soviets was to insist that this would actually harm the Soviet Jews themselves: "Senator Edmund S. Muskie [said] that Soviet emigration policy constituted a 'major roadblock' to expanded East-West trade. An official Soviet response came the next day. Georgy Arbatov, reportedly the Politburo's principal adviser on American questions, said at a briefing session for both press and trade conferees that if 'normalization of trade relations between the U.S. and USSR is frustrated by the Congress,' it would prove 'a harmful thing for Soviet-American relations' as a whole.

[12] T. Hays, "Ghanaian Who Claimed to Be a Princess Found Guilty," *Associated Press Newswire*, 16 January 2003.

Should the Jackson–Vanik legislation be adopted, Arbatov warned, it would, among other things, 'revive anti-Semitism in the Soviet Union.' Arbatov's threats evoked an outraged response from Senator Ribicoff, who received word of them while holding hearings of the Senate Subcommittee on International Trade, of which he was chairman. 'I am using this platform to tell Mr. Arbatov to mind his own damned business,' he said."[13] The United States, of course, passed the Jackson–Vanik Amendment, which remained in effect until the early 2000s. The effects of that amendment are complex, but it is worth noting that the initial response of the Soviet government to its passing was a slight reduction in the number of exit visas allowed.[14]

In both of these examples, the United States declared that particular people are entitled to particular rights of migration because of the perceived abuse they are suffering at home. In both of these examples, moreover, it is at least possible that the ultimate effects of these migration rights are not uniformly positive; the effects on those who are *not* seeking rights of migration might have been quite negative. The women of Togo, like the Soviet Jews, might have experienced renewed persecution, simply because of the expressive message of American legal decision-making. The explanation for these type costs seems to begin with the distaste states feel at being told that they are persecutors – even when, of course, they are *accurately* so described. Neither of these examples is perfect. In the case of Fauziya Kasinga, the negative impact of her asylum claims is largely speculative. I believe that the effects of the Kasinga case *were* likely negative, for some women who continued to be resident within Togo, but I can offer no proof of this proposition. The second case, further, focused not on the Israeli decision to offer asylum to the Soviet Jews but on the American decision to pressure the Soviet Union into abandoning its policy against emigration. These complexities are important. The structural worry, though, remains. What offers benefits to one person might well offer difficulties, if not worse, to those who are not so benefited. Robert Nozick once condemned an idea he called *normative sociology*: the thought that a given good thing is both compatible with and caused by

[13] W. Korey, "Jackson-Vanik: A 'Policy of Principle,'" in M. Friedman and A. D. Chernin (eds.), *A Second Exodus: The American Movement to Free Soviet Jews* (Boston: Brandeis University Press, 1999), p. 100.
[14] F. Lazin, *The Struggle for Soviet Jewry in American Politics* (Lanham, MD: Rowman and Littlefield, 2005), p. 51.

other good things.[15] Normative sociology is a standing danger in moral theorizing. Most of us are – I hope – possessed of the belief that the Jewish citizens of the Soviet Union, and the women of Togo, were treated unjustly by the social and political institutions of their society. We are therefore inclined toward approving of the particular claims for migration made by such individuals. The difficulty – and it is a wrenching one indeed – comes when one comes to believe that helping some of the set of victims may involve making things worse for others in that same set.

What, though, should our response be to these structural issues? I think there are – at least – three possible responses. Two of these involve the models of asylum Price himself discusses. We might defend these models, and show what moral values allow us to do so. I do not think, however, that either model is – as stated – perfectly up to the task of helping us deal with the ethical problems discussed above. I should be clear, at this juncture, that I am not discussing whether or not these are adequate models, full stop; I am interested in whether or not they can adequately respond to the distinct moral challenge described above. I do not think they can. I therefore suggest a third model, in which we regard the task of those who administer a system of asylum as a potentially *tragic* task. When one seeks to help the needy, by offering refuge, one must face up to the fact that one might end up making things worse for some people even as one helps others. This fact, though, might be taken to mean that there is, in the end, *no* adequate account of asylum, in which all parties are given what they are due, and no ethical costs remain after asylum is granted. Instead, on this *tragic* vision of asylum, we may face ethical dilemmas in which no choice is open to us that does not make us culpable in wrongdoing – and, as a result, rightly ashamed.

Before I discuss this model, though, I want to discuss what might be said for the two models discussed by Price – and why those two models may be inadequate in the face of the structural possibility described above.

I   The Palliative Model

The adherent of the palliative model, as above, wants the state to restrict its moral attention to the individual presented to it: to the individual person,

---

[15] Nozick introduces the idea with reference to bad things, rather than good ones: "*Normative sociology*, the study of what the causes of problems *ought to be*, fascinates us all. If X is bad, and Y which is also bad can be tied to X via a plausible story, it is very hard to resist the conclusion that one thing causes the other. We *want* one bad thing to be caused by another." R. Nozick, *Anarchy, State, and Utopia* (New York: Basic Books, 1974), p. 247.

that is, who is making the claim of asylum. The decision-making of the state should be focused only on that person – and not on any downstream consequences that might flow for individuals possessed of those characteristics that have led to the individual person's persecution. Why, though, should we restrict our attention in this way?

There are, I think, any number of justifications that might be given. One distinction that might be made is between the actual and the hypothetical; the *actual* person seeking refuge has a claim on us, we might think, that is distinct from the sort of claim that could be made by the person who lives abroad who *might* be persecuted by the foreign state. Or, if we prefer, we might want to focus on the fact that the asylum claimant exists in a particular relationship with a particular state against which she claims a right – whereas the one resident abroad has, as it were, a symmetrical claim against all states of the world. Perhaps we can restrict our attention to the one directly before us, then, by referring to the fact that she is, indeed, *before us* in a way that other vulnerable people are not.

I think there is some power in these ideas. We do, rightly, differentiate between what is owed to people who are at the border and what is owed to people who are not. I do not think, though, that this distinction is quite enough to justify a focus solely on those who present themselves to us as asylum-seekers. If we are to use the palliative model of asylum, we are implicitly setting the interests of those who are present and brought to our attention as *vastly* more significant than the lives and interests of identical people who have not successfully made it to our borders. Even if we accept that those who are presented to our attention have more weighty claims than others, it seems difficult to accept that we should take the claims of outsiders to be set at *zero*. Imagine, for instance, that an evil government tells a country of refuge that it will kill one hundred of its own (innocent) citizens, if an admittedly innocent foreign citizen seeking refuge is not extradited to her death. We might well choose to admit the one, knowing full well that this will lead to the death of the hundred. But in making this choice, we should rely on materials more robust than the fact that the one is *present*. The others are, perhaps, theoretical and hypothetical; the evil government might not have even chosen them yet. But they will be real individuals soon enough, and the deaths they suffer are as bad for them as the death of the one would be for her.

If there is a justification for the palliative conception, it would have to involve more than presence. One way of supplementing these ideas is by looking to some conception of *role morality*. We accept – and, indeed, expect – people who inhabit particular roles to have particular moral rights and duties. The physician is licensed to do things to the body that are generally prohibited; she is also expected to use those skills in particular ways, for the benefit of those she treats. That means, though, that perhaps a narrowing of focus – a focus, that is, only on the one person before us – might be an appropriate response to issues such as these. Arthur Applbaum describes this well:

> A defense attorney has a role-relative reason to argue for the acquittal of a factually guilty client that the prosecutor does not share, and the defense attorney is not to count in her moral deliberations the social consequences of setting a dangerous criminal free. A business executive has a role-relative reason to maximize the profits of his company that competitors do not share, and he is not to count the miseries of unemployment as a reason not to close an unprofitable factory.[16]

What is common to all of these permissions is the thought that the *role* we play in a particular system may demand that we restrict our moral attention; we are not called on to think about how to make the world the best place it can be, that is, but *to do our jobs*. Thus, the defense attorney focuses on serving his client, rather than on ensuring that guilty criminals receive just punishment. Similarly, the judge focuses on what the criminal deserves, rather than on the pain that criminal's incarceration will undoubtedly cause to his children. Perhaps the one administering a system of asylum might say the same thing? If so, it would seem at least somewhat akin to what is said by the attorney or the judge. My job, goes the argument, is not to think about the big picture. My job is this person, before me, right now.

This is tempting, but I do not think it can work. The problem is that staying *within* the role is permissible only when we are convinced that the system itself is justified, in virtue of the justice it creates. Arthur Applbaum, again, makes this nicely clear. He discusses cases such as that of Lemuel Shaw, who worked simultaneously as an abolitionist and as a judge, whose ambit was the administration of the Fugitive Slave Acts. Shaw thought he was bound, as a judge, to do *only* what was within the role of the judge: to administer the law before him. Applbaum makes the case that Shaw's sort of obedience is profoundly wrong.[17] A judge in a legal system that is *justified* can rest confident that she is allowed to focus only on her role within that system. But the law of the Fugitive Slave Acts was

---

[16] A. Applbaum, *Ethics for Adversaries: The Morality of Roles in Public and Professional Life* (Cambridge, MA: Harvard University Press, 1999), p. 63.

[17] Ibid., pp. 71–74.

unjust, and profoundly so, and Lemuel Shaw should have used his legal role to make the administration of that law more difficult for all involved. These ideas relate to asylum, I think, in the following way: we are allowed to restrict our attention to the case at hand only when we are confident that *someone else is taking care of the other cases*. A judge who sentences a father may worry that she is causing pain to that man's children, but she can at least rest assured that those children have legal rights to guardians and to public protection. The price of limited attention is the assurance that other people are paying attention to what we ignore. It is precisely this, however, which is missing in the case of asylum adjudication. We can look exclusively at what is before us only when what we do ensures something like justice in the administration of basic rights. Otherwise, argues Applbaum, obedience to role reflects an "empty, destructive formalism." This formalism was wrong for Lemuel Shaw; we might think it is equally wrong for those charged with the administration of asylum.

2 The Political Model

Price's chosen vision of asylum law is the political model. On this model, states are allowed to take into account the effects of their declaration of asylum on the internal politics of other states. The granting of asylum is a move in international politics, and the morality of that politics is relevant in the morality of asylum. What can be said, though, in favor of the political model, in light of the structural problem I discuss here?

The response, I think, might be fairly simple: if we are in the business of using our migration law to respond to particular forms of evil, then we ought to be focused on reducing the frequency with which that evil appears in the world. We are, in other words, called on to make the world have fewer instances of persecution within it. I think something like what Nozick called a utilitarianism of rights nicely describes this vision. We are called on not simply to refrain from violating rights ourselves; we are, on this vision, called on to make the world have the fewest numbers of rights-violations we possibly can. On this account, while the individual person present before us may have the most significant claim to our assistance, it is always possible that the numbers might tell us to avoid providing that person with asylum. To return to the imagined example above: if the choice is between one unjust killing and a hundred unjust killings, we ought to choose the one. We are called on to respect rights, on this vision, by ensuring that disrespect of rights is as infrequent as we can force it to be.

Nozick raises the vision of a utilitarianism of rights, of course, only to reject it.[18] On his analysis, we are called on not to minimize the number of rights-violations but to view rights themselves as a constraint on what we are allowed to *do*. If I have rights, argues Nozick, that means that I cannot be used in certain ways – even if the world would have more of some good thing within it were I to be so used. That, we might think, is what the word "rights" really means. My claim to be free from being sacrificed for a good ought to persist even if the good is cashed out in terms of the rights-protection of others. If it is wrong to make my basic rights vulnerable to calculations about the well-being of others, so too it is wrong to make my basic rights vulnerable to the rights-protection of others. What matters, in both cases, is whether or not I can simply assert my rights, rather than waiting to see what the numbers say. You do not have a right to extradite an innocent woman to her execution – and this moral conclusion ought to persist, even when you might prevent others from violating rights, were you to so extradite her.

These ideas, I should note, are intended only to make vivid the thought that the political model of asylum has its own worries, in responding to the structural worries I discuss here. If we were to refuse to offer admission to a clearly persecuted person, because offering her admission would make things worse for other people still being persecuted in her country of origin, we might think that we have nonetheless wronged the one we have refused. Many of us – myself included – would find it difficult to turn someone over for an unjust execution, even when offered certain evidence that many more unjust executions would result from our refusal to extradite. Many of us, I suspect, would react with horror and misery to *either* of the two options: offer asylum or refuse asylum. The world seems to have brought us to a place where either option we might choose brings with it moral costs we might find it difficult to bear. Recognizing and acknowledging this fact, though, would take us beyond the palliative and political models, to a more tragic view of the world of political practice; it is to this model that I now turn.

3   The Tragic Model

The moral notion of tragedy begins with the recognition that we can sometimes find ourselves in circumstances in which no choice is open to us that does not entail serious wrong-doing. We may find our agency

[18] Nozick, *Anarchy, State, and Utopia*, p. 30.

constrained, in other words, such that the very best thing we can do involves doing particular acts that are rightly described as immoral. This is, to be clear, not merely a case in which one must do something difficult, or distasteful, in the name of morality; instead, in cases of moral tragedy, one may find that all choices involve *wronging* particular people, in ways that those people rightly consider immoral. This vision of tragedy involves more than the thought that one must sometimes do something presumptively wrong, in the name of a greater good. If I need to steal bread to feed my child, I may (morally) break the laws of property in the name of that child's survival; your right to property is less weighty than my child's right to life. What makes a dilemma tragic is the thought that the action we perform will *still* be wrong, even if it is the thing I ought to do.[19] My theft of bread is justified, I think; there is no sense in which I ought to regard myself as having done a wrong thing, when the circumstances make that theft morally defensible. In tragic cases, though, I ought to think that the presumptively wrong act is both the thing I ought to do and, at the same time, a *wrong thing*, such that I ought to regard myself as having stained my character by having done it.

It is hard to overstate how morally strange this vision is. It is difficult for us to accept this – not least because it seems as if we might become bad people, as it were, by bad luck. If these dilemmas are real, then I may find myself in a situation in which I have no choice but to do something profoundly wrong, whose wrongfulness ought to make me profoundly ashamed. This means, though, that we cannot become good because we choose to do the right thing. Doing the right thing might not be enough to make us good. We must, then, hope both for good character and for good luck; our ability to go through life without staining our character depends on fortunate circumstance, as well as our own moral judgment.

Despite its strangeness, many people are attracted to this vision of moral tragedy. Michael Walzer, in particular, uses ideas such as this to discuss why politicians are unlikely to be able to do their jobs well without committing serious wrongs in the process. Politicians cannot, simply because of the structure of the choices they must make, refuse to do things that not only seem wrong but actually *are* wrong. For the sake of our good, though, we require the good politician to wrong people, and to be aware that he is doing so:

---

[19] My account of tragedy is consonant with that of Martha Nussbaum, who has developed it in several articles. See, for instance, M. Nussbaum, "The Costs of Tragedy: Some Moral Limits of Cost-Benefit Analysis," *The Journal of Legal Studies*, 29 (2000), 1005–36.

> In order to win the election the candidate must make a deal with a dishonest ward boss, involving the granting of contracts for school construction over the next four years. Should he make the deal? He may simply think that the deal is dishonest and therefore wrong, corrupting not only himself but all those human relations in which he is involved. Because he has scruples of this sort, we know him to be a good man. But we view the campaign in a certain light, estimate its importance in a certain way, and hope that he will overcome his scruples and make the deal. It is important to stress that we do not want just anyone to make the deal; we want him to make it, precisely because he has scruples about it. We know he is doing right when he makes the deal because he knows he is doing wrong. I do not mean merely that he will feel badly or even very badly after he makes the deal. If he is the good man I am imagining him to be, he will feel guilty; that is, he will believe himself to be guilty. That is what it means to have dirty hands.[20]

What Walzer emphasizes here is an uncomfortable combination of demands: the politician *should* make the deal; the issues at stake make winning the election important. People's rights will be, we might imagine, at risk if the election is lost. But the politician, in making the deal, should be aware that he is doing wrong. He is wronging others – certainly, rival construction firms, and likely a great many other people. He is, moreover, engaging in action that mars his character; he should be ashamed. But the good politician must, says Walzer, learn how to be bad, in order to do good. He must tarnish his soul, or he is useless.

Why, though, is politics taken by Walzer to be so central in the discussion of tragedy? There are at least three reasons why the politician is more likely than, say, the gardener to encounter a moral dilemma. The first is that the politician has, in virtue of her role, power over other people. She must decide *for others*, in that her decisions will end up affecting the rights and interests of a great many other people. The second is that the politician acts both to serve others and to serve herself. Politics is, perhaps, a calling, but it is also a job – and the risk of bias and flawed decision-making is profound, given the incentives politicians have to deceive themselves about the effects of their decisions. (As Upton Sinclair once remarked, it is difficult to get a man to understand something, when his salary depends on his not understanding it.) The final reason is that the politician lives in a system in which others have significant power over

---

[20] M. Walzer, "Political Action: The Problem of Dirty Hands," *Philosophy and Public Affairs*, 2 (1973), 165–66.

her choices. The options that are open to her are constrained by the decisions of others. The candidate imagined by Walzer is not an all-powerful tyrant; he exists in a world peopled by crooked ward bosses, and worse besides. His agency must acknowledge, and work within, the possibility set imposed on him by the malignant agency of others.

Walzer uses these ideas to express the thought that politicians are, perhaps, morally worse than the rest of us. (Although, as he notes, this is the wisdom of "the rest of us.") Those who enter politics place themselves in situations in which they will face moral dilemmas. What I would argue, though, is that the same issues are likely to affect those who set up and create a system of asylum. They may or may not be politicians; the actual practice of asylum depends on the labor of any number of different professions. But they all face structural worries about their decisions that echo what Walzer discusses under the heading of politics. Certainly, those who determine asylum exercise power over others. The power of admission to citizenship is profound; the decision of whether or not to admit is a "gateway decision," as Joseph Carens has it, that affects all aspects of life.[21] The inequality of power between the asylum-seeker and the agent deciding on asylum, moreover, is even greater than that between the citizen and the politician. The citizen can, in theory, vote the politician out; the asylum-seeker is profoundly powerless, and can exercise no effective power over those determining asylum. (Indeed, her powerlessness is one reason she is seeking asylum.) The one who determines asylum, moreover, faces any number of reasons to be biased in her administration. The bias may come from simple cultural ignorance and misunderstanding, as it often does when legal agents in the United States fail to understand how persecution might work in foreign societies. Bias may emerge, though, because those who exercise power over asylum claimants are also subject to biases in how we interpret the actions of states friendly to us – and those of states we regard with more animosity. To take a simple example: in 1984, 60 percent of those claiming asylum from Iran were granted residency rights in the United States – while under 3 percent of those fleeing El Salvador, whose government was supported by the United States, were granted asylum.[22] The system of asylum adjudication, finally, begins with a world in which the choices of a good agent are conditioned and restricted by the agency

[21] J. Carens, *The Ethics of Immigration* (New York: Oxford University Press, 2013), p. 257.
[22] S. Gzesh, "Central Americans and Asylum Policy in the Reagan Era," *Migration Information Source*, 1 April 2006. Available at www.migrationpolicy.org/article/central-americans-and-asylum-policy-reagan-era.

and choices of malign agents. To return to the hypothetical example: the one who must decide whether or not to give refuge to the one innocent person, at the cost of one hundred executions, faces that choice only because she lives in a world where people like the murderous tyrant have power over others. The one administering the program of asylum cannot make the world what she would like it to be; she must accept the world as it is, structured in large part by the decisions and policies of very bad people indeed.

I think it is possible, then, that if dirty hands are to be found anywhere, they are to be found in those who create and administer a program of asylum. I do not think that those who operate that system are bad people; far from it. They are, indeed, doing what ought to be done, and we cannot escape from the phenomenon of dirty hands by withdrawing from global responsibility. I mean only to say this: if it is possible that those who administer that system may face genuine moral dilemmas, then they face a set of options in which no choice they make should leave them without a sense of profound wrong-doing. They will have to make a choice to help some – at the acknowledged cost of failing to help others, or perhaps even being complicit in the evils that befall them. Those who work to ensure the rights of others are better people than the rest of us. (Certainly, they do more for the world than political philosophers do.) But the work they do is morally *risky*, in the same sense that being a politician is morally risky. Choosing this work means throwing one's self into making decisions for others, with a recognition that one may eventually find that the best choice one can make is still one that ought to make one ashamed.

Calling a dilemma tragic, though, does not tell us much of anything about what we actually ought to do. The idea of tragedy, instead, tells us the *attitude* we ought to have toward the decision we make. When Walzer's politician makes a deal with the ward boss, she should recognize that she is complicit in wrongdoing, and she should bear the guilt of that decision. I believe something similar might hold true where there are tragic dilemmas about asylum cases. Those we are not able to help, because of the way that our choices here are constrained by the agency of others, continue to have claims against us; and we ought to feel, perhaps, the guilt that rightly comes from our choice to ignore those claims. Political philosophy, though, should not focus on the felt phenomenology of guilt. If the tragic model of asylum is useful, it should make some small difference in practice. What difference would it make, if we were to approach asylum with this vision in mind?

One difference that might be made, I think, is in the recognition that those who are not helped by our decisions regarding asylum might continue to have claims against us. Nussbaum writes, in this context, about the need for practices of apology and rectification. If circumstances were such that the very best thing we can do was to wrong a particular person, she argues, we should not pretend that we are justified in the eyes of that person. We are, instead, obligated to do what we can to bring ourselves back into moral rightness with the one we have wronged. We are not called on simply to feel bad about what we have done; guilt, as a feeling, is not as important as what we might do to expiate that guilt. We ought, in short, to do what we can for those we could not help. What we can do might be large; we ought to work for a world in which this sort of dilemma does not fall on us quite as often, perhaps, by seeking global reform. We might, more often, be unable to do much but apologize. But the recognition of tragedy might at least keep alive in our minds the recognition that the apology is merited.

There are, of course, other things that might emerge from this tragic model of asylum. The most practical advice it can offer, I think, is that we ought to do what we can to avoid *finding* ourselves in the tragic situation described. I have asserted that how we run our system of asylum ends up sending messages to other societies, and that these messages may sometimes lead us into those situations I have been describing. One way to avert this is to be aware of how our decision-making will be received by other states, and to adjust it accordingly. This does not mean simply being careful about the terms and concepts we use – although that is, to be sure, an important part of the story. It is possible, perhaps, that different methods for the protection of vulnerable people might have different sorts of effects as acts of speech; what is called complementary protection, for instance, might be received as rather distinct from a grant of asylum.[23] Responding well would also require us to be aware that different states are distinct in how their speech will be received by those who hear it. President Johnson's speech, for instance, brought with it the implicit threat of military intervention; his condemnation of Cuba was received, rightly, as the speech of the stronger power to the weaker. The Ecuadoran government, in contrast, was speaking from a position of relative weakness. They sought to use Assange to condemn the laws and politics of the United States. Their condemnation, though, was that of a comparatively stronger state, by a comparatively weak one. The effects of speech do not depend solely on political power, but it does not seem implausible to suppose that

[23] Matt Lister makes the case that complementary protection ought to be provided with its own moral analysis, rather than one simply derived from the morality of asylum law. See Chapter 11 in this volume.

stronger powers have greater reason to be more careful with what they communicate, if only because of the greater vulnerability of weaker powers to the decisions and acts of the stronger. The effects of speech, further, can be counted on to be distinct, depending on the particular agency who is doing the talking. Throughout this chapter, I have been imagining that a single agent is charged with setting up and administering a system of asylum adjudication; this is, of course, not so. When Chris Armstrong condemned the judge who granted asylum to Denise Harvey, he brought to the forefront the recognition that different agents within a political system might approach the question of asylum in radically different ways. One way of interpreting Armstrong's speech is that he is speaking in his role as elected official – and, indeed, as an elected official who must frequently work with officials from the United States. The judges spoke as a judges, whose primary responsibility was to focus on the case before them. Armstrong spoke as politician, whose primary responsibility is to ensure the stability and national interest of Canada within the global community. I have, above, rejected the idea that role morality allows the *system* of asylum adjudication to focus solely on the one who stands before us, claiming asylum; we cannot do this, without wronging those who are left behind in the process. But I have not said that all agents *within* that system must speak in the same way. If we are worried – as we should be – about the effects of our speech, we might begin to inquire about the ways in which distinct sorts of agents differ in how their speech is understood by those who listen to their words.

I offer these ideas only as a way of showing that the tragic model of asylum might help us in some practical ways. I confess, though, that it cannot offer us much by way of practical advice. The tragic model, indeed, won't even tell you how to choose, when you face the sorts of dilemma I have described above. This might be taken as a reason to reject this model. I think that would be a mistake. The tragic model should remind us, I think, that the world in which we are working is a profoundly unhappy one, in which the choices open to us are formed because of the malign choices of other people. If politics is a morally risky realm, in which one cannot do good for the world while keeping one's hands clean, then it seems only right that asylum should be recognized as equally risky. Those who create and administer our systems of asylum, like those who engage in politics more broadly, are admirable people. They are also people who may have to get their hands dirty, in Walzer's sense of that word. We should welcome them, and recognize the fact that world *needs* people willing to do this sort of work. (Were they to cease to do this work, indeed, the rest of us would have to pick up their slack; as things are, our hands are clean only because theirs are dirty.) The only point I want to make in the present chapter is that the practice of asylum is necessarily done in a deeply flawed world, in which one cannot always do what must be done without wronging others in the process. The practice of asylum is morally necessary, in that flawed world; precisely because of that world's flaws, though, those who administer that system of asylum cannot hope to avoid becoming tarnished themselves.

CHAPTER 4

Border Rescue

Kieran Oberman[1]

Every year, thousands of refugees and other migrants die trying to cross borders. The dangers are many. Migrants die from exhaustion crossing deserts, freeze on mountain passes, drown at sea. One way states can save lives is by undertaking rescue operations. This chapter asks whether receiving states have any special duty to do so. The idea of a 'special duty' here can be brought out with the following question: Do receiving states owe a duty to rescue migrants at borders that they do not owe all people in need? In answering this question, the chapter starts with an important yet easily overly looked point: crossing borders is not inherently dangerous. Migrants die crossing borders because receiving states restrict migration. This fact, in itself, does not mean that receiving states have a special duty to rescue, but it does mean they cannot claim that border deaths are nothing to do with them. The question we need to ask is whether receiving states bear *moral* responsibility for border deaths as well as *causal* responsibility. The chapter goes in search of, and finds, arguments for why receiving states are morally responsible. States cannot treat border deaths like any other misfortune without changing their immigration policies.

I Special and General Duties to Rescue

In 2013, the Italian Navy, funded in part by the European Union, undertook Operation Mare Nostrum, aimed at rescuing migrants in the Mediterranean. It ended in 2015. What replaced it was Operation Triton, executed by the European Border and Coast Guard Agency (Frontex),

[1] Work on this chapter received funding from the European Union's Horizon 2020 research and innovation programme under the Marie Skłodowska-Curie grant agreement No 842176. I presented the chapter at workshops in Edinburgh and Oxford and received extremely helpful feedback. For this, I would like to thank the organisers: Ali Emre Benli, Elizabeth Cripps, Guy Fletcher and Matthew Gibney. Particular thanks are owed to David Miller, Christine Straehle and an anonymous reviewer for excellent written comments.

aimed principally at border protection, not rescue. Many human rights organizations decried this change. They argued that thousands would drown as a result.[2]

Are receiving states obliged to fund operations like Mare Nostrum? In a recent article, Eugenio Cusumano and James Pattison claim so.[3] They offer several arguments, but the simplest is humanitarian. States owe duties to assist people in need. Migrants at borders are people in need. Therefore, states owe duties to assist migrants at borders.[4]

This argument seems plausible, but there is something striking it leaves out: reference to anything about migrants in particular. There are, after all, millions of people in need. Most are not migrants. Cusumano and Pattison's humanitarian argument applies to them all. The other arguments offered – which refer to various ideas from the global justice literature – are no different in this respect. They show why migrants are among the millions to whom a general duty to rescue is owed. They do not show that states owe a *special duty* to engage in border rescue.[5]

This chapter argues that states do owe a special duty to engage in border rescue. States owe this duty because they are causally and morally responsible for causing dangerous migration. States are causally responsible since they impose restrictions that make migration dangerous. They are morally responsible when they impose restrictions (1) in violation of a duty to admit and/or (2) unnecessarily. States would have to admit many more migrants before they could treat border deaths like any other misfortune.

In arguing for a special duty, I hope to do some work toward justifying the special concern that some activists and scholars (including Cusumano and Pattison) have shown for border rescue. In the absence of a special duty, this concern seems puzzling. Why pick out migrants ahead of anyone else in need? The idea of a special duty to engage in border rescue cannot entirely answer this question. Special duties are not absolute duties; there could be reasons to prioritize others in need, all things considered. But if

---

[2] For an excellent summary of events, see C. Heller and L. Pezzani, 'Death by Rescue', *Forensic Architecture Agency* (2016).

[3] E. Cusumano and J. Pattison, 'The Non-governmental Provision of Search and Rescue in the Mediterranean and the Abdication of State Responsibility', *Cambridge Review of International Affairs*, 31 (2018), 53–75.

[4] Ibid., 57–58.

[5] Ibid., 56–57. To be fair to Cusumano and Pattison, their main focus is not the grounding of a duty to rescue but defending the view that governments must fulfil this duty rather than NGOs. I shall not address here the question of whether NGOs should be involved in rescue, nor the alarming trend toward criminalizing NGOs that are involved. While these are crucial issues, they fall beyond the scope of the chapter.

states owe special duties to engage in border rescue, we at least know there is more to weigh in their case than the mere opportunity to save lives.

Moreover, the reasons this chapter identifies as grounding a special duty are, I think, in line with many people's emotional reaction to this issue. There is a sense of anger; a sense that when bodies wash up on beaches or skeletons are found in deserts, something has seriously gone wrong with our immigration system. Migration should not be this dangerous. The fact that it is indicates a lack of respect for migrant lives. This chapter seeks to explain and justify this emotional reaction. People are right to be angry. Something has seriously has gone wrong. States are morally responsible for dangerous migration. They are obliged to engage in border rescue to mitigate the damage they have caused.

The chapter has ten sections. Section 2 refutes the argument that border rescue encourages dangerous migration. Sections 3 and 4 show that receiving states bear causal responsibility for border deaths and that migrants themselves cannot be blamed. Section 5 argues that receiving states are morally responsible for endangering migrants when states violate a duty to admit migrants safely. This leads to a discussion – Sections 6–8 – over the breadth, grounding and demandingness of a duty to admit. Section 9 offers a further argument for why states may be morally responsible, one from unnecessary harm. Section 10 concludes by explaining why all states owe special duties to engage in border rescue, not just states at dangerous frontiers.

Before embarking, let me make three preliminary points. First, it is important to distinguish a duty to engage in border rescue from a duty to admit. Satisfying the former involves merely rescuing migrants imperilled at borders. Satisfying the latter involves admitting migrants to a state's territory. When migrants are rescued, they can subsequently be admitted by the state that rescues them, returned to where they came from or sent to some third country. The two duties are morally connected, as I shall argue below, but they are not identical.

Second, the duty a receiving state has to engage in border rescue is not necessarily a duty to rescue migrants at its own borders. Consider, again, the Mediterranean case. Cusumano and Pattison believe that the EU should have continued to fund sea rescue in the Mediterranean. But why the EU and why the Mediterranean? One could imagine an alternative system under which sea rescue was left entirely to the Mediterranean states. Conversely, one could imagine a system in which the EU chose to fund rescue elsewhere in the world; Malaysia-bound migrants in Andaman Sea, perhaps, rather than the EU-bound migrants in the Mediterranean. There is, in short, a question about *where* border rescue must take place; whether states must rescue migrants at their own borders or whether they could (or should) do so elsewhere. Call this the 'Andaman question'. We shall return to it in Section 10.

Finally, as can be discerned from the terminology used, the chapter focuses on all migrants at risk at the border, not just refugees. But why this focus in a book on refugees? The answer is simple and controversial: I do not think there is anything ethically distinctive about refugees. There might be something ethically distinctive about migrants who are in need, but that category extends beyond the category of refugees, at least as 'refugees' are conventionally defined. Indeed, challenging the idea that refugees are ethically distinct constitutes a further contribution of the chapter (see Sections 4 and 6).

2 Border Rescue Does Not Cause Border Deaths

Before making the argument for border rescue, let me address a prominent objection: the claim that border rescue causes border deaths. This claim was advanced by the UK and German governments when seeking to justify Mare Nostrum's termination. The logic is this. If migrants think they have a high chance of being rescued if they engage in dangerous migration, they are more likely to engage in dangerous migration. The more migrants that engage in dangerous migration, the more deaths.

The argument raises interesting ethical questions. It seems to assume that there is no reason to rescue migrants in current danger other than the more general reason of preventing deaths. This might be challenged. In analogous cases, such as drug overdose, people do think there is special reason to rescue those in current danger. Even if rescuing people from drug overdose encouraged more drug taking, causing more deaths overall, few would endorse a policy of simply letting overdose victims die.

The real problem with the argument, however, is empirical. Border rescue does not increase border deaths; it reduces them.[6] The story of Mare Nostrum offers good evidence of this. When Mare Nostrum ended, the number of migrants did not decrease, but deaths rose dramatically. While sixty migrants drowned in the Mediterranean in the first four months of 2014, 1,687 drowned in the first four months of 2015.[7] The dramatic increase in deaths led European Commission President Jean-Claude

---

[6] Ibid., 64–65.   [7] Heller and Pezzani, 'Death by Rescue'.

Juncker to admit, 'It was a serious mistake to bring the Mare Nostrum operation to an end. It cost human lives.'[8]

Note, no one need deny that border rescue could have an incentive effect. Perhaps the danger of migration is one of the factors migrants consider when deciding whether to migrate.[9] Rather, the point is that border rescue, by definition, has a rescue effect. Border rescue saves a greater number of lives overall because the rescue effect swamps any incentive effect.

3   States Cause Border Deaths

Why do people die at borders? An initial thought one might have is that some border areas, such as seas and deserts, are naturally dangerous. No one can cross them without risk.

This answer is wrong, as is clear after a moment's reflection. Modern transportation permits safe and secure journeys across all borders, whatever the natural environment. For anyone with a visa and a ticket, seas and deserts are no threat. One can take a ferry across the Mediterranean, from Turkey to Greece or Morocco to Spain. The journey is practically risk free. A trip from Mexico to the United States – by coach or plane – is just as safe.

One's next thought might be that safe travel is expensive. Migrants choose dangerous routes to save costs. Wrong again. Migrants pursuing dangerous migration almost invariably employ smugglers. Smugglers charge thousands; conventional transport companies do not. A migrant who has enough to migrate dangerously has more than enough for a regular ticket.

So why are borders dangerous? Because states make them dangerous. States deny certain people the visas they need to ride a conventional ferry, coach or plane. At the same time, states erect guards and razor wire in those places where crossing without authorisation would otherwise be easy and safe. The effect is that unauthorised migrants are forced out into hostile environments, resorting to unconventional and unsafe transport, as their only means of entry. The seas and deserts where migrants perish may be natural, but the policies that direct them there are not.[10]

---

[8] Quoted in Heller and Pezzani, 'Death by Rescue'.

[9] Although there are many others; see H. Crawley et al., 'Destination Europe? Understanding the Dynamics and Drivers of Mediterranean Migration in 2015', *MEDMIG Final Report* (2016).

[10] W. A. Cornelius, 'Death at the Border: Efficacy and Unintended Consequences of US Immigration Control Policy', *Population and Development Review*, 27 (2001), 661–85; T. P. Spijkerboer, 'The Human Costs of Border Control', *European Journal of Migration and Law*, 9 (2007), 127–39. Much the same point is made, with characteristic simplicity and style, by Hans Rosling in his video for the Gapminder Foundation, 'Why Boat Refugees Don't Fly!' (2015), available at www.youtube.com/watch?v=YOoIRsfrPQ4.

That borders are not dangerous in themselves is obvious and yet frequently overlooked or understated. Cusumano and Pattison say almost nothing regarding it. Their analogy is with the famous example of a child accidentally drowning in a pond. That's the wrong analogy.[11] Or consider how refugee scholars Alexander Betts and Paul Collier in their book *Refuge* treat Mediterranean deaths. The villain of their book is Angela Merkel. They blame her for encouraging refugees to make dangerous journeys from Turkey to Greece by offering refuge to those who reached Germany. Betts and Collier say little as to what made these journeys dangerous except to note in passing that 'the offer of refuge in Germany did not come with any legal means of getting there'.[12] This is hardly a trivial detail. The deaths in the Mediterranean occurred because receiving states – including Germany, but not only Germany – prevented safe migration. In this context, singling out Merkel makes little sense. Why blame her for encouraging dangerous migration but not all receiving states for making migration dangerous in the first place?

Receiving states are causally responsibility for border deaths.[13] This is the first point that goes to explain why they have a special duty to engage in border rescue. It does not, however, take us all the way. Further points must be established.

4 Dangerous Migration as Forced Migration

One further point that needs to be established is that migrants embarking on dangerous migration are typically forced migrants. This point is important because it blocks one way by which receiving states might seek to deflect responsibility for dangerous migration: by blaming migrants themselves. If someone voluntarily runs headlong into my brick wall, I can hardly be held responsible for the harms they suffer. Likewise, if dangerous migration was entirely voluntary, it might seem inappropriate to blame receiving states. The argument that states are morally responsible for dangerous migration thus seems to depend on the claim that dangerous migration is forced or, if not entirely forced, then, at least, short of voluntary.

---

[11] Cusumano and Pattison, 'Non-governmental Provision of Search and Rescue', 57. Later, on page 60, Cusumano and Pattison do note that it is EU immigration rules that 'ultimately force refugees to risk their lives to illegally enter'. But given the importance of this point – and the fact that it applies to other states besides EU states and other migrants beside refugees – it is surprising how little they make of it.

[12] A. Betts and P. Collier, *Refuge: Transforming a Broken Refugee System* (London: Allen Lane, 2017), p. 108.

[13] Are *all* receiving states responsible? One might think that only states bordering dangerous frontiers, such as the Mediterranean, are implicated. One would be wrong; see Section 10.

Someone is forced to do something if she does it due to a lack of reasonable alternatives.[14] One can lack reasonable alternatives because other human beings have so conspired. Muggers, for instance, conspire to leave their victims with no reasonable alternative to relinquishing their valuables. One can also lack reasonable alternatives because of some natural misfortune. People have no reasonable alternatives to fleeing an erupting volcano. The volcano does not intend this effect – it does not intend anything – but that is the effect nonetheless.

Among migrants who are forced to migrate are those who meet the 1951 UN Convention definition of a refugee. The Convention defines refugees as people who are forced to migrate due to a 'well-founded fear of being persecuted for reasons of race, religion, nationality, membership of a particular social group or political opinion'.[15] Convention definition refugees are forced to migrate because persecution leaves them with no reasonable alternative. Convention definition refugees are not the only forced migrants, however. People fleeing war, generalized violence and natural disasters also lack reasonable alternatives.

What about economic migrants, that is, people migrating to improve their economic circumstances? Economic migrants are sometimes contrasted with refugees on the assumption that they migrate voluntarily. It is true that some economic migrants do migrate voluntarily. The category is a broad one. It includes people who migrate to pursue further opportunities even though they enjoy decent conditions at home. But not all economic migrants migrate voluntarily. Some are forced to migrate to escape poverty so severe it threatens their access to food, medicine and other basic goods. A life of such severe poverty is not a reasonable alternative to migration.

We have established that many migrants are forced to migrate. But why think that those migrants who are undertaking dangerous migration fit this description? Two reasons. First, data. We know that migrants pursuing dangerous routes across the Mediterranean and the US–Mexico border tend to come from countries experiencing the problems identified above, particularly war, generalized violence and desperate poverty. In the case of US–Mexico, gang violence in Central America is a major threat.[16] In the

---

[14] G. A. Cohen, 'The Structure of Proletarian Unfreedom', *Philosophy and Public Affairs*, 12 (1983), 3–33; S. Olsaretti, 'Freedom, Force and Choice: Against the Rights-Based Definition of Voluntariness', *Journal of Political Philosophy*, 6 (1998), 53–78.

[15] UNHCR, *Convention and Protocol Relating to the Status of Refugees* (Geneva: UNHCR, 1996), Article 1 (A).

[16] S. Bermeo, 'Violence Drives Immigration from Central America' (2018), available at www.brookings.edu/blog/future-development/2018/06/26/violence-drives-immigration-from-central-america/.

case of the Mediterranean, large numbers come from war zones such as Syria and Afghanistan and poor countries such as Mali and Guinea.[17] Second, logic. People tend not to expose themselves to significant risk unless they are in a desperate situation.

The idea that dangerous migration is mostly forced migration will seem obvious to many, but it is nevertheless worth considering a few commonly made claims that might seem in tension with it. Let us consider three claims. All three appear in one book: *Refuge*, by Betts and Collier. The first is that migrants are typically better off than the people who stay home. After all, they are able to cross borders. Betts and Collier describe African migrants crossing the Mediterranean as 'disproportionately risk-taking, namely young men and disproportionately affluent'.[18] Betts and Collier do not claim that this makes them voluntary migrants, but some might draw this inference. A second claim is that migrants pursuing dangerous migration often have other motivations besides desperation. For Betts and Collier, motivation is critical. For them, it lies at the 'core' of the distinction between genuine refugees and voluntary migrants. While genuine refugees are 'fleeing fear', voluntary migrants 'hope for honeypots', that is, the wealth and opportunities available in rich countries.[19] A final claim is that people who migrate through 'safe third countries' cannot be described as forced migrants. Betts and Collier make this claim about Syrians migrating to Europe through Turkey. Syrians are forced leave Syria, but in leaving Turkey they were 'making an economic decision to migrate'.[20] They had effectively switched categories, from refugees to voluntary migrants.

Do these claims put pressure on the idea that dangerous migration is mostly forced migration? The first is simply irrelevant. Someone is forced to do something if they lack a reasonable alternative to doing it. Whether they are better off than others is immaterial. When I flee a burning building, I am forced to leave, though I am better off than anyone trapped inside. The second claim is also irrelevant. People can have multiple motivations for doing what they are forced to do. If you offer me $1,000 to leave a burning building, I have two motivations for leaving: to escape the fire and receive the $1,000. Perhaps, I am a hopeful person and it is the $1,000 that is foremost in my mind as I flee. Still, I am forced to leave the building. Betts and Collier are wrong then to think that motivation is a

[17] UNHCR, 'Refugees Operational Data Portal: Mediterranean Situation' (2018), available at http://data2.unhcr.org/en/situations/mediterranean.
[18] Collier and Betts, *Refuge*, p. 68.   [19] Ibid., p. 30.   [20] Ibid., p. 199.

good, let alone 'core', criterion for distinguishing forced from voluntary migrants. Forced migrants can be motivated by hope as well as fear.

What about the third claim? Do migrants who travel through 'safe third countries' become voluntary migrants? If life in a third country is a reasonable alternative to onward migration, then yes, onward migration is voluntary. Indeed, the same would be true of people who never stepped foot in the safe third country but could have migrated there rather than their preferred destination. Dangerous migration to a preferred destination is voluntary whenever life somewhere else is a reasonable alternative.

The question we need to ask is: How often is life in a third country a reasonable alternative? In relation to some countries, the answer is clear. Take Libya, a country through which many migrants travel on their way to Europe. Libya is unsafe. Migrants are subject to detention, enslavement, rape and torture. Indeed, one of the most disturbing developments of recent years has been EU funding for the Libyan coast guard to intercept migrants despite knowing how migrants are subsequently treated.[21]

What about Turkey, the country Betts and Collier cite? Turkey is not Libya, but the situation there is still more complicated than Betts and Collier suggest. NGOs have accused Turkey of serious violations of refugee rights, including forced return.[22] Syrians in Greece have appealed in court against Turkey's classification as a safe third country, sometimes with success.[23] So, matters are empirically complex. They are also philosophically complex. When people need to migrate to survive, then clearly they are forced migrants. But what of cases in which people must migrate to escape severe hardships that do not threaten survival? Life in Turkey is hard for Syrians. The farcical nature of the work visa scheme effectively forces them into illegal work. The wages are low; the hours long. They are exploited and discriminated against.[24] They find it difficult to access basic services. Up to 40 per cent of Syrian children remain out of school.[25]

---

[21] M. Baldwin-Edwards and D. Lutterbeck, 'Coping with the Libyan Migration Crisis', *Journal of Ethnic and Migration Studies* (2018), 1–17; UNHCR, '"Detained and Dehumanised" Report on Human Rights Abuses against Migrants in Libya' (2016).

[22] Amnesty International, 'Turkey: Illegal Mass Returns of Syrian Refugees Expose Fatal Flaws in EU–Turkey Deal' (2016), available at www.amnesty.org/en/press-releases/2016/04/turkey-illegal-mass-returns-of-syrian-refugees-expose-fatal-flaws-in-eu-turkey-deal/.

[23] M. Gkliati, 'The Application of the EU–Turkey Agreement: A Critical Analysis of the Decisions of the Greek Appeals Committee', *European Journal of Legal Studies*, 10 (2017), 81–123.

[24] F. Baban, S. Ilcan and K. Rygiel, 'Syrian Refugees in Turkey: Pathways to Precarity, Differential Inclusion, and Negotiated Citizenship Rights', *Journal of Ethnic and Migration Studies*, 43 (2017), 41–57.

[25] B. Frelick, 'Syrian Refugee Kids Still Out of School in Turkey' (2017), available at www.hrw.org/news/2017/01/23/syrian-refugee-kids-still-out-school-turkey.

In such a context, there are, I think, two things one might say. One is that forced migration extends beyond cases of mere survival. Syrians leaving Turkey should be deemed forced migrants, even if they could stay in Turkey and survive. Life without legal employment, education for one's children and other such basic rights is, by itself, too high a cost to expect anyone to bear. The other thing one might say is that the dichotomy between forced and voluntary actions is too sharp. There are occasions in which someone does something that they might not be exactly forced to do but, given the pressures they are under, cannot be held entirely responsible for doing. We may, on such occasions, talk of 'partial responsibility'.

In the Syrian case, I think the former view is correct: Syrians are forced to flee Turkey for reasons other than mere survival. But the latter view might prove apt in other cases. Were a migrant to bear partial responsibility for engaging in dangerous migration, receiving states would likely share responsibility for their plight.

One final point regarding forced migration. Everything I have said so far has concerned adult migrants, but not all migrants are adults. When children are dependent on their parents, they lack a reasonable alternative to accompanying their parents. If parents migrate – voluntarily or involuntarily – their dependent children are forced to migrate with them.

5 Moral Responsibility as Duty Violation

We have shown that states share in causal responsibility for dangerous migration and that, since dangerous migration tends to be forced migration, few, if any, migrants can be held morally responsible for the dangers they face. Is this enough to show that states have a special duty to engage in border rescue? Some might think so, but I am sceptical.

Suppose a pedestrian accidentally pushes a stranger over in the street. At the same time, some other stranger falls over accidentally. The two strangers are an equal distance from the pedestrian and in equal need of her assistance. If you think that the pedestrian has a special duty to help the stranger she pushed over, then I have probably already said enough to convince you that receiving states have a special duty to engage in border rescue. Causal responsibility for harm triggers special duties; you break it, you fix it. But this is not my view. To my mind, the pedestrian owes nothing more to the stranger she pushes, than the second stranger who falls. What separates the two is merely physical, not moral.

If you agree with me that causal responsibility is insufficient to trigger special duties to assist, then more needs to be said to show that receiving states have special duties to engage in border rescue. We need to ask why receiving states bear moral, and not merely causal, responsibility for dangerous migration.

The first answer I wish to pursue is that receiving states can become morally responsible for dangerous migration by violating duties to admit. If states owe duties to admit, migrants should be allowed to migrate freely. If states instead impose restrictions, they wrongfully endanger migrants. Having wrongfully endangered migrants, states must seek to mitigate the damage by engaging in border rescue.

Duty violation, then, is one way states can incur a special duty to engage in border rescue. But now we need to ask: When do states owe duties to admit migrants? The question can be broken into three further questions: (1) Which migrants have a claim for admittance? (2) Why do these migrants have a claim for admittance? (3) Under which circumstances are states required to meet those claims? The first question is about the breadth of the duty, the second about grounding and the third about demandingness.

6 Breadth: Why All Migrants in Need Have a Claim to Admittance

When it comes to breadth, there are at least four plausible answers as to who has a claim to admittance:

(A)   Convention definition refugees.
(B)   Migrants whose basic needs *cannot* be alleviated without admission.
(C)   Migrants whose basic needs *will not* be alleviated without admission.
(D)   All migrants.

My view is (D). Everyone has a human right to immigrate whether or not they are in need. I have presented the argument for that view in other work.[26] I will not do so here. Instead, I shall defend (C). Wherever one stands on the question of whether there is a human right to immigrate, all should agree that some migrants have particularly pressing claims for admission. The task here is to show that the people who have particularly strong claims are all who fit under description (C) rather than (A) or (B).

---

[26] K. Oberman, 'Immigration as a Human Right', in S. Fine and L. Ypi (eds.), *Migration in Political Theory: The Ethics of Movement and Membership* (Oxford: Oxford University Press, 2016), pp. 32–56.

Indeed, defending duties of admission only to (A) or (B) is bound to fail. Logic forces us from (A) to (C).

Let us start then with (A). Convention definition refugees are at risk of persecution. It seems clear that they have a claim to admission, but why? The most compelling answer is the most obvious: they are in need of admission. But if that is the answer, then many others must have a claim to admission as well. Think, for instance, of the people referred to in Section 4: people fleeing war, generalized violence, natural disasters and poverty. They too are in need of admission.

There are several ways defenders of (A) might respond to this point. One is to deny that need is the sole basis for refugee admittance. Perhaps a further grounds is the opportunity to condemn persecuting states. When receiving states admit refugees, they acknowledge the persecution the refugees have suffered. In acknowledging the persecution, they condemn the persecutors.[27]

This response fails. It might be true that condemning persecution is of inherent value, but whatever value it has pales in comparison to the value of safeguarding those in need. If one could either express condemnation of persecution by admitting one refugee or save more lives by admitting other migrants, then, all else being equal, one should save more lives by admitting other migrants.

To this, it might be said that the value of expressing condemnation is not inherent but instrumental: it induces repressive regimes to change.[28] This instrumental argument, while interesting, rests on a questionable empirical hypothesis. We have no reason to accept that hypothesis without evidence. Admitting Convention definition refugees may have little or no effect in changing regime behaviour. It may even prove counterproductive, allowing repressive regimes to rid themselves of opposition forces and/or use the threat of refugee flows to exert power over receiving states.[29] Moreover, if we are to take instrumental considerations into account, then we should do so for all migrant categories. The instrumental benefits of admitting poor migrants, for instance, in increasing remittances and reducing poverty, must be allowed to weigh in their favour.

An approach that seeks to downplay need alleviation is, to my mind, a non-starter. Let us consider another tack. Some defenders of (A) argue that, while need alleviation is what we ultimately care about,

---

[27] M. E. Price, *Rethinking Asylum: History, Purpose, and Limits* (Cambridge: Cambridge University Press, 2009).

[28] Ibid., pp. 69–85.

[29] K. M. Greenhill, *Weapons of Mass Migration: Forced Displacement, Coercion, and Foreign Policy* (Ithaca, NY: Cornell University Press, 2010).

Convention definition refugees are distinct because their needs cannot be alleviated without admission. Other migrants, the argument goes, can be assisted in situ. Poor migrants, for instance, can be assisted by means of aid, trade or investment.[30]

The first thing to note about this second response is that it cannot defend (A). The distinction between Convention definition refugees and other migrants does not track the distinction between those whose needs can and cannot be alleviated by other means. It is not true that no Convention definition refugees can be assisted by other means. Some refugees can be safeguarded against persecution if effective diplomatic or military action is taken. Nor is it true that all other migrants can be assisted by other means. In some cases, problems such as violence and corruption render outside help impossible. The category 'those whose basic needs cannot be alleviated without admission' is a distinct category to that of Convention definition refugees, a point that some, adopting this line of argument, have been wise to concede.[31] We have moved, in other words, from (A) to (B).

But (B) is also unacceptable. There is no reason to admit those whose needs *cannot* be alleviated without admission over those whose needs *will not* be alleviated without admission. What matters is whether people's needs are alleviated, not whether they could be in theory. A receiving state cannot justify excluding poor migrants on the mere grounds that it *could* assist them in their home country by means of aid, trade or investment. If that aid, trade or investment is not forthcoming, the migrants have an equal claim to admission as anyone in equal need.

To see the implausibility of (B), imagine an analogous healthcare policy. The policy distinguishes patients who require hospital admission from those who could be treated at home. Home treatment is never actually provided, but patients who could be treated at home are, nevertheless, excluded from hospitals. Such a healthcare policy is clearly ludicrous. An immigration policy based on (B) is no less so.[32]

---

[30] M. Lister, 'Who Are Refugees?', *Law and Philosophy*, 32 (2013), 645–71; M. Cherem, 'Refugee Rights: Against Expanding the Definition of a "Refugee" and Unilateral Protection Elsewhere', *Journal of Political Philosophy*, 24 (2016), 183–205.

[31] D. Miller, *Strangers in Our Midst: The Political Philosophy of Immigration* (Cambridge, MA: Harvard University Press, 2016), pp. 82–83.

[32] For further debate on this issue, see K. Oberman, 'Reality for Realists: Why Economic Migrants Should Not Just "Go Home and Wait for Assistance"', *European Political Science*, 17 (2018), 658–61, and D. Miller, 'A Response to Song, Stilz and Oberman', *European Political Science*, 17 (2018), 661–66.

This then is how we move from (A) to (C). In so doing we have addressed the question of breadth. All migrants in need have a claim to admittance if their needs will not otherwise be alleviated.

One last issue. If (C) is the right answer, should we not expand the definition of a 'refugee' accordingly? Should 'refugee' be defined as a migrant whose basic needs will not be alleviated without admission? I have no answer to this question. I raise it only to forestall confusion. The normative question of who has a claim for admittance is often addressed alongside the conceptual question of who is a 'refugee'. But this has been a mistake. It has encouraged people to think the two questions are identical. They are not. There may be good non-normative reasons – historical or linguistic perhaps – for maintaining the Convention definition, but such reasons have no place in an answer to the normative question. In what follows, I shall refer to 'migrants in need' to mean (C) and leave it to others to judge whether that group warrant description as 'refugees'.

7 Grounding: Dangerous Migration as a Further Grounds for a Duty to Admit

In addressing the breadth question, we have already done much to address the grounding question. The primary reason why states owe duties to admit migrants in need is to enable them to alleviate those needs. There is, however, a further reason why states owe duties to admit: to avoid dangerous migration. If states prevent migrants in need from migrating legally, some will attempt to migrate dangerously. By permitting migration, states make migration safe.

One might think this second reason redundant. If states already owe duties to admit migrants in need, because they are in need, what work is done by noting that admission also prevents dangerous migration? In some cases, it is true, this second reason will prove redundant, but not in all. Imagine the following: receiving state R receives migrants from two sending states, S1 and S2. Migrants from both states are in great need, but, before they migrate, migrants from S1 are in moderately more need. If other things were equal, R should prioritise the admission of S1 migrants. Other things are not equal, however. R can maintain a firm border against S1 but not S2. If S1 migrants are excluded, they stay home. If S2 migrants are excluded, they attempt dangerous migration. Suppose, once the costs of dangerous migration are included, the citizens of S2 are, on average, at greater risk than the citizens of S1. R would then have reason, all things considered, to prioritise the admission of S2 migrants.

This is a stylised example, but the lesson to draw from it is that the two reasons to admit migrants in need can come apart. Preventing dangerous migration is a further grounds for a duty to admit migrants in need and it is not always redundant.

8   Demandingness: Admitting Migrants Is not Costly

The question of demandingness is not settled by breadth nor grounding. States may owe duties to admit migrants in need, but these duties are limited by cost. When the costs of admittance rise beyond a certain threshold, states have no duty to admit more.

I will not debate where the cost threshold lies. There is already work on that issue. The point I wish to make here instead is that wherever the threshold lies, states will likely be obliged to admit large numbers of migrants. This is for a simple empirical point: admitting migrants is often not costly.

That migration is often not costly is a point that is routinely ignored. Consider the story of a recent draft report, commissioned by the Trump administration, into the fiscal cost of refugee admissions. The administration was intent on restricting admissions. No doubt, it commissioned the report with the hope of justifying that decision. What did the report find? That refugees, over a ten-year period, make a net *contribution* of $63 billion.[33] Perhaps this should not have been surprising. Migrants work and pay taxes; they are not passive consumers of state benefits.

The draft report was never published. We have it only because it was leaked to the *New York Times*. Clearly, it was an embarrassment. It suggested that in restricting admissions, the US government would miss an opportunity to both save lives *and* make itself richer.[34]

Now the report concerned only the *fiscal* effects of *refugee* admission, but when we look at the broad *economic* effects of *migration in general* we find similar results. Migration – high skilled and low skilled – benefits receiving state economies. The debate among migration economists is not whether migration has this effect, but how large the benefit is.[35]

---

[33] Department of Health and Human Services, 'The Fiscal Costs of the US Refugee Admissions Program at the Federal, State and Local Levels, from 2005–2014' (2017), available at www.nytimes.com/interactive/2017/09/19/us/politics/document-Refugee-Report.html.

[34] I thank Serena Parehk for alerting me to this story. Discussion with her, and Patti Lenard, inspired this section.

[35] E. Boubtane, J. C. Dumont and C. Rault, 'Immigration and Economic Growth in the OECD Countries 1986–2006', *Oxford Economic Papers*, 68 (2016), 340–60; G. J. Borjas, 'The Economic Benefits from Immigration', *Journal of Economic Perspectives*, 9 (1995), 3–22.

We might still worry about distribution. Migration can benefit society overall and still leave poorer citizens worse off.[36] But even if migration does have a negative effect on those at the bottom of the labour market, that problem can be addressed by domestic transfers. It is unnecessary to restrict migration.

What about other kinds of costs besides economic costs? Is it not relevant, for instance, that many citizens prefer low immigration? Should we not add these 'subjective costs' to objective costs when determining the extent of the duty to admit? Actually, no. For we must ask what explains citizen preferences. One possibility is very little. They are *mere* preferences, much like preferences for, say, tea over coffee. If so, they are too insignificant to deserve inclusion. Receiving states can only exclude migrants in need if they have a good reason for doing so. A mere preference for having fewer immigrants around does not cut it. (Compare: 'Don't haul him into the lifeboat. I like the sense of space.') The greater danger, however, is that opposition to immigration is not a mere preference but grounded in either ignorance and prejudice. We know people poorly grasp the effects of immigration, tending to exaggerate or entirely invent the costs and under-estimate the benefits.[37] We also know that opposition to immigration correlates with prejudicial attitudes toward either particular ethnicities[38] or outgroups in general.[39] Given this evidence, we should be slow to include 'subjective costs' in our calculations. The duty to admit cannot be limited by ignorance or prejudice.

This is not to argue that the cost threshold will never be reached. There are, no doubt, important non-economic objective costs, such as environ-mental degradation, and the economic gains cannot go on indefinitely. At some stage, migration will have significant net costs. My point is merely that, given the benefits, states will likely be obliged to admit large numbers no matter how high or low we place the cost threshold. In a world in which admitting migrants produces either net gains or low net costs, even a seemingly undemanding duty to admit will yield radical results.

---

[36] G. J. Borjas, *Heaven's Door: Immigration Policy and the American Economy* (Princeton, NJ: Princeton University Press, 1999).

[37] For some nice examples of the perception/evidence mismatch, see J. Hidalgo, 'The Case for the International Governance of Immigration', *International Theory*, 8 (2016), 140–70.

[38] R. Ford, 'Acceptable and Unacceptable Immigrants: How Opposition to Immigration in Britain Is Affected by Migrants' Region of Origin', *Journal of Ethnic and Migration Studies*, 37 (2011), 1017–37; J. W. Ayers et al., 'Is Immigration a Racial Issue? Anglo Attitudes on Immigration Policies in a Border County', *Social Science Quarterly*, 90 (2009), 593–610.

[39] D. R. Kinder and C. D. Kam, *Us against Them: Ethnocentric Foundations of American Opinion* (Chicago, IL: University of Chicago Press, 2010), pp. 125–50.

9 Moral Responsibility as Unnecessary Harm

Having offered some thoughts on the breadth, source and demandingness of the duty to admit, let me repeat the general argument. The general argument is this: when states fail to admit migrants that they have a duty to admit and this causes dangerous migration, states are morally responsible for dangerous migration. Because they are morally responsible for dangerous migration, they owe a special duty to engage in border rescue.

But now suppose a state has discharged its duty to admit. Would it cease to have a special duty to engage in border rescue? Not necessarily. While violating a duty to admit is one way a state can become morally responsible for dangerous migration, there might be others.

Consider this: if a state has alleviated its duty to admit, then it is permitted to impose restrictions, but the permission to impose restrictions is not a requirement to do so. If a state is permitted but not required to impose restrictions, then it is permitted *not* to impose restrictions. If the state nevertheless chooses to do so, it endangers migrants by denying them a reasonable alternative to dangerous migration. This is a form of unnecessary endangerment. It seems plausible that states can have special duties toward those they unnecessarily endanger.

To understand this argument better, consider a set of analogous examples involving (once again) a street collision.

Push 1: Pedestrian pushes Stranger without justification. Pedestrian is required not to push Stranger.

Push 2: Pedestrian's daughter is in danger. To save her, Pedestrian must run across the street. Doing so involves pushing Stranger. Pedestrian is required to save her daughter, so she is required to push Stranger.

Push 3: Pedestrian's wallet is stolen. Pedestrian is permitted but not required to chase the thief. Doing so involves pushing Stranger. If pedestrian is permitted but not required to chase the thief, she is permitted but not required to push Stranger.

In which of these cases does Pedestrian have a special duty to assist Stranger? *Push 1* is analogous to those cases, discussed at length, in which states violate a duty to admit. Duty violation is certainly grounds for a special duty to assist. *Push 2* is tricky, but my view is that Pedestrian has no *special* duty to assist Stranger in this case. The harm Pedestrian causes Stranger is morally necessary. She is thus casually but not morally responsible for Stranger's injuries. It is like our first case, in Section 5, involving an accidental collision. No doubt some will disagree with this judgement, but if so they should certainly agree with me in relation to *Push 3*. In *Push*

3, morality does not require Pedestrian to push Stranger but only permits her to do so. If Pedestrian nevertheless chooses to push Stranger, I think she has special duty to assist Stranger. She is morally responsible for Stranger's injuries because she harms her unnecessarily.

Now, for unnecessary harm to be a further grounds for a special duty to engage in border rescue there has to be cases like *Push 3*. States must be, at least sometimes, permitted but not required to impose migration restrictions against migrants in need. While I will not assess here whether this is in fact so, the possibility of 'discretionary admissions' is consistent with most accounts of refugee and migration ethics. It seems particularly plausible if one assumes that the duty to admit is not especially demanding.

A different challenge: if a state lacks a duty to admit migrants in need, why would it have a duty to engage in border rescue? If admission is too costly, would not border rescue also be too costly? Not necessarily. Admission and border rescue may impose different kinds of cost. Consider one of the costs referred to above: environmental costs. A state might be permitted to exclude to prevent environmental costs, but these environmental costs would not permit a failure to engage in border rescue. And remember, rescue need not result in admission. A state that rescues migrants (or finances their rescue) might send them elsewhere.

10 The Andaman Question and the Moral Importance of Aeroplanes

Let us turn finally to the Andaman question: the question of whether states owe duties to rescue migrants at their borders in particular. The arguments that Cusumano and Pattison offer for a duty to engage in border rescue offer no reason to think so. As we have noted, their arguments support a general duty to rescue, and a general duty to rescue does not distinguish migrants from others in need, much less migrants in a particular location.

At first glance, one might think that this chapter delivers the opposite conclusion. The argument that I have offered is from state responsibility for dangerous migration and one might think that only receiving states at dangerous frontiers, such as the Mediterranean, the Andaman and the Sonoran desert, are responsible for dangerous migration. After all, when migrants are imperilled, they are trying to avoid restrictions imposed by these frontier states: the United States, Malaysia, Italy, Greece and so forth. Canada, Germany and other states that lie beyond the frontier might seem to avoid responsibility.

In fact, the responsibility argument I have offered also implicates non-frontier states. One reason for this is that non-frontier states can play a critical role in setting and enforcing restrictions at the frontier. The EU offers a clear example; Mediterranean restrictions are the product of decisions made in Berlin and Brussels as much as in Rome or Athens. But there is a more basic reason why non-frontier states are implicated: aeroplanes. Aeroplanes offer safe transport to all states in the world. If non-frontier states capable of hosting migrants would allow migrants to migrate by plane, those migrants would have a reasonable alternative to dangerous migration. They would not have to cross the Mediterranean, the Andaman, the Sonoran desert or some other dangerous frontier. The problem is non-frontier states routinely deny migrants the visas they need to fly to, and settle within, their territory. A migrant who lacks a reasonable alternative to dangerous migration is therefore forced to migrate by *all* receiving states that are capable but unwilling to host her, not just the frontier state to which she flees. Since all receiving states are in the exclusion game, all receiving states share responsibility for dangerous migration.[40]

Now, there might be contingent reasons why duties to rescue should fall on the nearest states. That is the legal convention and one that fits well with norms concerning sovereignty.[41] So perhaps local rescue can be justified on the basis of these contingent reasons. Still, it is striking that there is no deep moral reason for doing things this way. Many migrants imperilled in the Andaman would have flown to EU countries instead but for EU restrictions. Absent convention, there is no reason why the EU should rescue migrants in the Mediterranean ahead of these Andaman-imperilled migrants. To some, this might seem like an odd result, but, on reflection, I am not sure it is. States have special duties to engage in border rescue if they are morally responsible for leaving migrants with no reasonable alternative to dangerous migration. To avoid this duty, they should admit more migrants. If they fail to do so, it is not odd to think that they have a special duty to rescue all those they have failed. On the contrary, it would be odd if states had duties to rescue only those migrants who had reached their borders and not those further away.

[40] Which is not to say that all receiving states are responsible for *every* case of dangerous migration. Admittedly, there will be some cases in which particular migrants cannot safely migrate to particular states for reasons outside those states' control.

[41] On legal convention, see Cusumano and Pattison, 'The Non-governmental Provision of Search and Rescue', 58.

CHAPTER 5

Selecting Refugees

David Miller[1]

1 Introduction

In this chapter I examine the criteria that it is legitimate for liberal states to use when selecting refugees for admission. My aim is not to provide detailed policy guidance. Refugee policy, like immigration policy generally, is a complex matter, and states have evolved different selection practices to suit their particular circumstances and the demands for admission that they face. Nevertheless, we can readily agree that some selection criteria are inadmissible – selection on grounds of race, for example. In particular, I want to explore whether in setting their policies, states have simply to respond to the weight of the moral claim that each refugee can make to be admitted, or whether they also have some scope to shape these policies to reflect the preferences and interests of their own citizens. In relation to the former, what gives one refugee a stronger claim than another to be granted admission, on either a temporary or a permanent basis? In relation to the latter, how far, if at all, is it permissible for states to allow considerations of national culture, economic advantage, social cohesion and so forth to influence their refugee selection policies?

Some readers may find the very idea of refugee *selection* disturbing. Don't all refugees have a *right* to be admitted, under the long-established principle of *non-refoulement*, which prohibits their return to the place that has made them into refugees – or indeed any place where they face persecution, or some other unavoidable threat to their human rights?[2]

[1] Earlier versions of this chapter were presented to the workshop on Feasibility and Immigration, Australian National University, 23–24 April 2018, the conference on Refugees and Minority Rights, University of Tromso, 14–15 June 2018, and the conference on Refugees, Borders and Membership, University of Malmo, 24–26 October 2018. I thank the participants in all three events for their penetrating comments and criticisms, and also Patti Lenard, Serena Parekh and Christine Straehle for their advice and suggestions.
[2] I will not say anything more here about how 'refugee' should be defined, a question discussed at length in the Introduction. The arguments I make in the chapter should apply regardless of whether

So why the talk of selection, which implies that some will be turned away? But here I believe a small dose of realism is unavoidable. We might imagine a first-best world in which all states treated their citizens with respect, and made a good-enough job of protecting their human rights. In that world, plainly, there might still be a need for immigration policy, but there would be no refugees. We could also imagine a second-best world containing a few rogue states that produced refugees, though in small enough numbers that no state would be burdened by admitting everyone who applied to it in search of asylum. But we are living in a third-best world where the number of people with valid claims to refugee status is so high that states can justifiably set limits to the numbers they will accept, preferably under a burden-sharing scheme that divides their collective responsibility to aid refugees fairly between them.[3] Indeed the key document establishing a right to claim asylum under international law – the 1951 Geneva Convention – also recognizes the problem that admitting such a right may pose when it acknowledges that 'the grant of asylum may place unduly heavy burdens on certain countries' and that a solution must involve international cooperation.[4] The UNHCR was established in part as an instrument for managing refugee flows in such a way that no country would have to bear such burdens single-handed. In other words, while the right to asylum was recognized by the international community acting through the UN in the post-war period, it was also acknowledged that the

a wider or a narrower definition is preferred. My own position is set out in D. Miller, *Strangers in Our Midst: The Political Philosophy of Immigration* (Cambridge, MA: Harvard University Press, 2016), ch. 5.

[3] For discussion of such schemes, and the criteria that might be used to determine what each state's refugee quota should be, see P. Schuck, 'Refugee Burden-Sharing: A Modest Proposal', *Yale Journal of International Law*, 22 (1997), 243–97; J. C. Hathaway and R. A. Neve, 'Making International Refugee Law Relevant Again: A Proposal for Collectivized and Solution-Oriented Protection', *Harvard Human Rights Journal*, 10 (1997), 115–211; A. Hans and A. Suhrke, 'Responsibility Sharing', in J. Hathaway (ed.), *Reconceiving International Refugee Law* (The Hague: Martinus Nijhoff, 1997), pp. 83–109; A. Suhrke, 'Burden-Sharing during Refugee Emergencies: The Logic of Collective versus National Action', *Journal of Refugee Studies*, 11 (1998), 396–415; T. Kritzman-Amir, 'Not in My Backyard: On the Morality of Responsibility Sharing in Refugee Law', *Brooklyn Journal of International Law*, 34 (2009), 355–93. I do not mean to underestimate the practical difficulty in getting states to sign up to such schemes, given that they will have their own internal estimates of the real costs of admitting and integrating refugees, which may not correspond to the economic burden calculated on the basis of objective criteria such as population size or per capita GDP – for example, they may claim that it is particularly costly for them to have to admit refugees from certain ethnic groups. I believe, nonetheless, that there is an obligation both to help establish and to join them.

[4] UNHCR, *Convention and Protocol Relating to the Status of Refugees* (Geneva: UNHCR, 1996), p. 15.

exercise of that right would in practice require countries to cooperate in responding to large-scale refugee crises.[5]

Once we accept that states are justified in establishing limits to the number of refugees they will admit in any given time period, we cannot avoid confronting the selection issue. States may also have a responsibility to tackle the refugee problem at the source, helping to move the third-best world toward second-best and ultimately first-best configurations, but meanwhile they need to have ethically justified policies for deciding which refugees should be given priority for admission within those limits. What principles should guide them here? We can approach this question from the side of the refugee, asking what factors might contribute to the strength of his claim to be admitted to a particular state. But we can also approach it from the side of the receiving state, noticing that the costs and benefits of admitting different refugees may vary considerably: some will contribute a lot and need little support from the state, whereas for others the opposite may be true. But is it acceptable for a state to take these costs and benefits into account when it decides on its admission policy? In the case of refugees, unlike other immigrants, some may think it impermissible. I examine the refugee's perspective first before turning to the receiving state's perspective.

To get our question into proper focus, it is important to distinguish analytically between two categories of refugees. The first covers those who are admitted on a short-term basis in the expectation that they will be able to repatriate to their home countries after a few months or years, when the crisis that has turned them into refugees has passed. These will typically be people escaping from collapsed states or civil wars who cannot for the time being be protected in their homelands. I shall describe refugees in this category as candidates for *sanctuary*. The second covers those who are applying to remain in the receiving state on a long-term basis, because they have no realistic prospect of returning home safely. This might be because they are certain to face persecution on grounds of race or religion if they attempt to do so, or because the place they might otherwise return to has been so transformed meanwhile that they could no longer make a life there. Typically, refugees in this second category will already have spent

---

[5] In this chapter, I am going to set aside the large policy question of how states should best respond to such crises – how far they should respond by admitting refugees, or on the other hand by providing funding for purpose-built refugee camps or investing in enterprise zones where refugees can find employment in third countries. For discussion of these alternatives to admission, see especially A. Betts and P. Collier, *Refuge: Transforming a Broken Refugee System* (London: Allen Lane, 2017). I assume simply that admitting *some* refugees to liberal democracies must be part of the solution.

some years in countries of first asylum, eking out a living in refugee camps, cities or rural settlements. I shall describe refugees in this category as candidates for *resettlement*.

As indicated, the distinction between sanctuary and resettlement is an analytical one. In any concrete case, it may be difficult to know whether a refugee who seeks admission should be treated as claiming sanctuary or as claiming resettlement, because it is hard to tell in advance whether the situation she is fleeing can be resolved quickly enough to allow return within the time limit for which sanctuary is granted. We must also recognize that there is a length of time, difficult to specify precisely, beyond which a claim for sanctuary will turn into a claim for permanent resettlement, because the refugee has put down sufficiently deep roots in the receiving society that it would breach his human rights to require him to return to his society of origin. Here I am endorsing what is sometimes called the 'social membership' argument, which holds that once a person has lived in a society for a number of years, forming social ties and contributing productively through working, paying taxes and so forth, that person has a right to become a permanent resident and in due course a citizen.[6] This is regardless of the terms on which he or she entered the society initially. But although for these reasons the distinction between sanctuary and resettlement may be blurred in practice, it will turn out to be important when we begin to evaluate selection criteria. I will argue that some factors that may properly be taken into account when judging claims for resettlement may not be used when only sanctuary is being sought. It is also a distinction that is drawn in practice by many states, when they offer some asylum-seekers temporary residence visas that expire after three or more years unless renewed, and others permanent residency.[7] So although it may prove difficult to devise a policy that exactly captures the morally

---

[6] For the fullest defence of this argument, see J. Carens, *The Ethics of Immigration* (New York: Oxford University Press, 2013), ch. 8. See also R. Baubock, *Transnational Citizenship: Membership and Rights in International Migration* (Aldershot: Edward Elgar, 1994), ch. 6; R. Rubio-Marin, *Immigration as a Democratic Challenge: Citizenship and Inclusion in Germany and the United States* (Cambridge: Cambridge University Press, 2000), chs. 2 and 5; A. Shachar, *The Birthright Lottery: Citizenship and Global Inequality* (Cambridge, MA: Harvard University Press, 2009), ch. 6; and my own defence in Miller, *Strangers in Our Midst*, ch. 7. For the influence of this principle in US law, see H. Motomura, *Americans in Waiting: The Lost Story of Immigration and Citizenship in the United States* (New York: Oxford University Press, 2006), ch. 4. For a critique, see K. Oberman, 'Immigration, Citizenship, and Consent: What Is Wrong with Permanent Alienage?', *Journal of Political Philosophy*, 25 (2017), 91–107.

[7] This is common practice within the EU, for example, and also applies in Australia and New Zealand. In the United States, refugees become eligible to apply for permanent residency after one year. For a fuller discussion (and defence) of such practice, see Chapter 11 in this volume.

relevant distinction between refugees whose vulnerability is a short-term condition that will end with the cessation of conflict or a change of regime in their home country, and those for whom it is likely to last indefinitely unless they are given the chance to make a life in a new place, we need to use that distinction in a discussion of selection criteria, as will shortly become apparent.

2   Selection by Lottery?

Let's begin with the simple case in which a state is receiving more asylum applications than it is willing to accept, whether these are being lodged by refugees arriving at its borders, or through embassies or from camps in third countries. Once it has been determined that the applicants do indeed qualify as refugees, a selection needs to be made. One possibility would be to select via a lottery. This might seem to have certain advantages. A lottery is strategy-proof, in the sense that no one can gain an advantage by misrepresenting their situation. It also rules out partiality, say on the grounds of race or gender, on the part of the selectors. The lottery gives each refugee an equal chance of being chosen.[8] There are precedents for using lotteries to select immigrants. The best-known example is the US green card lottery, which each year awards immigration visas to 50,000 applicants out of a pool of nearly 10 million. Canada gives 10,000 family reunification places by lot to people wishing to bring in parents or grandparents. These programmes have their supporters, but they are also fiercely attacked by critics who object to someone's life-chances being determined in such a direct way by the luck of the draw. It's also relevant that these lottery mechanisms make up only a small part of the overall immigration regimes of the countries in question, allowing defenders of the green card lottery, for example, to argue that it serves to offset the bias of the system as a whole in favour of the highly qualified.[9]

---

[8] For a defence of lotteries that emphasizes their imperviousness to strategic behaviour on the part of the prospective beneficiaries, see J. Elster, 'Taming Chance: Randomisation in Individual and Social Decisions', *Tanner Lectures on Human Values*, 9 (1988), 107–79. Elster does, however, also provide a plausible explanation of our reluctance to allow important decisions to be decided by a random procedure such as a lottery.

[9] As one put it: 'This is the only instance where an average Joe, housewife or a mechanic, just an ordinary person – not a PhD holder, not a Harvard professor, not an engineer – could apply. And that continues to be the beauty of it. . . . Nowhere else are you going to find ordinary people, from different parts of the world, feeding the American melting pot and enriching the lives of Americans in the way this program does.' Available at www.theguardian.com/us-news/2017/may/02/green-cardlottery-us-immigration-trump-agenda.

It would be hard, however, to defend selection by lot in the case of refugees. A lottery system might be defensible when it is handing out golden tickets to a few, which seems to be the way the US green card lottery is usually regarded, but not when what is at stake is offering protection to people whose human rights are under threat. The lottery necessarily discards a great deal of information relevant to assessing a refugee's claim for admission, so unless reliable information is impossible to come by, not merely difficult to obtain, it's unacceptable as a selection mechanism. Even though by definition a refugee is someone whose human rights are under threat, the immediacy and severity of the threat will differ markedly from one person to another. The principle behind it – that each claimant should have an equal chance of success – should be set aside once we recognize that refugees are not all alike, and some will have stronger claims on our protection than others.[10]

3 Vulnerability as Grounds for Admission

So what are the factors that should determine the strength of a refugee's claim? Given that the source of the claim is the threat that the refugee faces to her human rights, it seems obvious that her degree of vulnerability must be the main factor. What we need to ask is whether it is the *only* one. Moreover, what 'vulnerability' means is less than clear-cut.[11] What makes one refugee more vulnerable than another? There appear to be two dimensions to this judgement: one is *urgency* – how *immediate* is the threat to the refugee's human rights if she remains where she is – and the other is *depth* – how serious is the harm she will suffer if not given

---

[10] John Broome has defended the use of lotteries in some cases where claims are unequal in strength on the grounds that this is what fairness requires: everyone should have some chance of getting the good that is being allocated. However, he concedes that this looks most plausible when the differences of strength are not too great. See J. Broome, 'Fairness', *Proceedings of the Aristotelian Society*, 91 (1990–91), 87–101. It may also be relevant here that the case for a lottery looks strongest when the allocation takes the form of a single unrepeated event; whereas in the case of refugees, those who are not selected in any one time period may have the chance to reapply at some later time, and this reinforces the case for selection on grounds of relative vulnerability, as I suggest below.

[11] For the purpose of this chapter, 'vulnerability' is to be understood as the threat to the refugee's human rights imposed by her own state or by other third parties. In a different sense, a refugee might be described as vulnerable to the decision of the state that is now considering her for asylum, since her life prospects in general will depend on whether or not her application is granted (for this wider conception of vulnerability, see R. Goodin, *Protecting the Vulnerable* [Chicago, IL: Chicago University Press, 1985], ch. 5). Vulnerability in this second sense does not in itself constitute grounds for admission, but it does impose a special duty of care on the state that is assessing her application. For a fuller discussion of this point, see Miller, *Strangers in our Midst*, pp. 83–85.

protection. Combining these dimensions gives a criterion that seems compelling: if there are refugees who are in imminent danger of losing their lives, or being tortured, for instance, then they should be given top priority for admission.

But now we must look at some complicating factors that qualify the judgement that refugees should be selected only on grounds of relative vulnerability. One is that while vulnerability may be the main criterion to be used when refugees are being considered for sanctuary, it is less obvious that it can do all of the work when selecting refugees for resettlement. In many cases resettlement will be offered to those who have already moved across an international border and are now living in a third country – perhaps in a city, perhaps in a purpose-built refugee camp. Although their human rights are not fully secure, they are not directly vulnerable to the severe threats in their country of origin that have turned them into refugees.[12] So if a person's vulnerability is measured by the immediacy and depth of the threat to their human rights, it may be very difficult to discriminate on such a basis between refugees in that category. If a selection for purposes of resettlement is going to be made, therefore, it seems that it has to be on grounds other than relative vulnerability – for example, how likely it is that the refugee will be able to repatriate safely in the near future or, alternatively, integrate successfully in the country that has so far provided her with asylum.

A second issue is about the source of vulnerability. What should we say about refugees who have special needs – special medical needs, for example – when these needs are not connected to the persecution that has turned them into refugees? Do they have stronger claims because they are more vulnerable overall, even though part of that vulnerability is due to

---

[12] It is difficult for those not directly involved in working with refugees to form an unbiased judgement about conditions of life for those who have crossed a border and settled in the global South, whether in a camp or elsewhere. The picture seems to vary considerably from one country to the next. Because those who are contained in camps are often prohibited from finding work outside, staying for more than a short period is likely to be a miserable experience. On the other hand, there are forms of local settlement, such as those sponsored by the Ugandan government, that give refugees more autonomy. For analysis, see Betts and Collier, *Refuge*, chs. 5 and 6; O. Bakewell, 'Encampment and Self-Settlement', in E. Fiddian-Qasmiyeh et al., *The Oxford Handbook of Refugee and Forced Migration Studies* (Oxford: Oxford University Press, 2014), pp. 127–38. The bleakest description of the condition of refugees in Kenya and Uganda, written from a confessedly partisan perspective, is G. Verdirame and B. Harrell-Bond, *Rights in Exile: Janus-Faced Humanitarianism* (New York: Berghahn Books, 2005). For a helpful synthesis, see S. Parekh, *Refugees and the Ethics of Forced Displacement* (New York: Routledge, 2017), ch. 1. For purposes of this chapter, I assume only that there are a substantial number of refugees who qualify for resettlement on the grounds that they have no decent future in the places they are currently settled, but whose basic human rights are not immediately at risk.

factors other than persecution? The UNHCR, in listing its grounds for resettlement, offers as one criterion a person's having severe medical needs that cannot be treated in the country of asylum; however, it also gives special weight to the claims of those who have been victims of violence or torture, suggesting that needs that arise directly from persecution may be treated differently from others.[13] So the underlying question here is whether we see the international refugee system as something established as a specific response to human rights threats posed by rogue or collapsing states, or whether we see it more broadly as discharging one part of a wider global responsibility to meet all human needs.[14] If we think that refugees make special claims of us by virtue of being refugees, then we are taking the former view, and this means that our obligations toward them *as* refugees are limited to counteracting the human rights threats they face, by providing refuge in one form or another. That means discounting medical or other needs that have arisen for independent reasons as grounds for selection. Of course there is no ban on doing more for the refugees who are accepted for admission, but this should not be a factor that affects the selection process itself.

This question about different possible ways of measuring vulnerability is also connected to a third issue, namely, whether besides considering vulnerability itself, we should also look at how far granting admission is likely to improve a person's situation. Obviously, removing someone directly from a danger zone is always going to improve their life chances very markedly. But if the question is where they are going to be offered sanctuary or resettlement – in one particular Western state – then how they are likely to fare in different places seems relevant at first sight. Someone who is illiterate, or who has very few work-related skills, may find it difficult to find proper employment if they are granted residence in a developed society. They may still be better off materially than they would be living in a refugee camp, but perhaps not much better off. Whereas someone who has professional skills is likely to find that their life chances improve very substantially, especially if they are offered the opportunity to resettle permanently.

There are parallels here to the debate in medical ethics over whether, with limited resources, we must always give priority to the patients who are currently worst off or whether we should also consider how effectively

---

[13] See UNHCR, *UNHCR Resettlement Handbook* (Geneva: UNHCR, 2011), ch. 6.
[14] The contrast between these two perspectives is further developed in the Introduction to this volume and in Chapter 1.

different patients can be treated. This might mean practising a form of triage whereby we prioritise those whose condition can be significantly improved, regardless of how ill they were initially. Presented with that dilemma, most people opt for an intermediate position which takes account of both how badly off patients are to start with and how far their condition can be improved with the resources available.[15] In more abstract terms, the question is whether when considering how to respond to people in need, we should take account only of the relative depth of their initial need, or also of how far that need can be relieved given our capacity to respond. You do not have to be a strict consequentialist to think that the second factor should play some role in our practical reasoning. But does the same form of reasoning also apply in the refugee case?

It does, but only with an important qualification. The refugee's claim for sanctuary or resettlement is based on the threat to her human rights. So all that should count is the extent to which her human rights situation can be improved by being admitted. Increasing opportunities over and above that basic standard – opportunities for higher education or a professional career, for example – should not. Suppose we consider two stylised characters – one, a person who is illiterate and the other, a trained medic – and ask who has the stronger claim to be resettled. We know that the medic will do far better than the person who is illiterate overall if resettlement is granted. The worry here is that if we select in favour of the medic for that reason, we are resolving a human rights dilemma on grounds that have nothing essentially to do with human rights. It may seem unfair that the medic should be advantaged *in this context* by allowing the fact that we can do much more to advance her higher interests to determine the outcome. In other words, while it might be relevant that one person's *human rights* situation can be improved more than another's by granting them admission, it is not relevant that one person's *overall* situation can be improved more than another's if the expected human rights improvement is similar in both cases.

Once again, the underlying issue here is whether when developing criteria for use in refugee selection, we should ask how much we can help each refugee overall, or how much we can help each refugee overcome the specific human rights deficits that have made her into a refugee. As we saw, the same question arises in relation to the problem of medical needs that

---

[15] For relevant evidence, see J. Hurley et al., 'Nonmarket Resource Allocation and the Public's Interpretation of Need: An Empirical Investigation in the Context of Health Care', *Social Choice and Welfare*, 49 (2017), 117–43.

have arisen independently of refugeehood. If Aziz has developed cataracts for genetic reasons, but is now housed in a refugee camp where specialist treatment is unavailable, should that count in favour of resettling him in Canada? (Assume that human rights are not immediately at stake: Aziz's sight is deteriorating, but only slowly.) From a general humanitarian perspective we may be inclined to say Yes, but if we are thinking strictly about Aziz's claims *as a refugee*, then we should consider only factors that are relevant to his status *as* a refugee, which disqualifies the cataracts.

So long as we are looking at the selection issue entirely from the refugee's perspective, therefore, severe vulnerability to human rights abuses, where it can be established, remains the paramount consideration. But there may be factors other than vulnerability that can help to bolster an admission claim. One such factor is family reunification, meaning here bringing back together immediate family members, that is, spouses and/or dependent children. This counts as a legitimate reason for a state to grant preference in immigration policy generally, and it also adds weight to a refugee's claim, since involuntary separation from one's family members by reason of state action breaches the human right to family life.[16] In this case the breach has presumably been caused by the actions that have turned one or both parties into refugees.[17] So the grant of sanctuary or resettlement can be seen as providing a remedy for a rights violation over and above the violations that have made the person into a refugee in the first place.

In the case of family reunification, what gives the refugee an additional claim against a particular state is simply the ongoing presence within that state of a relevant family member. But there are also cases in which the existence of a prior relationship between the refugee and the state itself adds weight to his claim. I have referred elsewhere to people in this position as 'particularity claimants'.[18] A case in point is where the receiving state has helped to create the conditions that have turned the person into a refugee – say, through an armed intervention that goes wrong and leads to

---

[16] For a fuller analysis and defence of family unification as grounds for admission, see M. Lister, 'The Rights of Families and Children at the Border', in E. Brake and L. Ferguson (eds.), *Philosophical Foundations of Children's and Family Law* (Oxford: Oxford University Press, 2018), pp. 153–70.

[17] What if one party has moved *voluntarily* to the receiving state, perhaps in anticipation that this would help strengthen the claim of her refugee partner or child? Well, first, clearly the family cannot be reunited in the state from which the refugee has fled, so long as the threat to his human rights persists there. But, second, what of the case where the refugee is seeking resettlement from a camp or some other place in a third country? Could it be argued that the family can be reunited if the voluntary migrant also moves to that third country? But this might involve, for example, swapping a secure life in Germany for an insecure life in Lebanon.

[18] Miller, *Strangers in Our Midst*, pp. 113–16; D. Miller, 'Justice in Immigration', *European Journal of Political Theory*, 14 (2015), 401–3.

social breakdown.[19] Here the refugee has a reparative claim at least for sanctuary and in most instances for resettlement if the breakdown persists. Similar considerations apply when a person has been forced to seek refuge as a result of having previously helped the state to which he is now claiming admission – say, as an interpreter or translator for an occupying force. I don't suggest that particularity claims of either kind should outweigh extreme vulnerability – where someone is in imminent danger of being killed or tortured if she is not granted sanctuary, that should be the decisive factor in prioritising her admission. But in third-country resettlement cases, these other factors should count. Recall that we are envisaging a situation in which states have each agreed to admit a certain refugee quota, and the issue is which refugees in particular are going to be offered sanctuary or resettlement. States, I believe, are obliged to take account of the effects of their own past actions when making these decisions.

4   The Receiving State's Perspective

Up to this point I have been examining the selection issue from the refugee's side, asking what factors might strengthen or weaken her claim to be admitted. But we also need to examine the issue from the perspective of the receiving state, where a different set of factors may seem relevant. Some refugees are likely to be costlier than others to receive and integrate, and equally some can be expected to create greater benefits than others as they contribute productively or culturally to the society they have joined. When a refugee quota is established, either unilaterally or through an agreement made between states, an estimate will have been made of the overall cost–benefit effect of taking in a certain number of refugees. Nevertheless, the state and its citizens still have a clear interest in selecting those refugees from whom they expect to derive the greatest benefit at least cost, using whatever metric of benefit and cost citizens deem to be relevant. Fulfilling the fair refugee quota is an obligation, but as with obligations generally, it is permissible to try to discharge it in the least burdensome way. The question is, are these considerations of cost and benefit legitimate grounds on which states can choose which refugees to admit?

They are not legitimate when refugees are being admitted, for either sanctuary or resettlement, as a result of an immediate threat to their human rights – in other words, they are moving directly from the state

---

[19] See the more extensive discussion in J. Souter, 'Towards a Theory of Asylum as Reparation for Past Injustice', *Political Studies*, 62 (2014), 326–42.

where their rights are under threat to a Western state. In these circumstances, the only selection criteria that can justifiably be used are those already discussed – the refugee's degree of vulnerability, together with special factors that already link her to the receiving state. Now when refugees are admitted in these circumstances, they are likely to be legally entitled to more than basic rights protection. Returning to the case of Aziz, for example, it may well be that if he is chosen, he will qualify to have his cataracts removed. So, accepting him will impose higher than average costs on the medical system. But it would be wrong to discriminate against him on that basis. When considering his claim, I argued that it was not strengthened by having greater needs when these needs had nothing inherently to do with his condition as a refugee. But nor I think should he be penalised at the point of selection because our medical system operates in such a way that he will in fact receive the same attention as a citizen would. In principle, it would be legitimate to limit the benefits available to those offered only sanctuary, even though it would certainly also be mean-spirited. Their claim is to have their human rights adequately protected, not to enjoy all of the benefits that a state provides for its own citizens. Since that is all we are morally obliged to offer, it would be wrong to disfavour Aziz at the point of selection on the grounds that in practice we will provide him with more, at some cost. In sanctuary cases, then, selection should be special-needs blind.

The position looks rather different, however, in resettlement cases where the human rights of the person being granted that status are not under immediate threat. For here what is being offered goes considerably beyond the protection of basic rights. The refugee is being given the opportunity to join the implicit social contract that the arrangements of a liberal democracy embody. He will in due course have access to the full set of social and political rights that other citizens possess. It therefore seems reasonable to ask, as with immigrants generally, whether he is likely to be a net contributor to the scheme or a net liability. This will depend on factors such as the talents and skills he already has or will be able to acquire, and conversely on the demands he can be expected to make on the welfare state. Assume that the state is discharging its international obligations by taking in N refugees, its quota under a fair distribution of responsibility. If it is going to offer permanent settlement to some $n < N$ of these, why shouldn't it be allowed to select the n by considering the net contribution they are likely to make, while choosing the remaining $N - n$ on grounds of immediately vulnerability?[20]

---

[20] As one illustration of this approach in practice, consider Robert Vineberg's proposal that in the case of Government-Assisted Refugees in Canada, there should be a 50–50 split between those who are

The problem with this proposal comes into view, however, when we think about the distribution of refugees between states. For what is being proposed is in effect that state S should be allowed to cherry-pick the n resettlement candidates whose human rights are not immediately at risk. If a burden-sharing scheme for refugees is going to be fair, quotas must be set on the basis that the overall profile of the refugees going to each state will be approximately the same – the numbers will vary according to the capacities of the receiving state, but the make-up of the group will be similar. So, if a state begins to cherry-pick on cost–benefit grounds, it is imposing an unfair burden on other states, who will have to take in a disproportionate number of more costly refugees – those who are low skilled or who have special needs, for example. If, in response, other states also begin to cherry-pick, then what happens will depend on the preferences of the favoured refugees who can expect to receive multiple offers – with no guarantee that the outcome will preserve fairness between countries.

Note, though, that this objection to selection on grounds of expected net contribution assumes that all states will use the same criteria when assessing contribution. But this need not be so. Some features are likely to be prized by only a minority of states. Language competence is perhaps the clearest example. Only a few states will value the ability to speak German; similarly with Portuguese. There may also be specific occupational skills of which the same is true. In that case the objection to cherry-picking, that it leaves other states with a disproportionate number of more socially costly refugees, is dissipated. If Germany is permitted to favour German-speakers and Portugal to favour Portuguese-speakers, this does not seem unfair to other countries (unless language competence is strongly correlated with some other feature such as level of education).

One might take this further, and advocate what has been called a matching system for refugees.[21] The proposal here is that when states are cooperating under a burden-sharing scheme, they should be asked to specify the characteristics that they value in refugees, while the refugees themselves should be allowed to rank-order the countries in which they

most in need of refuge and those who are most likely to establish themselves in Canada within a year (i.e., integrate successfully). See R. Vineberg, 'Canada's Refugee Strategy: How It Can Be Improved', *University of Calgary School of Public Policy Publications*, 11 (2018), available at https:// d3n8a8pro7vhmx.cloudfront.net/cdfai/pages/3533/attachments/original/1523488412/Canadas_ Refugee_Strategy.pdf?1523488412.

21 See W. Jones and A. Teytelboym, 'Matching Systems for Refugees', *Journal on Migration and Human Security*, 5 (2017), 667–81; W. Jones and A. Teytelboym, 'The International Refugee Match: A System That Respects Refugees' Preferences and the Priorities of States', *Refugee Survey Quarterly*, 36 (2017), 84–109.

might be given the right to settle. A computer algorithm would then determine the optimal allocation of particular refugees to particular countries, given the overall quotas that had already been agreed. Defenders of this proposal point to its efficiency when compared with a random system of allocation, and the fact that it gives some weight to the preferences of the refugees themselves (without of course guaranteeing that every refugee is offered resettlement in their top-choice country).

These are important virtues of a matching system, but the issue of fairness remains, unless we assume that refugees' preferences are quite heterogeneous, in which case we might expect that each country will be allocated a sizable number of refugees who would be ranked highly by its own criteria. If refugees' country rankings converge, on the other hand, then the system will assign the most-favoured countries the refugees they are most keen to accept, which, we can assume, will often be the ones who are easiest to integrate, are expected to be most economically productive, and do not have special needs. So there will unavoidably be trade-offs between efficiency, sensitivity to the agency of the refugees themselves in choosing their country of resettlement, and fairness between the receiving states who have agreed to participate in the matching scheme.[22]

5   Why Some Selection Criteria Are Inadmissible

What this discussion has revealed more generally is that, in resettlement cases, there may be good reasons to allow states to select refugees on grounds other than relative vulnerability, subject to considerations of fairness *between* states when a burden-sharing scheme is in place. In this last section of the chapter I want to look more closely at the selection criteria that might be used in this context. Intuitively, some seem more acceptable than others, but what explains this?

We have little difficulty in understanding why selection on grounds of race is unacceptable: it merely bows to the prejudices of some citizens, while failing to capture any feature of the applicant that is relevant to her entry into the social contract. Nor, on the other hand, do we have a problem in explaining why it should be legitimate to select people for permanent settlement when they can show that they have skills that are in

---

[22] To tackle the fairness issue, a monetary compensation scheme might be proposed for states that find that they are allotted a disproportionate number of 'expensive' refugees. Although this would not require putting a price on the head of individual refugees, it might still be accused of stigmatising groups of refugees, whereas it is a claimed virtue of the matching scheme itself that no monetisation of refugees is involved.

high demand: there are benefits to both sides in using this as a criterion. The difficult cases are those that involve features that are de facto relevant to the refugee's capacity to integrate successfully, such as their ethnic or religious background, but that we may still feel are illegitimate as selection criteria.

Note first that these features may well be morally relevant when they correlate with special vulnerability – that is, when people are being oppressed in their home country precisely on account of their ethnic or religious affiliation. That could justify selecting them ahead of others for either sanctuary or resettlement. The problem arises with cultural attributes that are not in themselves relevant sources of vulnerability, yet affect their bearer's capacity to function well in the society he is joining. What explains this? One reason might be the norms of behaviour embedded in the refugee's home culture, which may be closer to, or more distant from, the norms of the receiving society. Norms governing how men and women should behave to one another are an oft-cited example. Someone who arrives with strongly held patriarchal values will find it harder to adjust to a society where equality between the sexes is the proclaimed norm, if not always the reality. A patriarchal father may be unwilling to allow his wife to find paid work, or his daughters to complete their education, with obvious implications for equality of opportunity and social mobility. Another reason may be the presence or absence within the host society of groups with the same cultural background as the refugee. We know empirically that immigrants of all kinds tend to do best when they are able to interact with denizens who share their cultural background, and immigration choices will often reflect this. For both these reasons, a refugee's cultural background is likely to determine how easy it is for her to integrate, measured by markers such as learning the local language and finding a job. So if, as I am assuming, 'ability to integrate' is a legitimate reason when considering candidates for resettlement (though not for sanctuary), then we may be tempted to conclude that cultural selection is sometimes permissible.

Yet we may still feel uneasy about this conclusion. Cultural selection just sounds wrong. One reason for thinking so is that it might serve as a proxy for racism, if the culturally favoured groups happen also to be largely white. That is no doubt a real possibility in practice, but it can be set aside here on the grounds that most criteria of selection, however defensible in themselves, might be adopted for indefensible reasons. I will also set aside a second challenge to cultural selection, namely, that if we select refugees on this basis, we seem simply to be embracing the status quo – that is, we are favouring those whose cultural norms are closest to the ones we happen to have already, and/or those who belong to cultural groups who are already well represented in our society, and these, it might be argued, are merely arbitrary facts, open to change. However, although the present cultural configuration of our society is indeed in one sense arbitrary, it is still a hard fact, unchangeable in the short term, and therefore relevant to how refugees from different backgrounds will actually fare. In other words, although it may be an accident of history that our society already hosts a thriving community of Sikhs, say, it is surely relevant to the question whether incoming Sikhs are likely to integrate successfully, as compared with other immigrants.

The real problem with cultural selection, I believe, lies elsewhere. To understand what is wrong with it, consider by analogy racial profiling – practices like police stop-and-search operations aimed at members of groups known to have a higher than average likelihood of carrying drugs or concealed weapons. Profiling of this kind is objectionable because it targets individuals on the basis of a statistical fact about the group they belong to – membership being assigned externally by skin colour – rather than on the basis of pertinent facts about them as individuals. It attaches a significant burden – being regularly stopped by the police in a way likely to cause significant anxiety and distress – on the basis of an assumption that in the case of any particular individual may be entirely false.[23] The analogy, I suggest, is that if a person is disadvantaged in refugee selection by virtue of belonging to a cultural group that is perceived as less likely to integrate successfully, this also imposes an unfair burden on them as an individual.[24] After all, they might be eager to throw off their inherited culture, or adapt it creatively so as to fit more easily into the society they are joining. Of course, we have no reliable way of knowing that in the case of any particular refugee, but this just shows that we should not make selection decisions on the basis of guesses about how easy or hard it will be for a person to integrate culturally. The contrast here is with job-related skills, where a selection agency can often determine reliably enough

---

[23] For conflicting views about the level of harm that racially profiled groups such as African Americans will suffer as a consequence of police profiling, see M. Risse and R. Zeckhauser, 'Racial Profiling', *Philosophy and Public Affairs*, 32 (2004), 131–70; A. Lever, 'Why Racial Profiling Is Hard to Justify: A Response to Risse and Zeckhauser', *Philosophy and Public Affairs*, 33 (2005), 94–110.

[24] Notice also that there are no offsetting benefits that accrue to the members of the disadvantaged group, unlike the social order benefits that Risse and Zeckhauser suggest will mitigate the harm that blacks suffer from racial profiling by the police, in their (qualified) defence of the practice.

whether a person has the skills and qualifications that will enable her to find paid work in the society she has applied to join.

6 Conclusion

To conclude, I have been exploring the grounds on which liberal states may select refugees for admission, on the assumption that selection will be unavoidable in the third-best world we currently inhabit. The distinction between offering (notionally short-term) sanctuary and (notionally permanent) resettlement turned out to be important. I considered briefly the idea of selection by lot, but claimed that this was unacceptable where we have clear evidence about the relative strength of refugees' claims. I argued that when sanctuary alone was being offered, the main ground of selection should be vulnerability – the depth and urgency of the threat to the refugee's human rights – though some weight may also be given to personal factors linking the refugee to a particular state. But when resettlement is being offered to refugees currently living elsewhere but whose rights are not immediately at risk, it is reasonable in addition to consider their capacity to integrate and become contributing members of the society they join, so long as this does not involve 'skimming the cream off the milk' at the expense of other refugee-receiving societies. And finally I suggested why selection by cultural background was wrong, even though we may have statistical evidence about how refugees from different backgrounds are likely to fare if admitted.

My hope is that these proposals can pass the twin tests of ethical acceptability and democratic legitimacy. As citizens, we have a legitimate interest in preserving social cohesion and the conditions for what Rawls called 'a well-ordered society'. But we also have obligations to help protect the human rights of outsiders, especially those whose own states deprive them of the opportunity for a decent life. These two imperatives can perhaps never be perfectly reconciled, but a refugee selection policy of the kind I have described responds to them both, and offers a resolution.

CHAPTER 6

Refugees and the Right to Remain

Adam Omar Hosein

1 Introduction

Governments have often used deportation to limit their populations of refugees and asylum-seekers. The purposes of deportation include preventing people from filing asylum claims at all, removing those whose claims have been rejected, transferring responsibility for refugees to other countries, and repatriating refugees who have already been living in a country for some time.

The different forms of deportation just mentioned, I will argue, raise quite different moral issues. I will begin by considering situations where states remove asylum-seekers fairly quickly after their arrival. I will then turn to asylum-seekers and refugees who are likely to spend, or have already spent, a substantial period in the receiving country. I will ask whether these people are owed a 'right to remain', which grants them the legal assurance that they can live in the territory indefinitely. I will contrast three approaches to this right, the Samaritan approach, the affiliation approach, and the autonomy approach, arguing that the autonomy approach provides the strongest basis for a right to remain.

Let me first explain some background assumptions of the chapter. First, I will assume that states, as a default, have moral discretion over who is permitted to enter their territories. This is mainly because the central discussions of refugees, in politics and the law, in addition to political theory, take place against that background: international law, for instance, includes no general requirement on states to admit immigrants, and refugee treaties are intended to carve out an exception. All the same, my arguments will also be of interest to 'open borders' theorists, who believe that states are morally required to admit each person that wishes to immigrate. The open borders view entails straightforwardly that all asylum-seekers should be admitted and permitted to remain indefinitely. But in a world of significant political constraints on the admission of immigrants and grants of the right to remain, open borders theorists must consider whom to prioritize, and the arguments here will help to answer that question by exploring when asylum-seekers and refugees have especially weighty claims to remain in a territory. I will also narrow my inquiry in a second way: I will be considering what states are permitted to do *unilaterally*, in the absence of substantial global cooperation in distributing refugees across territories. This will allow me to set aside large institutional questions about what such cooperation would look like and also means that the discussion will be more relevant to present circumstances, where such cooperation is relatively weak. Finally, I will assume that states have *some* non-trivial reasons to want to avoid admitting refugees or allowing them to settle indefinitely. This assumption is clearly controversial, especially given the evidence that, at least in the medium to long term, refugees can bring large economic and other benefits to a country. But it is worth making here since political debates about the right to remain generally occur in a context in which some parties believe there are such reasons. Now some (though certainly not all) philosophers will say that this assumption is far too concessive to those who want to deny the right to remain, since those people are, these philosophers will say, exaggerating the costs of granting the right. I am sympathetic to the views of these philosophers, but I suggest that it is still worth seeing whether it is possible to make an argument under my assumptions since, as Rawls points out, 'one task of political philosophy – its practical role, let's say – is to focus on deeply disputed questions and to see whether, despite appearances, some underlying basis of philosophical and moral agreement can be uncovered'.[1]

2 Refugees, Refoulement, and Asylum

Most discussions of deportation of people seeking asylum have focused on when those people should count as refugees, a matter of ongoing debate discussed in detail elsewhere in this volume. For present purposes, let us just say, crudely, that to count as a refugee someone must be 'under threat' in their home country, leaving open the question of what this threat must look like (for instance, whether, say, potential starvation counts, or just persecution on the basis of a protected category).[2] And let us also say that

---

[1] J. Rawls, *Justice as Fairness: A Restatement* (Cambridge, MA: Belknap Press of Harvard University Press, 2001), p. 2.
[2] I also set aside further definitional questions such as just how likely it must be that the person will be persecuted in their home country for them to count as under threat.

to count as a refugee they must be displaced from their country of origin to another territory, which we will call the 'receiving country'.

What happens when an individual can show that they were under threat in their home country? The basic legal protection this person is guaranteed – for instance, by the 1951 UN Convention – is *non-refoulement*: the right that they not be returned to the place where they were under threat (or removed to any other country where they will be under threat). The right to *non-refoulement* does not include any entitlement – sometimes referred to as a 'durable solution' – to participate fully in the receiving society. For instance, the displaced individual need not be given the opportunity to work, or receive social assistance, or travel freely within the receiving country. Most crucially for our purposes, it does not imply any right to remain: to live in the receiving society indefinitely, without fear of removal. For while respecting *non-refoulement* prevents the receiving country from sending a refugee back to their home state, it is compatible with, for instance, sending them to some *other* state (assuming they will not be under threat there also).

Though the UN Convention makes clear that states must not return refugees, it leaves them much freer to withhold asylum within their own territory. People who entered the state without legal permission – such as the tens of thousands of Central Americans entering the United States via the US–Mexico border without prior authorization – need not be granted asylum there even if they can show that they are under threat in their home countries. The conditions for when asylum should be granted have remained disputed and often vague. This gap was exploited by, for instance, the German government in 1993, which introduced new constitutional provisions allowing the government to deport asylum-seekers to other 'safe' countries – places where they would not be under threat – that they had already passed through on their way to Germany.[3] (Though of course in recent years the German government has been relatively generous to asylum-seekers and refugees.) When states do grant asylum within their own territory, the Convention leaves them relatively free to choose which mix of rights to grant the migrants beyond a minimum of rights to police protection, access to the courts, and so on. For example, in the late 1990s Australia announced that people who had entered without authorization, but gone on to prove that they were refugees, would be given only

---

[3] M. J. Gibney, *The Ethics and Politics of Asylum: Liberal Democracy and the Response to Refugees* (Cambridge: Cambridge University Press, 2004), pp. 100–106.

temporary visas, allowing them to work but withholding the opportunity to bring their families or the security of a permanent right to remain.

We thus need to disaggregate the package of rights that might come with asylum. In this chapter, I will focus specifically on the right to remain. In addressing this issue, we will see, it is important to keep separate some different categories of asylum-seeker and different conditions of removal or potential removal. I will begin by considering removal of people who have only recently entered a territory and then turn to my main focus: people who will be, or have been, present in a territory for a longer period.

3   Swift Removal

Some states have tried to enforce their borders by immediately removing asylum-seekers. The 1993 German example cited earlier was like that: the goal was to remove the arrivals as soon as possible – a second-best option to preventing them from arriving in the territory at all. The typical goal of these measures is both to reduce the number of asylum-seekers whose claims are processed in the territory and to reduce the number of people who are ultimately admitted as refugees.

When are these policies permitted? *Non-refoulement* constraints of course require that the refugee be sent to a genuinely safe country. A gay refugee fleeing discrimination in Uganda would not be protected in the United Arab Emirates, which maintains the death penalty for 'homosexual activity'. Likewise, when a Swedish student in 2018 attempted to prevent an Afghan man from being deported back to his country of origin, her argument was that 'people [in Afghanistan] are not sure of any safety', while the government's argument was that civilians were no longer under serious threat. These disputes turn ultimately on who counts as genuinely under threat in a particular country.

What if someone is deported to a safe country? Does this violate their rights? The *sheer* fact of someone's qualifying as a refugee does not seem to entitle them to remain in any *particular* state. Let us briefly consider two broad approaches (I will not try to adjudicate between them here).[4] The first approach says that the obligation to admit refugees is ultimately a humanitarian one. Refugees are simply people in need, or perhaps people

---

[4] For a more detailed discussion of these approaches, see Chapter 1 in this volume.

in need who can be helped only by admission to another country.[5] An alternative approach says that obligations to admit refugees are *political*: they arise because we live in a world of separate states and because of the need to justify this global institutional arrangement to each person. Refugees are people who are denied the right to live under a legitimate government, something that the global order ought to secure for everyone.[6] On each of these theories, responsibilities to refugees are, in the first instance, collective: the obligation on humanity as a whole to ensure that each individual has their basic needs met or the obligation on the international order of states to ensure that each individual lives under a legitimate government, which is to say a government that has the right to rule over those under its jurisdiction. These duties are satisfied as long as each refugee is admitted *somewhere* other than their home country where their needs are met, and so a refugee cannot demand that they be admitted to some particular country. Thus, a state that deports refugees to a safe country is not denying a refugee their fundamental entitlement: to be in *a* country where they are not under threat.

Still, we might ask whether said state is failing to do its part in contributing to the collective goal of helping refugees. *Fairness* seems to matter here: it is unfair to expect any individual state to discharge in its entirety a duty that falls on the collective, and it also seems unfair for states with lesser capacity to admit more refugees than those with greater capacity.[7] Now, we have been discussing people who qualify as refugees. But what about those whose status is uncertain: asylum-seekers who might not qualify and whose claims have yet to be adjudicated? States deport asylum-seekers partly to limit their refugee populations, but also to avoid the burden of processing asylum claims. States – including those in Europe and North America – have often insisted on returning asylum-seekers to third countries where they could have filed a claim, insisting that their claims must ultimately be processed in those countries. These steps are consistent with the language of the Convention, which protects from removal only those who enter the country without authorization but

---

[5] See M. Lister, 'Who Are Refugees?', *Law and Philosophy*, 32 (2013), 645–67, for an argument that we need to include the 'can only be helped' qualification. Myself, I prefer a slightly different standard of 'can best be helped', but this complication can be set aside for present purposes.

[6] For a much more detailed explanation of the differences between these two approaches and their respective merits, see my book *The Ethics of Migration: An Introduction* (London: Routledge, 2019).

[7] For a discussion of fairness in the context of humanitarian duties to refugees, see D. Owen, 'Refugees, Fairness and Taking Up the Slack: On Justice and the International Refugee Regime', *Moral Philosophy and Politics*, 3 (2016), 141–64.

directly from countries of persecution. Issues of fairness also arise when such steps are taken. If there is a collective duty to make sure that refugees are admitted to safe countries, there is also a collective duty to identify which people qualify as refugees, and the burdens of this identification process, the establishment of institutions, the funding of officers, and so on should be shared fairly.

It is, of course, difficult to determine exactly what fairness demands in the processing or admission of asylum-seekers: Should a state's responsibilities be determined by its GDP, population density, institutional stability, or some other factor(s)? I cannot answer that large question here, but I would like to explain the relationship between fairness and deportation. Suppose that we know what fairness demands and can say whether an individual state is admitting its fair share. What happens when some states are not pulling their weight?

Removal can be a way of enforcing requirements of fairness. Suppose that we have agreed to an apartment swap – you will use my place for the weekend while I use yours – yet I intentionally fail to leave you a key and you are stuck out in the cold. If you can get into the apartment anyway, perhaps by climbing in through a window, you are permitted to so (at least assuming that climbing through the window does not cause major destruction to the property). You would not be violating any property right of mine, since, given that I am under a duty to let you use it, I have no right against you that you not use it.

Likewise, if some safe countries are not admitting their fair share of refugees, then deporting refugees to those countries can be a way of compelling them to fulfil their duties of fairness.[8] States are under a duty to accept their fair share of refugees into their territory. They thus have no right against those refugees entering the territory or other countries deporting the refugees to their territory. Of course, such steps will be successful only if those countries in fact admit the refugees, but deportation is at least a method of putting pressure on those countries. Take, for example, Italy's late spring 2018 measures to prevent asylum-seeker boats from landing on its shores, ultimately resulting in the diversion of the boats toward Spain. Given its southern geographical position, Italy has – compared with many other European nations, including Spain – processed

---

[8] Of course, there is a potential disanalogy between the apartment example and the case of refugees: in the first case the original duty is acquired voluntarily, whereas in the latter case it is not. But this should not affect the analysis: the key general principle is that when you have a duty to ensure X you have no right against others ensuring that X occurs (at least assuming that the means they use do not cause excessive harm).

and admitted a disproportionate number of asylum-seekers crossing the Mediterranean, and the measure was ultimately successful in causing the Spanish government to accept the migrants. Now, there are multiple concerns that could be raised about these non-arrival tactics, including their risks for migrants who may be running out of provisions on their boats. My point here is just that one potential justification for them is enforcing fairness, and deportation can be viewed in a similar light.

According to a common line of thought in the literature – as in Wellman's account, for instance – states do not have to actually admit *any* refugees, even though they share in the global responsibility to protect refugees, and they can do their part in serving the world's needy by, for instance, contributing foreign aid instead.[9] We have been considering people who cannot be helped through aid because they are already displaced and would be at risk on return to their home countries. Must a state admit some share of these people? Here too Wellman might say that a state need only contribute to ensuring that they are admitted to some safe country, not necessarily into its own territory. Thus a state might say it is permitted to deport refugees to another safe country as long as it is willing to help offset the costs of resettling the refugees there. The trouble with this suggestion is that it would involve a strategy of 'cross and compensate': violating a right with the intention of correcting the wrong through compensation.[10] Although offering compensation is an appropriate remedial response to a rights violation, it does not render the initial rights violation justified. Compare again the apartment example. It would not be permissible for me to lock you out of the apartment but send a cheque at a later date to offset any costs and suffering you incurred that night as a result of having to find somewhere else to stay.

Let me briefly review my conclusions so far. We have seen when and why a state may deport a recently arrived asylum-seeker. Whether the asylum-seeker can be returned to their home country depends on whether they count as a refugee. Whether they can be removed to a 'safe' third country depends on whether it would be *fair* to expect the third country to process the asylum-seeker's claims and potentially admit them. Deportation can be a legitimate means of pressuring that country to admit its fair share of refugees and bear its fair share of the burdens of processing asylum-seekers.

[9] C. H. Wellman, 'Immigration and Freedom of Association', *Ethics*, 119 (2008), 109–41.
[10] The phrase comes from R. Nozick, *Anarchy, State, and Utopia* (New York: Basic Books, 1974).

4   Longer-Term Stays and the Right to Remain

Suppose that an asylum-seeker stays in the territory beyond their immediate arrival. We have already seen that *non-refoulement* provisions prevent a state from deporting an asylum-seeker who arrives at its borders to any country where they would be under threat: they must be granted refugee status. This provision applies beyond the point of initial arrival to any time during which the asylum-seeker is present in the territory. But as we have seen, a state can meet the *non-refoulement* requirement while still reserving the option of removing them at any time to a safe third country or back to their home country at a point when it has become safe for them. When should an asylum-seeker be fully shielded from this possibility, given assurance that they will never be removed? I will refer to a shield of this kind as a (legal) 'right to remain'. In the remainder of the chapter I focus on whether and when asylum-seekers who are present for a long period of time should be granted this right to remain, understood as a legal right to live in the receiving country indefinitely.

Let me begin by distinguishing a little more carefully between some different ways that an asylum-seeker or refugee can ultimately come to reside in a receiving country for a substantial period of time (without having an unlimited right to remain). One way is for there to be significant delays in the assessment of their application, especially once we factor in potentially lengthy appeals processes. Immigration courts often have (owing in part to lack of government support) significant lack of capacity to deal with large flows of asylum-seekers. For instance, in December 2015, United States Citizenship and Immigration Services conducted 2,000 asylum interviews and completed 2,300 cases. But there remained more than 128,000 pending applications.[11] In recent years, lengthy processing times have also often been combined with significant periods of detention while the applications are reviewed.[12] Another way asylum-seekers can have extended stays is for them to be granted asylum and given some form of permit to remain in the country for a limited duration, and for these permits to be renewed a sufficient number of times. Haitian nationals seeking refuge in the United States in 2010 following the severe

---

[11] T. Aleinikoff et al. (eds.), *Immigration and Citizenship: Process and Policy*, 7th ed. (St. Paul, MN: West Academic Publishing, 2011), p. 795.
[12] S. J. Silverman, 'The Difference That Detention Makes: Reconceptualizing the Boundaries of the Normative Debate on Immigration Control', in A. Sager (ed.), *The Ethics and Politics of Immigration: Core Issues and Emerging Trends* (London: Rowman and Littlefield, 2016), pp. 105–24.

earthquake were given eighteen-month permits, which were renewed several times by the Obama administration. A third source of a long-term stay is for a refugee to be granted a conditional right to live indefinitely in the country – where conditions might include refraining from committing certain kinds of crime – and for them either to remain in the country for a long period without violating those conditions *or* to violate the conditions but not be subjected to removal proceedings until some years later. For example, in the United States in 2018 the Trump administration relied on such conditions to deport some Cambodian refugees who had been admitted following the Vietnam War.[13] In many cases, the crimes used to justify deportation had been committed more than twenty years earlier.

We can also distinguish between two different perspectives on an asylum-seeker's length of stay.[14] First, we can think *prospectively* about the length of time for which an asylum-seeker is likely to remain in the country. Second, we can look *retrospectively* at how long they have already been present. While the latter is in principle a relatively simple inquiry, requiring assessment of documents and so on proving the length of stay, the former necessarily involves complicated assessments of probabilities. We have seen some different ways in which a stay might become extended, and we can consider these possibilities in advance. For instance, considering recent processing times, the number of immigration judges available, and so on can give us an idea of how long it will take for someone's asylum application to be assessed. We can also look at some further factors that are likely to increase the chance of an individual leaving (or being removed) more quickly. For example, the nature of the conditions in their home country will be relevant. The quicker those conditions are expected to become more favourable, the more likely it is that the individual will wish to return to their home country or for the state to be able to remove them in the near future without violating *non-refoulement* requirements.

Having distinguished the prospective and retrospective inquiries, we can also see two different ways in which a right to remain might be justified on grounds of a refugee's length of stay. They might be given a right to remain based on the *expectation* that they will be present for a longer period, or they might be given a right to remain based on their *history* of presence in

---

[13] K. Yam, 'The U.S. Just Quietly Deported the Largest Group of Cambodians Ever', *Huffington Post*, 7 April 2018. Available at www.huffingtonpost.com/entry/cambodians-deported-trump-immigration_us_5ac77dd9e4b07a3485e3da6c.

[14] These two different perspectives were first proposed to me by Adam Cox, and are mentioned in our joint paper. (A. B. Cox and A. O. Hosein, 'Immigration and Equality', unpublished manuscript.)

the country. In what follows I will consider how different theories – initially developed to deal with authorized migration – might justify a right to remain, based on either a history of substantial presence or an expectation of substantial presence. What counts as substantial? Let us assume at least ten years: enough time to count as a major chapter in a human life (the different theories we will look at will provide different reasons for thinking that time matters, and thus the precise length required will likely vary too).

The Samaritan Approach

One approach to the right to remain treats it as a required 'Samaritan' (in Michael Blake's words) response to crucial human needs, defined as those which must be satisfied for someone to lead a life of basic decency.[15] The ability to remain can become a crucial need because of the attachments people form to particular countries. When and why exactly is being able to remain a crucial need? Joseph Carens's familiar suggestion is that this need grows out of the fact that people put down roots when they live in a particular place:

> Connections grow: to spouses and partners, sons and daughters, friends and neighbors and fellow-workers, people we love and people we hate. Experiences accumulate: birthdays and braces, tones of voice and senses of humor, public parks and corner stores, the shape of the streets and the way the sun shines through the leaves, the smell of flowers and the sounds of local accents, the look of the stars and the taste of the air – all that gives life its purpose and texture.[16]

As should be clear, the Samaritan approach directs us to look retrospectively at a migrant's stay in a territory when deciding whether a state ought to grant the right to remain. The best proxy for how strong people's 'roots' in a place are, Carens emphasizes, is how long someone has already been present, and so the right to remain should be granted to asylum-seekers and refugees who have lived in a territory for a sufficiently long time. Certainly, refugees who are admitted into a country start to interact with its social life, physical space, and so on. And Carens is surely right that the effect is strongest for those who are admitted at a young age, since their

---

[15] M. Blake, 'Equality without Documents: Political Justice and the Right to Amnesty', *Canadian Journal of Philosophy*, 40 (2010), 99–122.

[16] J. Carens, *The Ethics of Immigration* (New York: Oxford University Press, 2013), p. 150.

basic self-conceptions, understandings of social interactions, and so on are formed then.

Does the Samaritan approach succeed in justifying a right to remain (for those who have been present in a territory for a substantial period)? Blake accepts that being removed will be a very significant disruption for the person who has put down roots, but questions whether the person removed will really face a life below the level of basic decency. After all, he points out, (post-)graduate students often spend many years in foreign countries, five to ten maybe, and few people think that when they return home they are living a life beneath human decency. Furthermore, one might add, many people are willing to bear those costs, to tear themselves out of a community, in order to take a job or other attractive opportunity in another country.

Is there a way to resurrect the Samaritan justification for a right to remain? Blake proposes a revised argument which says that while (typical) graduate students who must return to their home countries may not be suffering enormous harm, people from very poor countries who must return are facing such harm. In favour of adopting this approach here, we can note that asylum-seekers and refugees who are returned to their home countries typically face the *compound* harm of having to give up their ties to the host countries and having to live under difficult conditions (even if they are not, strictly speaking, 'under threat'). An agent who can alleviate significant harm to another while bearing only low costs, Blake argues, must do so. And, he suggests, it costs a receiving country relatively little to allow a migrant who has been present for a long period to remain.

This version of the argument still faces difficulties. Recall two assumptions that we are making here. First, we are assuming that the people deported are going to situations where – while they may not be very well off – they are still getting everything they are owed by the global community. This is true whether they are deported to their home countries or safe third countries. In other words, we are operating in a dialectical context where any harms associated with living in one of those countries are being downplayed. Second, we are also assuming that the receiving country faces non-trivial costs in granting the right to remain. Thus, the interests of the migrants must be weighed against the state's own interests. With these assumptions in place, it seems that the harms of being uprooted will have to do much of the heavy lifting in this argument: they will have to be substantial enough to make the total harm done to the migrant through deportation disproportionate to the relevant costs to the state. But, we have already seen, there are good reasons to question the scale of those uprooting harms.

I thus suggest that the revised argument is unable to support as a general matter granting the right to remain to asylum-seekers and refugees based solely on their length of stay. It is, however, I suggest, plausibly able to support granting a right to remain in a narrower set of cases. For example, a refugee whose family ties would be severed when they are removed (suppose my partner is unable to join me in my home country because they remain a suspected political dissident) faces very substantial harm. And someone who is relatively integrated in a country – linguistically, for instance – will be little or no burden (and indeed likely a benefit) to the host country. In cases such as these, the migrant's interests are likely to be sufficiently weighty relative to the interests of the state that it would be wrong to remove them. This conclusion is significant for current policy disputes. In the United States, for example, judicial discretion in removal proceedings – which would allow a judge to take into account a migrant's particular circumstances – has been highly circumscribed, and the considerations just raised tell in favour of loosening it.

In sum, the Samaritan approach does not seem able to support an across-the-board right to remain for all who have been present for a significant period of time, though it does provide a basis for an individualized assessment of particular individuals' circumstances, justifying a right to remain where the burdens of removal are especially high and the costs to the receiving society of granting the right to remain are relatively low.

The Affiliation Approach

According to the affiliation approach, the right to remain should be granted not because of a Samaritan duty on the state to help alleviate need in general, but because of a claim that specific people have against the state to remain.[17] Citizens and permanent residents have various special claims against the state – entitling them to vote, access public benefits, and so on – and so too, Hiroshi Motomura argues, some asylum-seekers and refugees have a special claim against the state: an entitlement to remain.[18] The people who have that claim are those who have become 'enmeshed'

---

[17] I use 'claim' here instead of 'right' to make clear that I am talking about a *moral* claim, as opposed to a legal right to remain.

[18] H. Motomura, *Americans in Waiting: The Lost Story of Immigration and Citizenship in the United States* (New York: Oxford University Press, 2006).

with a society by sharing interactions and bonds of identity. In the same
vein, Carens gives an argument (which we should distinguish from the
Samaritan approach, even though they rest on somewhat similar observations) that 'social membership' in a society gives one a claim to remain
there. Unlike the Samaritan approach, the affiliation approach focusses not
on individual needs but on the obligations and entitlements that come
with having certain relationships to other people and institutions. Relationships with family members, friends, members of a social club, and so
on all seem to trigger obligations and entitlements, and on the affiliation
approach having certain bonds with a society is a trigger for the entitlement to remain.

What exactly does it take to form the appropriate bonds with a society,
to become sufficiently enmeshed in it? The affiliation approach follows a
similar track here to the Samaritan approach in the relationships that it
focusses on (though the moral significance of these relationships is quite
different on the two approaches). Immigrants, as they become more settled
in a society, join churches, helping to run their fundraisers and participating in their ecclesiastical life, or they get involved with secular societies.
They go to community centres and political party meetings, make friends
at the corner shop and in sporting leagues. They become closer to the host
society with respect to their 'values, lifestyle, language, occupation, family,
and so on'.[19]

The appropriate way to measure these bonds, according to Carens and
Motomura, is to look at the length of time for which someone has been
present in a territory.

Why do these bonds matter, morally speaking? Here is a way to
motivate the approach. Suppose someone joins your cricket team. They
show up for games and play alongside the other members, and they also
help make the tea and tend to the grounds, participate in social evenings,
and come to identify with the club and adopt its culture – 'I'm a Queen's
Park player', they might say, 'so I always walk.'[20] As these shared interactions and identities become denser, it would be natural to feel a greater
sense of responsibility toward this person: to offer to help change their tyre
when their car breaks down or to bring them soup when they are sick. It
would also seem natural to feel that as a long-term member they have a
claim to be on the team in future years, even if there is a slightly better

---

[19] Carens, *The Ethics of Immigration*, p. 164.
[20] For those unfamiliar with cricket, 'walking' is a form of especially sporting behaviour (one that involves admitting when you are 'out', even if the umpire might not notice).

player who could be brought in from outside: past membership seems to generate some form of claim to continued membership.[21] The affiliation approach says that these considerations apply writ large: bonds of interaction and identity across a whole society also generate a claim to stay a member.

Applied to asylum-seekers and refugees, the argument again asks us to make a retrospective inquiry into how long they have been present, whether they have been waiting for their asylum status to be settled, renewing temporary permits, or present on a conditional basis. Those who have been present for long enough are entitled to remain.

Is this argument successful? In earlier work I have suggested that treating affiliation as an important basis for claims against the state is a mistake.[22] While it may be true that social bonds can generate obligations between people in the context of clubs and so on, it is far less clear that they are an appropriate basis for central *political* entitlements, of which the right to remain is one species. Affiliation comes in degrees. Some groups are more integrated into the main body of society than others. Compare, for example, the Presbyterian community in the United States with the Amish community, which conducts the education of its children, its business practice, and its social life in relative separation from the rest of the US population. It seems very implausible to say that the Amish are less entitled to state subsidies paid for by other groups in society than are Presbyterians. Surely it would not be permissible to give them lesser access to, say, unemployment insurance.

Another concern about the affiliation justification for the right to remain is that it gives the state significant leverage in determining whether an asylum-seeker or refugee who has just entered will ever in the future be entitled to the right to remain. Time spent in a territory is one proxy for how enmeshed someone is or will be in its society. But there are other factors than can be used as an indication of how enmeshed someone is

---

[21] Christine Straehle has suggested to me that since club membership is voluntary, it may not be a good model for explaining the affiliation approach: club obligations and entitlements are just determined by what is agreed to when someone joins. In response, I note that while some of the obligations associated with club membership might be directly related to whatever terms were agreed to when someone joined the club, others seem to be based more on the nature of the person's ongoing relationship with other club members. For example, no agreement is typically made to fix each other's tyres, nor is there generally a clause saying that more time spent at a club gives someone a greater claim to be on the team. Yet these obligations do seem to grow with someone's deepening connection to the club.

[22] A. O. Hosein, 'Arguments for Regularization', in A. Sager (ed.), *The Ethics and Politics of Immigration: Core Issues and Emerging Trends* (London: Rowman and Littlefield, 2016), pp. 159–79.

likely to be. The more time someone has spent in detention, the less opportunity they will have had to form relationships with others in that society. Another factor is the degree to which that person's future in the territory remains uncertain. Someone who lives under the cloud of potential deportation will be less likely to participate fully in society, an effect that is heightened with the degree of uncertainty: someone who is given no assurances that they are able to remain for any length of time will likely be even less enmeshed than someone given a temporary permit (a renewable two-year visa, say).

Thus, even if the basic affiliation approach to political rights can be defended, it gives a firm basis for the right to remain only for people who have not been substantially detained and have already been living under relatively stable conditions, such as refugees who have had a conditional right to permanent residence.

5   The Autonomy Approach

The final approach we will look at focuses on an individual's relationship with the state rather than their involvement in social or economic life in a society. Like the affiliation approach, it takes account not simply of individual needs but of the entitlements that come with being in certain relations with other people and institutions. Specifically, it takes account of the fact that states exercise *authority* within their territory, demanding that people under their jurisdiction obey their commands. The state makes rules governing property, taxation, contracts, marriage, and so on, and individuals must lead their lives in accordance with these rules, on pain of punishment. In this way, the exercise of authority threatens the ability of subjects to be *autonomous*: to make a life of their own choosing.[23]

What can make this demand acceptable? A plausible line of thought says that for this authority to be acceptable, the rules made by the state must themselves serve the purpose of *enhancing* individual autonomy, where that includes the ability to make not only day-to-day choices but also *plans*, which stretch out over time. And for this to happen the law must create a

---

[23] I draw here substantially on T. Nagel, 'The Problem of Global Justice', *Philosophy and Public Affairs*, 33 (2005), 113–47; and M. Blake, 'Distributive Justice, State Coercion, and Autonomy', *Philosophy and Public Affairs*, 30 (2001), 257–96. But my approach departs from theirs in various ways. Most centrally, they argue that the relinquishment of autonomy to the state is to be justified by the provision of resources to individuals under the state's jurisdiction. On my approach, the relevant 'trade' must be in the same coin: some autonomy is given up to the state for the sake of autonomy supporting steps on the part of the state.

degree of stability for individuals, allowing them to know which plans they can form and carry out without being interfered with by the state or other people. Thus, liberal theories generally insist that, for instance, the rules be publicly available, reasonably determinate, and reasonably stable over time so that individuals can make plans secure in the knowledge that they will be able to carry them out without getting penalized. The creation of stable property rights is also important because it enables individuals to make plans about how to use particular resources without having to worry that others will suddenly lay claim to them or steal them.

This framework can also give an explanation for why the right to remain is another core entitlement of citizenship.[24] Individual plans are frequently, indeed mostly, territorially bound. People invest time and resources into building places of worship in their neighbourhoods, developing skills associated with the industries in their regions, and so forth. Someone whose residence in a place is uncertain cannot securely make such plans: they may well have to leave behind an unfinished mosque or an incomplete training program. Now, of course some plans are sufficiently short-term that all someone needs to make and complete them is to have clarity about exactly how long they will be able to remain in a territory. But plausibly someone can be fully autonomous only if they at least have the option of making more long-term plans and thus an unrestricted right to remain. So a right to remain is an important form of support for individual autonomy and thus owed to citizens in light of their subjection to state authority.

Let us apply these findings to asylum-seekers and refugees. Asylum-seekers and refugees are subject to the authority of the state as soon as they enter its territory: they must obey its contract, criminal, and tort law; they must pay taxes; and so on. Their lives are thus immediately under the control of the state to some degree, and we should expect some degree of obligation on the part of the state to secure their autonomy. Their claim to remain, I will now argue, depends to a significant degree on the length of their stay in a territory.

First, notice that not all limitations on someone's ability to remain in a territory have a significant impact on their ability to plan. Take, for example, a tourist who is given a month-long visa. This person can still make longer-term plans in life: the fact that they are briefly elsewhere does not prevent them from building a career, religious community, and so on

---

[24] I developed an earlier version of this argument in A. O. Hosein, 'Immigration: The Argument for Legalization', *Social Theory and Practice*, 40 (2014), 609–30.

in their country of origin. They can treat the trip as a mere 'visit'. It also seems possible for someone to live for, say, a year under uncertainty about the length of their stay without there being any severe compromise of their control over their own life. They can defer any long-term plans for that relatively brief period.

Second, notice that control over someone's life surely comes in degrees. A person present briefly in a territory must tailor their behaviour somewhat to meet the receiving state's requirements, while someone present in a territory for decades must conform their entire life to those requirements. Someone who has resided in a territory for a significant period of time has been and is leading a life that has been very substantially shaped by the directives issued by the state. So if it is control over someone's life that triggers obligations on the part of the state, then those obligations grow stronger the longer someone is present in a territory. Someone who has been present for longer has, in effect, 'banked' a greater degree of autonomy relinquishment to the state and is thus due greater concern from the state for her present and future autonomy. Thus, we have a second reason for thinking that the longer someone's stay the more important it is to grant them a secure right to remain.

These two considerations suggest that we should look both prospectively and retrospectively at someone's length of stay when we are thinking about the strength of someone's claim to remain in a territory. Prospectively, the longer someone is going to be present, the more important it will be to give them the security of a right to remain, so that they can start to build a stable life. Someone who needs to wait only a month or two to have their asylum application adjudicated is in a much better position to make plans than someone who is likely to be in limbo for five years while their application is processed. In the latter example there is a stronger case for going ahead and granting the right to remain *now*, rather than waiting until they have already been present for many years without being able to properly control their own life. Retrospectively, the state should also take account of how long someone has been present as a guide to how much control it has already exercised over their life and thus its obligations to them.

Having given the main contours of the autonomy approach, I would like to explain now why I think it justifies a right to remain in a broader range of cases than the Samaritan or affiliation approaches. Unlike the Samaritan approach, the autonomy approach says that (some) individual people have a claim against the state to remain: they are not simply poorly off people that the state might support as one part of an attempt to help needy individuals in general. Such claims are harder to override with alternative considerations than are obligations to help the needy. For instance, it is much harder for the state to justify killing a foreign person for the sake of national security – a violation of a claim – than it would be for the state to invest in national security at the expense of life-saving foreign aid – a failure to satisfy need. So in cases where the Samaritan approach fails to justify a right to remain because it would be excessively costly to the state to grant one, the autonomy approach is likely to be more successful.

Turning to the affiliation approach, we saw earlier that there are steps the state can take to prevent people from developing strong ties to a society. For example, continued detention could weaken their ability to become enmeshed in society. On the autonomy approach, a lack of roots plays no role in determining their right to remain, so the time spent in detention does not weaken someone's claim to remain. If anything, subjection to detention should in fact *heighten* a state's responsibilities to an individual, since detention is an especially strict form of control over someone's life.

6 Conclusion

In summary, we have seen that it is important to distinguish two broad issues relating to deportation of asylum-seekers and refugees. The first concerns removal of people who have recently arrived in a territory. The relevant moral considerations are how to define the category of refugee and fairness in the distribution of refugees across receiving countries. The second issue concerns what rights people who stay beyond this initial period should get, in particular whether they should get a right to remain: a secure legal entitlement to stay in the country without fear of later removal. We looked at three ways to justify the right to remain, focusing on people who are expected to be, or have been, present in a territory for a significant period of time: the Samaritan, affiliation, and autonomy approaches. I argued that the last provides the strongest basis for that right and in the broadest range of cases. Most strikingly, perhaps, it shows us that we should look *prospectively* as well as *retrospectively* at someone's length of stay, taking account of the fact that for many refugees return to their home countries may not be possible for most of their lifetime, so only granting them the right to remain gives them a secure opportunity to build a new, autonomous life.

CHAPTER 7

The Duties of Refugees

Matthew J. Gibney[1]

What are the duties of refugees? Writing in 1970, Michael Walzer described refugees a possessing a peculiar and distinctive 'kind of freedom'.[2] The refugee, by virtue of being effectively stateless, is released from all the duties associated with citizenship, not least the duty to fight for the state. However, this, Walzer immediately noted, was a *poisoned* freedom, one that any refugee would gladly exchange for the bonds of citizenship. It was a freedom grounded in uncertainty and insecurity because the refugee's liberation from duties came with the disappearance of any state duties to the refugee.

This idea of the refugee as someone released from obligations does not chime well with the contemporary politics of asylum. Everywhere one looks one finds examples of refugees being publicly criticised for violating various moral norms, expectations and obligations. Refugees have recently been accused by European leaders of failing to respect national immigration controls, funding people smugglers, engaging in inappropriate sexual behaviour, of wantonly damaging immigration detention centres, and generally abusing the hospitality of their hosts. Justified or not, the political and moral language of the contemporary refugee politics revolves as much around the duties of refugees as it does the obligations of states. The perceived failure of refugees to fulfil their duties is often used to legitimise curtailing their rights through detention and measures that bar access to asylum.

[1] This chapter has been presented, in various forms, to audiences in Leeds, Southampton, Winchester, Munich, Berlin, Augsburg, Florence, Malmo, and Kalmar. Audiences at these workshops and seminars, and at home in Oxford, have provided me with extremely valuable criticism and comments. I have particularly benefitted from the observations of Chimène Bateman, Michael Blake, Rebecca Buxton, Georgia Cole, Cathryn Costello, Mollie Gerver, Colin Grey, Theo Kwek, David Owen, Blair Peruniak, Matt Ryan, Ben Saunders and James Souter. David Miller and Christine Straehle were, as one would expect, also intelligent and insightful readers.
[2] M. Walzer, *Obligations: Essays on Disobedience, War, and Citizenship* (Cambridge, MA: Harvard University Press, 1971), p. 147.

The interconnectedness of the perceived duties of refugees and the rights they enjoy was starkly evident in what became known as the 'Children Overboard' scandal in Australia in 2001. Asylum-seekers in a sinking boat on the open seas headed for Australia from Indonesia were (it later turned out falsely) accused by Australian politicians of throwing their children overboard in order to gain the attention of coast guard authorities who, they hoped, would take them to Australia.

The Australian government, already hostile to the arrival of refugees, seized on this version of events to label the refugees unfit for entry. The Prime Minister, John Howard, speaking on Australian radio at the time, observed: 'I don't want in Australia people who would throw their own children into the sea.... There's something to me incompatible between somebody who claims to be a refugee and somebody who would throw their own child into the sea. It offends the natural instinct of protection and delivering security and safety to your children.' This portrayal of the asylum-seeker as amoral and in breach of their basic obligations as parents helped generate public support for a government policy of preventing refugee boat arrivals on Australia territory.

In this chapter I will explore the question of refugees as duty holders and consider, in particular, what duties refugees have as refugees. I will undertake this task not by deriving a list of specific duties from a set of general moral principles. Rather (and somewhat less ambitiously), I will proceed by critically examining three particular duties – relating, respectively, to resistance, repatriation and cooperation – recently ascribed to refugees by European governments. While I accept that political leaders often use the language of refugee duties as a tool for their own political ends, I show that each of the three duties under consideration raises important moral issues. More generally, these duties force us to consider what characteristics the agents and institutions that govern the lives of refugees would need to have to be worthy of the moral respect of refugees.

I begin the discussion that follows with a historical interlude. I briefly illustrate how the duties of refugees were initially conceived in debates over the 1951 Refugee Convention, the main piece of international law applicable to refugees. But I will move quickly to the contemporary context and analyse three particular duties that have been ascribed to refugees in recent political debate. These are: the 'duty to fight', the 'duty to leave' and the 'duty to wait'. In the conclusion of this chapter, I consider the implications of the previous discussion for a broader account of the obligations of refugees, stressing in particular what we need to consider for a more adequate account of refugee duties.

For the purpose of this chapter, I follow David Miller in defining a 'refugee' as an individual 'whose human rights cannot be protected except by moving across a border, whether the reason is state persecution, state incapacity, or prolonged natural disasters'[3]. However, at various points, including my discussion of the legal duties of refugees, I will discuss the 1951 Geneva Convention definition which refers, more narrowly, to individuals facing a 'well-founded fear of persecution' on grounds of race, political opinion, religion, nationality or membership of a particular social group. When I write of 'refugee duties', I mean to specify moral obligations to perform or refrain from engaging in particular acts, which emerge specifically from the experience of displacement, such as the process of forcibly leaving one's country of origin, the act of seeking asylum in a host country and the enjoyment of refugee status. Throughout this chapter, I consider two types of duties: natural duties which individuals have simply in respect of our personhood and special or associational duties that individuals incur as a result of the particular relationships (family, citizenship, etc.) in which they are enmeshed in the course of their lives.[4]

It is important by way of introduction to defend my focus on refugee duties. There are, it is true, circumstances when it is almost obscene to talk about refugees having obligations, such as when they are risking their lives on sinking ships in the Mediterranean or struggling simply to keep their sanity in the midst of a mind-numbing and uncertain existence on Manus Island, effectively imprisoned there by the Australian government. Necessity, as the saying goes, knows no law.

Yet we should resist the spell of the idea that refugees are *only* victims, driven by considerations of necessity. While it is clear that refugees often find themselves in perilous situations, they also find themselves in relatively stable situations that range from permanent residence in host countries to the protracted limbo of refugee camps or detention centres. In these circumstances and others, refugees make choices and act in ways that illustrate their moral agency: they decide to send money home to compatriots or to testify against the regimes they have escaped; they pay smugglers; they lobby governments for the entrance of their compatriots through resettlement programmes; and they choose to obey or not to obey the laws of the society they have joined.

[3] D. Miller, *Strangers in Our Midst: The Political Philosophy of Immigration* (Cambridge, MA: Harvard University Press, 2016), p. 83.
[4] See J. Waldron, 'Special Ties and Natural Duties', *Philosophy and Public Affairs*, 22 (1993), 3–30; S. Scheffler, *Boundaries and Allegiances: Problems of Justice and Responsibility in Liberal Thought* (New York: Oxford University Press, 2001).

Unless we recognise the moral choices refugees make, we risk *de*humanising them, we risk reducing them merely to victims defined solely by immediate circumstances. Just as recognising people as rights holders may be a way of acknowledging their dignity, so, too, is recognising them as duty holders. That said, there are obvious dangers in leaving the content of refugee duties for states and political elites to define alone, not least in the current restrictive environment in which overblown fear of foreigners is a key feature of much electoral politics. Political leaders are often tempted to define – implicitly or explicitly – the duties of refugees in capricious and self-serving ways. It is the role of moral and political theory to subject dominant accounts of moral responsibilities to critical and reasoned scrutiny. This chapter is intended as a preliminary contribution to that task.

1   History

Before I turn to examine some recent public articulations of the moral duties of refugees, I want to spend a little time considering how the duties of refugees have been conceptualised in international law. The main instrument of international law pertaining to refugees is the 1951 Convention Relating to the Status of Refugees, signed by 148 of the world's states. The Convention's origins lay in a Europe recovering from the brutal devastation of World War II.

The Convention enumerates a range of rights for refugees and places a number of obligations on signatory *states*, the most important of which is the duty of *non-refoulement*, the obligation not to return refugees to countries where they would face persecution. However, the Convention has surprisingly little to say about the explicit duties of *refugees*. Indeed, discussion of refugee duties is limited to a terse statement prominently placed in Article 2:

> Every refugee has duties to the country in which he finds himself, which require in particular that he conform to its laws and regulations as well as to measures taken for the maintenance of public order.

This statement seems, on the face it, unexceptional. It suggests that refugee duties are virtually the same as those of any other foreigner residing in a state such as tourists and permanent residents. This kind of minimal conception of duties has a long history, and closely reflects Hugo Grotius's account of the duties of exiles in his *On the Law of War and Peace* of 1625. In that work, Grotius comments that:

a permanent residence ought not to be denied to foreigners who, expelled from their homes, are seeking a refuge, provided that they submit themselves to the established government and observe any regulations which are necessary to avoid strifes.[5]

The relatively unexceptional nature of the Convention's article, however, obscures the fact that in discussions over the drafting of this treaty, the duties of refugees were a matter of significant dispute among states.

The drafters of the Convention fell into two major groups on the question. One group, which contained the United States and the United Kingdom, saw it as unnecessary to write in law any special duties for refugees. They felt that a statement that refugees had (like other settled immigrants) a general duty to obey the law was sufficient. These countries were also concerned that, as refugees themselves were not signatories to the Convention, it was inappropriate to enforce special duties on them under it.

A very different view was held by a number of other countries, including France and Australia. The French authorities submitted a draft of the Convention that included a provision stating that 'states reserve themselves the right to restrict or prohibit political activity on the part of refugees'.[6] The French authorities believed that, because refugees were more likely to be politically active than other immigrants and that such activity could cause foreign policy problems, it was reasonable to demand that refugees refrain from political activity until they became citizens.

This proposal was criticised by other states as discriminatory. The French authorities responded to this charge by defending the provision as a reasonable 'security measure' designed to dissuade refugees from activities that would otherwise warrant their deportation.[7] The French provision was not the only special duty proposed. Some states wanted the Convention to include a duty of refugees to undertake military service in the country of asylum. The Australian government even suggested that refugees be obliged to work in sectors of the economy nominated for them by the government where they were resettled.

All of these special duties failed to make it into the Convention, though a concern about political order might be said to live on in the 'public order' provision, which requires, with some vagueness, that refugees conform to

---

[5] H. Grotius, *On the Law of War and Peace*, trans F. Kelsey (Washington: Carnegie Institution, 1913), Book II, Ch. 2, sect. 16.

[6] Quoted in A. B. Johnsson, 'Duties of Refugees', *The International Journal of Refugee Law*, 3 (1991), 579–84.

[7] Johnsson, 'Duties of Refugees', 580.

'measures taken for the maintenance of public order'. In the influential African Union convention on refugees, this requirement is even more closely aligned with Grotius's one, adding to the 1951 Convention definition the sentence that a refugee 'shall also abstain from any subversive activities against any Member State of the OAU'.

The challenge the states drawing up the 1951 Convention faced with going any further in explicitly specifying special duties for refugees was that any such duties would contradict the spirit of Convention – and the broader (newly inaugurated) United Nations Declaration of Human Rights – against arbitrary discrimination. Most signatories were hostile to the idea that refugees should be treated as holding a second-class status in the societies in which they found asylum. Indeed, the Convention made clear in several places that refugees were to be treated no less favourably than other resident aliens.[8]

Nonetheless, while the Convention is short on enumerated duties, a number of duties for those seeking and holding refugee status might be said to derive from it. For example, the requirement in Article 31 that that refugees should not be penalised for entering unlawfully under certain conditions suggests an obligation on refugees to apply for asylum without delay and, arguably, in the first country of asylum they settle in. The 'ceased circumstances' provision in Article 1C states that refugee status may end as a result of 'fundamental changes in the objective circumstances in the country of origin upon which refugee status was based (sub-paragraphs 5 and 6)'. One might infer from this provision an obligation on behalf of the refugees to no longer avail themselves of the status (and thus potentially return home or leave the asylum state).[9]

Finally, there may be an implicit legal duty to cooperate with refugee status determination procedures, for example, by being open and honest about one's nationality, route of entry, circumstances for leaving and identity consonant with determining one's eligibility for refugee status. Specifying these duties, however, is made somewhat tricky by the fact that the Convention itself says nothing about the procedures to be used for determining refugee status.

---

[8] J. C. Hathaway and M. Foster, *The Law of Refugee Status* (Cambridge: Cambridge University Press, 2014).

[9] G. Schneider, 'The Cooperation Duties of Asylum Seekers', available at www.ipw.uni-hannover.de/fileadmin/politische_wissenschaft/Dateien/luise_druke/schneider_541_570.pdf.

2 Duties Emerging from Politics

If we consider international law, then, the explicitly stated duties of refugees are quite modest. They are limited to the duty to obey the law in the country where the refugee finds asylum. Given that this is a duty that is commonly considered also to apply to citizens and non-citizens resident in the state, it seems largely unobjectionable, at least when the state concerned is legitimate and its laws are not manifestly unjust.[10] Even this duty of obedience to the law has an important caveat in the Convention. States themselves, as we have seen, have a duty not to return a refugee who would face persecution under the terms of the Convention in its *non-refoulement* provision. As a corollary, refugees are under no legal duty to respect the immigration laws of a state to the extent that these laws prevent them from escaping persecution or human rights violations.[11]

My primary aim in what follows, however, will be to examine not duties that are enshrined explicitly in law but those that emerge from politics. If the formal legal duties of refugees are relatively modest, the moral duties often ascribed to refugees in contemporary political debates across Europe are far more expansive, emerging as they do from a broader set of social and political understandings. In particular, I am going to highlight three different duties of refugees that have recently been articulated by political elites: the duty to return home to fight for one's country of origin, the duty to leave the country of asylum when refugee protection is no longer necessary, and the duty to wait for resettlement by queuing for entry into a European country.

There are of course other moral duties that one might examine. I focus on these three because of their recent political prominence. Refugees who fail to fight have been criticised as selfish; those who fail to leave as

---

[10] There are of course vexed and long-running debates concerning the problem of political obligation that are relevant here but I do not have the space to discuss (see, for example, C. Pateman, *The Problem of Political Obligation: A Critical Analysis of Liberal Theory* [Chichester: Wiley and Sons, 1979]; A. J. Simmons, *Moral Principles and Political Obligations* [Princeton, NJ: Princeton University Press, 1981]). The coerced circumstances of refugees' entry to states of asylum raises particular issues about their duty to obey the law in their country of asylum.

[11] The issue, as David Miller has rightly pointed out to me, becomes somewhat more complicated when the refugee has the option of going to other countries with their claim of asylum without risk. I consider some issues relevant to this question in M. J. Gibney, 'Refugees and Justice between States', *European Journal of Political Theory*, 14 (2015), 448–63, in a discussion of whether refugees have a right to choose their country of asylum. For a nuanced discussion of the general issue of whether refugees have a *moral* duty to obey the immigration laws of a (basically) just state when that law excludes them, see M. Blake, *Migration, Justice, and Mercy* (Cambridge: Cambridge University Press, forthcoming).

ungrateful; and those who fail to wait as unfair. These three duties also serve to spotlight the major communities to which refugees conceivably owe duties: the community of origin, the host country, and the international community or other refugees.

In what follows my focus will primarily be on duties recently ascribed to refugees by political elites. However, it is worth noting that the behaviour of refugees themselves would be hard to understand if one did not see refugees as subject to a range of moral duties (to family, compatriots, the societies they enter and other refugees). Moreover, the articulation of duties has on occasion been used by refugees for their own political purposes. For example, representatives of German expellees who fled Soviet forces at the end of World War II produced a charter of expellees in August 1950. In the charter, designed to reassure their hosts that they would be good guests, they publicly committed themselves to (1) 'renounce all thought of revenge and retaliation', (2) 'support with all our strength every endeavour directed towards the establishment of a united Europe, in which the nations may live in freedom from fear and coercion', and (3) 'contribute, by hard and indefatigable work, to the reconstruction of Germany and Europe'.[12]

3 The Duty to Fight

I will start with what I will call the 'duty to fight'. Soon after large numbers of refugees from Syria started to appear in Europe in 2015, voices arose in European states more or less openly accusing male Syrian refugees of shirking their duty to stay and fight against the forces destroying their society. The Czech President, Milos Zeman, noted in a Christmas address of December 2015 that 'a large majority of the illegal migrants [his term for Syrian refugees] are young men in good health and single'. He then asked rhetorically, 'I wonder why these men are not taking up arms to go fight for the freedom of their countries against the Islamic State?'[13]

Zeman's question was echoed by right-wing politicians across Europe and as far afield as the United States and Australia. Unfavourable parallels were drawn between the cowardly behaviour of the Syrian refugees and the actions of the displaced during World War II, who, it was argued, fought bravely against the Nazis to liberate their countries of origin.

---

[12] The charter is available online at www.westpreussen-online.de/html/charter_of_the_german_expellee.html.
[13] Quoted in *The Guardian*, 27 December 2015.

This moral criticism of Syrian refugees for evading their duties was deeply problematical. For a start, it was almost always levelled by politicians and observers who seemed hostile to accepting *any* Syrian refugees. Zeman prefaced his own comments with the statement that his country was facing an 'organised invasion and not a spontaneous movement of refugees'. Furthermore, comparing the Syrian crisis with the World War II was fatuous. Fighting for Assad is hardly the equivalent of fighting for the Allies. As many commenters have noted, the nature of fighting in the current conflict has had more the character of an all-in pub brawl than a conventional military battle. The difficulties of finding a 'side' with whom one has good reason to fight are thus enormous. Finally, the casual sexism of those advising refugees of their duties is hard to ignore. Why is it only *men* that have the duty to fight?

It is important to separate the message from the messenger, however. The question of whether refugees have a duty to fight to defend their state when it is possible and practicable for them to do so raises important issues. At the very least, it encourages us to reflect on the question of what responsibilities refugees have to the societies they have left behind.

It is worth starting consideration of this question by stating the obvious. The views of some right-wing politicians notwithstanding, most Western societies no longer expect their citizens to fight (and die) for the state. Modern armies are generally professional ones and military conscription has disappeared in the last few decades in all but a handful of countries.

Conscription has disappeared partly because citizen armies are no longer necessary due to the changing character of modern warfare,[14] but also because there is great resistance to the idea that people should be forced to risk their lives for their state, especially in foreign laws; in many countries military conscription would be considered a violation of basic rights.[15] Thus one objection to the claim of a refugee duty to fight emerges: there seems something deeply hypocritical in asking refugees to do something that people in our own societies seem no longer prepared to do (or are legally obliged to do.)

It might be replied, though, that this scepticism of a duty to fight applies most strongly to battles on foreign soil. Under circumstances where one's own state was invaded by a threatening external or internal power,

[14] P. Triadafilopoulos, 'Dual Citizenship and Security Norms in Historical Perspective', in T. Faist and P. Kivisto (eds.), *Dual Citizenship in Global Perspective: From Unitary to Multiple Citizenship* (Basingstoke: Palgrave Macmillan, 2007), pp. 27–41.
[15] R. K. Fullinwider, *Conscripts and Volunteers: Military Requirements, Social Justice, and the All-Volunteer Force* (Totowa, NJ: Rowman and Allanheld, 1983).

military enlistment may well be considered as obligation. This kind of situation is the one that often obtains in the countries from which some refugees come. Nonetheless, if we hold a social contract view of the state – as is common in liberal theory – the idea that we have a duty to fight even in these circumstances is questionable.

The reason is that in the social contract tradition, the citizen has certain duties because the state provides her with goods that she could not achieve on her own. Preeminent among these, as evident in the work of both Hobbes and Locke, is the good of security and the provision of a general social context in which the other rights of individuals can be protected.

The problem is that refugees exist just because this reciprocal agreement has broken down. Refugees emerge because, as Andrew Shacknove has argued, the state has failed to fulfil its end of the social contract due to weakness, ineptitude or malevolence. Asylum is a substitute form of protection when one's own state has *failed*.[16] But if the state has failed – if it is no longer living up to its end of the social bargain – there is no necessary moral reason why the citizen is obliged to protect the state or to fight on its behalf.[17] This is one reason why the political theorist Michael Walzer, writing in the late 1960s and early 1970s in the context of Vietnam War conscription in the United States, argued that a liberal state can never obligate a citizen to go to war. 'Indeed', he observes, 'the great advantage of liberal society may simply be this: that no one can be asked to die for public reasons on behalf of the state.'[18]

It might be, though, that the criticism of refugees for failing to fight is not really about defending the *state*. Those who call for refugees to return and fight typically talk about refugees having a duty to their *society* rather than their state. Most critics of refugees conspicuously avoid, for example, claiming that refugees should defend President Assad's regime. The implication is that even if refugees have no obligation to the state that has failed them, they might still have a duty to assist and protect their fellow *compatriots* (or other community members) from forces that would jeopardise their lives and security. To put it another way, even if the *vertical* contract between the individual and the state has broken, the *horizontal* contract between members of a society – be it based on

[16] A. E. Shacknove, 'Who Is a Refugee?', *Ethics*, 95 (1985), 274–84.
[17] M. Gross, *Bioethics and Armed Conflict: Moral Dilemmas of Medicine and War* (Cambridge, MA: MIT Press, 2016).
[18] Walzer, *Obligations*, p. 89.

citizenship, ethnicity, religion or kinship – may still hold and issue in moral obligations.[19]

There is little doubt that examination of the experiences of refugees from literature and history vindicates the power of such felt obligations. In the *Aeneid*, Virgil goes to great lengths to establish that Aeneas flees – or, significantly, 'is swept' – from the besieged city of Troy only after being after engaging in life-risking battle and with the imprimatur of the gods:

> Weeping, I set out from my country's shores,
> The plains where Troy had been. I swept to exile
> With my friends, my child, my clans' gods, and the great gods.[20]

In Jeremy Adelman's recent biography of German Jew Albert Hirschman, the morally conflictual nature of exile is also on display.[21] Hirschman fled Germany in the 1930s, but, as Adelman shows, he continued to support the community he had left behind by taking up arms against fascist forces in Spain and then Italy, and by assisting in the escape of refugees from France to Switzerland. When Hirschman finally sought the protection of asylum in the United States, he saw it as a kind of failure: 'I didn't want to leave. I wanted to fight.'[22]

A version of the same tension is alive across the world's refugee communities today. A recent article in the *New York Times* poignantly documented the heartbreak of a Syrian family resettled in Canada who left family members behind in camps in Lebanon. Daily phone calls between Toronto and Lebanon testified to the feeling that they had deserted their family members.[23] Everywhere one looks, asylum's connection with guilt is as common as its association with deliverance.

Of course, the traumatic events that generate refugees sometimes *dissolve* the horizontal contracts between the members of a society, and their associated duties. Judith Shklar has argued that even after the destruction of the Nazi state in 1945, the Jews who fled Germany had no 'conceivable obligations' to the German people: 'both contracts had been broken', she wrote, 'the first between members of society, as well as the second between

---

[19] See M. Walzer, 'The Moral Standing of States: A Response to Four Critics', *Philosophy and Public Affairs*, 9 (1980), 209–29.

[20] Virgil, *Aeneid: A Prose Translation*, trans. D. West (London: Penguin Classics, 1995), Book III, line 10.

[21] J. Adelman, 'Hirschman's Choice: Exiles and Obligations of an Anti-Fascist', *Transatlantica: American Studies Journal*, 1 (2014). Available at https://journals.openedition.org/transatlantica/6864.

[22] Quoted in Adelman, 'Hirschman's Choice', p. 15.   [23] *New York Times*, 22 October 2016.

citizens and the state. [The Jews] were betrayed at both levels, excluded from civil, no less than from political society.'[24]

It is not difficult to think of analogous situations. The case of the persecuted Rohingya in Burma is a contemporary one. But many refugees emerge because of state fragility or incompetence rather than state malevolence, and in such situations the broader society may not be complicit in a situation where a lack of rights forces departure. Furthermore, even when a community is implicated, loyalties and responsibilities to other communities that partially overlap with (but may not be the same as) citizenship sometimes remain. Hirschman retained a commitment to German socialists, for example, as well as to German Jews.

Can we say, then, that, albeit in some situations, refugees simply have a *duty* to stay and fight for members of their society left behind, a duty, in effect, to eschew asylum? I do not think so. The major problem is that it is hard to see anyone as having a *duty* to risk their life for others (even if there might be circumstances when it is morally admirable to do so). There are certainly situations when someone might be reasonably expected to make great sacrifices for the sake of associative duties. Parents are often viewed as having an obligation to risk their own lives (and, more often, their own happiness) for the welfare of their child. Yet the family is a poor analogy for other kinds of group membership. It is a more intimate, exclusive and (often) more mutually dependent association; it is reasonable to think that our duties to fellow citizens are not as onerous as those we may have as parents.

Thus, while refugees, like all of us, have duties to assist their compatriots and even to help preserve just institutions when doing so can be done without more than modest risk to themselves, a duty to engage in military battle is a step too far. To stay and to take up arms – in contemporary Syria or elsewhere – is virtually always to put one's life directly on the line.

Fortunately, when we look closely at the experiences of actual refugees we see that a simple contrast between exile and staying and fighting is dubious anyway. Hirschman fought for those communities in Germany he felt duty-bound to help while he was *in exile* in France, Spain and Italy. Many Syrians who have found refuge in Canada today lobby government authorities and their sponsors to open up resettlement places for their displaced relatives, friends and community members. Sri Lankan Tamil and Bosnian refugees have used remittances from abroad to support communities – and even to further the war – at home. With contemporary

[24] J. N. Shklar, 'Obligation, Loyalty, Exile', *Political Theory*, 21 (1993), 181–97.

technologies, the idea that warfare itself requires physical proximity seems somewhat passé.[25]

Even Aeneas, as the epic goes, spun his exile into gold by embarking on a journey that laid the foundations for a new Troy in the form of Rome. Refugees may be able to do more good to help their community abroad than they could at home. For a mixture of principled and pragmatic reasons, then, it is difficult to imagine the circumstances when a refugee would be obliged to stay and fight.

4   The Duty to Leave

A second duty that refugees are commonly perceived to have is a 'duty to leave' their host country once conditions in their country of origin improve. Asylum, in other words, should not be claimed by refugees for longer than the circumstances that forced the refugee to flee exist.

This idea draws some support from a section of the 1951 UN Refugee Convention in Article 1C which, as I showed earlier, refers to situations where refugee protection may no longer be necessary 'because the circumstances in connexion with which he has been recognized as a refugee have ceased to exist'. More generally, a duty to leave has implicitly underpinned the growth of asylum as a temporary status across many Western states, including Australia and the United Kingdom, in the last couple of decades.

In 2002, David Blunkett, the British Home Secretary, encouraged Kosovan refugees in Britain to return home now that the Serbian forces had been defeated: 'If [refugees] are dynamic and well-qualified', he stated, 'they should get back home and recreate their countries that we freed from tyranny.'[26] In 2016, Angela Merkel told Syrian refugees currently in Germany that: 'If there is peace in Syria and Isil is defeated in Iraq, we expect you to return to your homelands, with the knowledge of what you have received from us.'[27]

As is apparent in these quotations, the duty to leave is sometimes conceptualised as a duty owed to one's country of origin. The refugee is obliged to return to help one's compatriots rebuild or 'recreate' the broken society which they were forced to leave. This account is consistent with Blunkett's emphasis on the duty of the 'well-qualified' to contribute. However, the duty can also be understood as an obligation owed to the

---

[25] D. Gregory, 'From a View to a Kill: Drones and Late Modern War', *Theory, Culture and Society*, 28 (2011), 188–215.
[26] *The Guardian*, 18 September 2002.   [27] *The Daily Telegraph*, 31 January 2017.

host country for what it has given the refugee. This is evident in Blunkett's reference to Britain 'freeing their countries from tyranny' and Merkel's emphasis on the 'knowledge you have received from us'. In this latter sense return exhibits a *duty of gratitude* owed the host country.

This duty of gratitude is typically grounded in the idea that providing asylum is an act of hospitality by a state; the refugee is a guest and, like any guest, can outstay her welcome given that hosting can be taxing, in terms of both emotional and financial resources. As Julian Pitt-Rivers notes, reflecting on the rules of hospitality, 'the courtesy of showing a guest to the door or the gate both underlines a concern for his welfare as long as he is a guest, but it also defines precisely the point at which he ceases to be so, when the host is quit of his responsibility'.[28] The refugee's return marks the end of responsibility and allows the political community in question to get back to the way things were; it releases resources and effort spent on accommodating the individual in need of protection.

It is also possible to see the duty to return as a duty the refugee *owes to other refugees*. When refugees leave, it might be argued, they free up the state to accept other refugees by reducing claims on its resources, infrastructure and public generosity. This can enable the state to be hospitable to other guests – that is, new refugees – in the future. Temporary protection, as the international law scholar Jim Hathaway has argued, may (when it works) be a way of 'renewing asylum capacity' among states.[29]

One reason to be sceptical about whether refugees actually have a duty to leave is because of concerns about whether conditions have *really* improved (or improved enough) in the country of origin. European countries have recently been sending refugees back to Afghanistan. As part of the return agreement, these states have encouraged the Afghan state by offering, among other things, to build a new terminal at Kabul airport to accommodate the returnees.

It has long been a criticism of human rights groups that European countries, like the United Kingdom and Germany, are often so keen to see refugees return that they are insensitive to the human rights conditions prevailing in the countries of origin. Given that the states of asylum are usually the primary judges of when conditions are safe for return, they have something of a conflict of interest, to say the least. But let us put aside for the time being the issue of judging when it is safe to return.

[28] J. Pitt-Rivers, 'The Law of Hospitality', *HAU: Journal of Ethnographic Theory*, 2 (2012), 514.
[29] J. C. Hathaway (ed.), *Reconceiving International Refugee Law* (The Hague: Martinus Nijhoff, 1997).

It does not seem like an unsurmountable problem if the right processes are put in place.

What are we make of a duty to leave? To the extent that this involves a duty to return to *one's country of origin*, it strikes the same problems as the duty to fight. In particular, it is hard to argue that anyone can have a duty to return to rebuild a society that has persecuted them. The bonds of connection between an individual and the state are no longer strong enough to issue in duties. There may be good reason for Rohingya refugees in Pakistan to return to Burma over the next year. But it is hard to see that these refugees have a moral duty to go back after the suffering they have endured.

To be sure, the issue is more complex for those who have fled for reasons of the generalised and indiscriminate violence of war or in situations where a harmful regime has been replaced by a relatively benign one. Refugees often face the question of returning to a state that has simply been incompetent or where those who abused their power have been overthrown. These distinctions are of moral importance. Incompetent regimes are different from malicious ones; and new regimes cannot necessarily be held responsible for the crimes of old ones. Nonetheless, a state that fails a citizen so egregiously as to make fleeing the state the only serious option is not entitled, as a matter of right, to demand the trust of its exiled citizens. Refugees may have good reason to return their country of origin, but they have no duty based on state allegiance to do so.

It still might be said, mirroring the discussion above of the duty to fight, that duties to fellow citizens or co-ethnics left behind rather than the government or broader state are relevant to the question of return. By not returning, refugees might damage the prospect of their compatriots rebuilding their society or their co-ethnics becoming a group large or influential enough to make sure its interests are taken into account (and thus to guarantee its future security). Refugee returns, for example, can be a way of reversing attempts to ethnically cleanse populations and thus combatting egregious injustice[30]; the return of refugees with certain skills (e.g., political leadership) may be highly significant to a society's future. It is possible that returning may be the only effective way of helping one's compatriots. I am thus reluctant to say that refugees could never have a duty to return for the sake of one's compatriots.

What about a duty to leave grounded in gratitude to the *host* state? The existence of this duty relies in part on whether or not we view asylum

---

[30] See Chapter 8 in this volume.

through the lens of *hospitality* as opposed to an *entitlement* of refugees. Some have argued that Convention refugees (those who have suffered persecution), in particular, have a right to be admitted to citizenship in the country of asylum. For Matthew Price, the act of persecution by rending asunder any contract between the individual and their state of origin makes a new citizenship essential.[31] In other cases, a duty to rectify harm weakens considerations of gratitude. A state may find itself hosting refugees who exist in part because of its own actions: refugees may be the product of foreign military intervention (e.g., Iraq since 2002) or civil conflict that is subsidised, encouraged or facilitated by third-party state powers. When relationships of harm like these exist, the obligation of a state to grant asylum may most appropriately be understood as a reparative obligation, and there is little reason why a refugee ought to feel grateful.[32]

However, even if we view asylum as hospitality for which the refugee should feel grateful, a number of considerations would seem to undermine the case for a duty of leave. One is the fact that a refugee's gratitude might be fulfilled in ways other than departure, for example, by benefitting the new society through charitable works, becoming a good citizen, etc. Furthermore, after several years of asylum, the individual may have a strong moral claim to remain in the host society built on what Joseph Carens has called the principle of 'social membership': the factual integration of the individual into the community.[33] In the case of refugees this claim is particularly powerful because the coercive circumstances under which they originally entered make it hard to argue that they truly consented to stay temporarily when they first arrived. This right to remain might, in principle, issue in a situation where refugees simultaneously have a moral entitlement to remain in the host state and a duty to return owed to compatriots in the state of origin.[34]

Finally, there is a duty to leave *owed to other refugees*. The force of any such duty is, of course, going to depend on whether the state concerned is truly committed to regenerating its asylum capacity, that is, whether it is likely that resources and capacity will be freed up and actually used to help other refugees. The behaviour of many Western states in recent years does not give one reason for optimism. Nonetheless, the possibility of such a

---

[31] M. E. Price, *Rethinking Asylum: History, Purpose, and Limits* (Cambridge: Cambridge University Press, 2009).

[32] See J. Souter, 'Towards a Theory of Asylum as Reparation for Past Injustice', *Political Studies*, 62 (2014), 326–42; Miller, *Strangers in Our Midst*.

[33] J. Carens, *The Ethics of Immigration* (New York: Oxford University Press, 2013).

[34] I am grateful to David Miller for bringing to my attention this possibility.

justification – if, for example, states pledged to make a new asylum place available for every returning refugee – should not be ruled out.

It is worth noting that many of the world's refugees evidently *do* feel an obligation to return to the countries from which they were displaced. Refugees often live in countries neighbouring the one from which they fled. A large number would like nothing more than to return home as quickly as possible when they adjudge conditions to be safe, and indeed do so when the opportunities arrive. Moreover, as Megan Bradley has intelligently noted, there are real ethical dangers in assuming that the political relationship between refugees and the countries from which they have fled is permanently severed once asylum has been granted.[35] Clearly, refugee return is often desirable, though it is only under certain exceptional conditions (for example, when it is beneficial to other refugees seeking asylum) that it might be said to be obligatory.

5   The Duty to Wait

The final duty I want to discuss is what we might call the 'duty to wait'. During the refugee controversy in the early 2000s, the Howard government in Australia, hostile to the arrival of boats, began to characterise arriving refugees as 'queue jumpers'; that is, people who pushed in front of other refugees waiting to come to Australia by legal means. This was an inspired move by a government eager to convince the public that harsh policies against refugees were justified.[36] The 'queue jumper' label portrayed the boat arrivals as violating a duty *to their fellow refugees*, while distracting attention from the government's own dubious actions. By not adhering to the duty to wait, the boat arrivals were characterised as those who unfairly elevated their claim to asylum above those of other desperate refugees.

The duty to wait has found its way to Europe in the last few years. The British government has used the queue-jumping argument to justify its policy of not resettling Syrian refugees who make it to Europe under their own steam in favour of resettling 'more vulnerable' individuals who remain in camps in Turkey, Lebanon and Jordan. A version of the argument has also been affirmed by Peter Singer, who, bemoaning the irrational distribution

---

[35] M. Bradley, 'Rethinking Refugeehood: Statelessness, Repatriation, and Refugee Agency', *Review of International Studies*, 40 (2014), 101–23.
[36] W. Maley, *What Is a Refugee?* (Melbourne: Scribe Publications, 2016).

of responsibility for refugees globally, has stated that the current refugee regime provides incentives for people 'somehow to jump the queue'.[37]

What should we make of this duty to wait? It is, in my view, a deeply flawed conceptualisation of refugee obligations in the current system. The idea that there exists a *queue* for asylum in Australia or any European country is completely fictional. Some refugees are indeed resettled in countries of the global North through orderly programmes. But in Europe, the number that arrive on such schemes is risibly small and opportunities are sporadic. Britain, for example, under much pressure committed itself in 2015 to take 20,000 refugees from the Syrian region before 2020; however, in the first ten months of the scheme only around 2,000 arrived. Worldwide, only around 80,000 refugees were given resettlement places with UNHCR assistance in 2015. This is a tiny number compared with the numbers that need asylum in Europe. Regardless of how long most refugees wait, they will not be getting resettled.

It is also worth noting that the conditions under which refugees do wait can be extremely harsh. Refugees started heading to Europe from Turkey, for example, in 2015 only after it became obvious that opportunities to work, to get their children an education and to eke out a decent existence were not going to be on offer anytime soon. Refugee camps can be places of great insecurity; they are typically also places of limbo. The refugees therein can become vulnerable to labour and sexual exploitation, smugglers, traffickers and destitution. For the host countries, the politics of aiding refugees typically becomes trickier over time, with hostility and resentment among the public likely to grow.

These are, of course, practical criticisms of the duty to wait. What if a more just system for allocating asylum to refugees was actually in place and the stability of this system depended on the orderly movement of refugees? Imagine a hypothetical scenario, one in which European states, displaying a hitherto unseen level of cooperation on refugee issues, have in place a workable system for sharing responsibilities for refugees fairly among themselves. This system enables European states dramatically to increase the availability of asylum in Europe. Suppose also that this system's effective working requires refugees to queue, to wait in a third country, say, Turkey or Morocco, for a period. This queueing makes sure that refugees are fairly distributed in the order they arrive and that refugees with special needs are prioritised.

Would refugees faced with such a system have a *duty to wait* rather than head to Europe on their own steam and proceed to a country of their

---

[37] *INews*, 10 June 2016.

choice? I think it is highly plausible that the answer is yes, providing a number of conditions are met. These conditions would include but not be limited to (1) the requirement that refugees' basic rights would not be jeopardised by staying in the transit state in which they waited; (2) that the offer of a resettlement place for her is genuine and realistic; (3) that the waiting period involved is short; (4) that the resettlement system makes a serious attempt (taking into account the goals of maximising asylum places) to accommodate a refugee's request to go to the European country of their choice[38]; and (5) that other refugees are also waiting and thus participating in the scheme.

It is conceivable that an effective and asylum-maximising scheme of responsibility sharing might also impose other duties on refugees. I have already alluded to one of these. Refugees who no longer need protection might have a duty to leave their country of asylum and go to another country as an immigrant or return home if doing so was necessary for maximising the availability of asylum.

How might we ground this refugee duty to cooperate with responsibility-sharing schemes? One answer lies in John Rawls's idea that we all have a natural duty of justice to 'support and comply with just institutions that exist and apply to us'. According to Rawls, this duty 'also constrains us to further just arrangements not yet established, at least when this can be done without too much cost to ourselves'.[39] The five requirements I have offered are a way of ensuring that the responsibility-sharing scheme does not impose huge costs on refugees.

But there is another way of expressing the duty here. The duty to act in ways that facilitate responsibility sharing is a duty that refugees owe to other refugees. In their search for asylum, refugees vindicate their support for the institution of asylum. But what they claim for themselves they cannot reasonably deny to others with similar needs and in similar situations. Hence, *if refugees can further an equitable and inclusive system of protection* by making changes to their behaviour, like waiting, at low cost to themselves, they have a duty to do so.[40]

---

[38] It is clear that points three and four seem to hold only if we assume that refugees have a right (or at least a strong moral interest) in choosing the country in which they will find asylum. I believe they do have such a strong moral interest and I make the case for this in Gibney, 'Refugees and Justice between States'.

[39] J. Rawls, *A Theory of Justice* (Cambridge, MA: Harvard University Press, 1971).

[40] Georgia Cole has rightly suggested to me that one can also infer from the behaviour of refugees refusing to wait or stay in various countries of first asylum that they do not see all protection as equal. The actions of refugees, that is, do not simply vindicate the value of asylum but also testify to the necessary conditions for its effective provision.

6 Clarifying Refugee Duties

What can we draw from the discussion of these three duties? First, it is evident that despite emerging from the febrile atmosphere of current immigration politics, none of these duties (to fight, to leave or to wait) is completely baseless. The duty to fight, for example, is one that has a long history, and has often been keenly felt by refugees themselves. In many circumstances, refugeehood quite evidently does not entirely undermine the belief that there are duties to those left behind or even to the state of origin. The duty to leave, on the other hand, is often seen as grounded in the commonplace view that asylum is an act of hospitality by the host state and should not be called upon by a refugee for any longer than it is necessary for their protection. Finally, any organised and functioning system of refugee protection seems likely to require the cooperation of refugees for its success. Hence, it is likely that a duty to wait will be a necessary element of a coordinated system of international refugee protection.

That said, a number of difficulties undermine the attempt to articulate these as compelling moral duties for refugees. Three challenges can be drawn from the preceding discussion. First, it is not always clear what form of action adherence to a particular duty requires for refugees. This was apparent in the case of the duty to fight. Contra Mr Zeman, a duty to fight (assuming one exists) does not necessarily require that refugees engage in military combat. If we interpret the purpose of fighting as resisting an oppressive regime or an aggressive actor, refugees might fulfil this duty through a range of other actions, including giving testimony to atrocities or sending remittances to support armed resistance at home. The duty is thus not necessarily incompatible with the enjoyment of asylum.

A second challenge involves the problem of identifying the appropriate beneficiary of a duty. As we saw, the duty to leave might be conceptualised as owed to the host community, to the community of origin, to other refugees (in pursuit of asylum) or, potentially, to all three. The existence of different beneficiaries might simply make a particular response morally over-determined. But it is also possible that different beneficiaries will lead to conflict in the action required. For example, if the duty to leave is owed the country of origin, the expectation will be that the refugee concerned with return (repatriate) back to their country of origin presumably will assist in the country's recovery. If the duty is owed to the host community, however, all that may be required of the refugee is that she leave the country in question; where she goes is immaterial as long as they ease the 'burden' on the host state. If the duty is owed to other refugees, it would be satisfied if they migrate as non-refugee immigrants to a state that does not accept refugees. A further difficulty is to reconcile potential conflicts of duties. A duty to fight owed to one's compatriots exercised by sending remittances from abroad may be in tension with laws in the host country that forbid funding foreign conflicts. Equally, waiting passively for asylum, as required by the duty to wait, may be in tension with fulfilling a (expansively understood) duty to fight by proceeding directly to a country where refugees can most effectively assist their compatriots left behind.[41]

The final and, in many ways, most fundamental challenge to conceptualising refugees as duty holders concerns whether the beneficiary of the duty is *worthy* of being the recipient of the obligation. This concern emerged in a number of different contexts in the preceding discussion. For example, while there are certainly duties of gratitude, it is not obvious that refugees have them (or at least always have them) to their host state. Clearly, when a host state is implicated in a refugee's need for asylum (for example, by having contributed to the harm that has resulted in need for protection), gratitude may be inappropriate (the state is giving the individual nothing more than they deserve). But, more generally, given that states often go to great lengths to prevent the arrival of refugees at their territory, it is hard to understand why refugees who manage slip through these barriers (often risking their lives to do so) and gain protection ought to be grateful to the state concerned.

The issue of whether the beneficiary is deserving was also evident in the duty to fight. Here, the question concerned what a refugee owes to a state that has persecuted or otherwise failed her in the past. The traditional assumption that refugees would take up the citizenship of the host state on gaining refugee status (on grounds of persecution) illustrates a widespread assumption that ties to the country of origin had been severed. Finally, the question of desert emerged in the duty to wait. In this case, I suggested that a coordinated system of protection could obligate a refugee to wait *only* if it was characterised by certain features (for example, if the refugee's human rights were protected during the wait; the system improved the protection opportunities for refugees overall).

This last challenge suggests that any convincing account of the duties of refugees requires an assessment of the legitimacy of the agents, practices and institutions that govern the lives of refugees. If refugees have duties to return, to wait, to obey or to fight, they do so only under certain

---

[41] I am indebted to Christine Straehle for this point.

circumstances and with certain conditions. Refugee duties are often asserted by political leaders simply to justify the exclusion of refugees, in order to legitimise practices and policies that prevent the arrival of refugees or to facilitate their departure. But a proper examination of the duties of refugees must turn the mirror back on states and ask what makes (or would make) these entities or institutions worthy of the moral respect of refugees.

I have given one example here of what might make institutions deserving: the fact they promote the interests of refugees in gaining asylum. This was evident in my discussions of the circumstances in which one could talk of a duty to wait and a duty to return. Refugees cannot deny the good of maximising the availability of asylum. But it is much less obvious that refugees have obligations to the state from which they have fled and the state which has granted them asylum. This not least because refugees are, by definition, those who have been persecuted or failed by the former and they are (in practice) often poorly treated by the latter, by being (increasingly) subject to forms of social, political and economic exclusion.

7 Conclusion

It is clear that I have only scratched the surface of the issue of refugee duties in this chapter. I hope, however, to have at least pierced the view that political philosophers interested in refugees can safely ignore this topic. Talk of the duties of refugees can obviously be manipulated by political elites to engage in unfair moral criticism of refugees in order to justify their exclusion and the violation of their rights. But a more systematic focus on the duties of refugees can serve to foreground the question of what our social and political institutions would need to look like for such marginalised, neglected and maltreated people to have any responsibilities beyond those of ensuring their own survival. I have attempted to make some inroads into answering this question here.

CHAPTER 8

Is Return the Preferred Solution to Refugee Crises?
Exploring the Moral Value of the Right of Return

Megan Bradley[1]

Voluntary return is hailed as the 'preferred' solution to displacement by many actors in the refugee regime, including states, international organizations such as the Office of the UN High Commissioner for Refugees (UNHCR) and often by refugees themselves. Many political leaders use the rationale that refugees' presence is only temporary, and that they will eventually return to their countries of origin, to justify to their sceptical constituents the decision to shelter thousands of beleaguered foreigners. However, obstacles such as ongoing conflict currently impede large-scale returns to countries like Syria, Iraq and South Sudan. This leaves millions in protracted limbo as other so-called durable solutions to refugee situations, such as resettlement to third countries or local integration and the acquisition of citizenship in asylum states, are simultaneously becoming increasingly rare. When refugees do return, voluntarily or otherwise, they commonly face impoverishment and violence, sometimes resulting in repeated displacement.

Given these conditions, many scholars and advocates have been understandably sceptical of the claim that return is the preferred avenue, practically or theoretically, for resolving refugee situations.[2] Some concede that states' rhetorical insistence that refugees will eventually return plays a useful role in preserving the institution of asylum, but the possibility that there may be other, compelling moral reasons for supporting return as a preferred solution to displacement remains under-examined. When normative arguments pertaining to return movements are explored, there is an unfortunate tendency to focus on narrow or overly reductive interpretations of the right of return – the legal and moral principle underpinning

---

[1] This research was supported with grants from the Social Sciences and Humanities Research Council of Canada (SSHRC). I would like to thank Blair Peruniak for his helpful suggestions.
[2] See, e.g., B. S. Chimni, 'The Meaning of Words and the Role of UNHCR in Voluntary Repatriation', *International Journal of Refugee Law*, 5 (1993), 442–60. In this chapter, I use 'repatriation' and 'return' largely as synonyms.

repatriation movements. For instance, the right of return is often framed disjunctively, or exclusively defined in terms of 'domicile return,' an interpretation whereby the right of return is understood to have been upheld only if exiled individuals not only reenter their countries of origin, but more specifically reclaim their lost homes and lands, and resume living there on a permanent basis. This effaces the much broader range of ways in which refugees themselves have interpreted and advanced this right – practices that illuminate the potential moral value of repatriation for refugees themselves, and reasons why return may in some senses at least be normatively preferable over other approaches to resolving displacement.

Accordingly, in this chapter I identify and preliminarily examine some key arguments that may be forwarded to support the stance that return is the normatively preferable solution to refugees' displacement. I begin by situating the discussion in relation to historical and social science research on return movements and the dynamics of the international refugee regime. I then parse out the actors involved in claiming the right of return, some of the different ways in which this claim can be interpreted and instantiated, and the values associated with these stances. Following this, I explore four interlinked senses in which return may be understood to be morally valuable and in some cases even normatively preferable: first, that the right of return may serve as a means of upholding housing, land and property rights; second, that it may more broadly affirm and advance the equal rights of all citizens; third, that it embodies opposition to the perverse logics of ethnic cleansing and genocide; and fourth, that it may be an important form of redress for refugees. As this discussion demonstrates, under the right circumstances return can advance morally valuable outcomes that other approaches to resolving displacement do not. However, I contend that while some persuasive arguments may be made for promoting return as the 'preferred solution' to displacement, this should not translate into restrictions on the claims of individual refugees to pursue other solutions, such as local integration in the countries and communities where they have sought shelter. Further, I argue that even if refugees attain other solutions, they retain a legitimate claim to return to their countries of origin. In this sense the *possibility* of return is a requisite to the comprehensive resolution of refugee situations, even if it is not uniformly preferable.

Some clarifications: my focus is on voluntary, peaceable returns. The conditions under which returns may be considered truly voluntary, and the legitimacy of involuntary returns, are among the few aspects of return that have been analyzed in detail by scholars concerned with normative aspects of migration.[3] Rather than intervening in these debates, I aim to draw attention to moral and normative aspects of return that have been less commonly addressed. While I concentrate primarily on refugees who have fled across international borders, this discussion is also relevant in varying degrees to those displaced within their own countries. There are of course massive philosophical literatures on how preferences matter morally; much of this work is relevant to this discussion of return as the 'preferred solution' for refugees.[4] However, my aim is not to engage in depth with a particular philosophical approach but to use empirical (and, to a lesser extent, legal) examination of how the right of return has been understood and advanced – particularly by refugees themselves – as a springboard for more pertinent theoretical inquiry on this subject, and to provide a foundation for such inquiries by fleshing out some of the broad normative concerns and values associated with the promotion of refugee returns.

1   Grounding the Debate: Durable Solutions and Return as the 'Preferred' Solution to Displacement

Political theorizing on refugees and migration more generally has been preoccupied with outbound movements from the global South to the global North. Debates have focused on issues such as the obligations of liberal democracies toward those seeking shelter, and states' contested right to control their borders.[5] While certainly important, these debates are largely peripheral to the predicament of the vast majority of the world's refugees – some 85 per cent – who remain in the global South and will, to the extent that they can, seek out solutions to their predicament there. Even theorists who explicitly address dynamics in the global South typically concentrate on questions surrounding the stop-gap institution of asylum, rather than the resolution of refugee situations.[6]

---

[3] See, e.g., M. Gerver, 'Refugee Repatriation and the Problem of Consent', *British Journal of Political Science*, 48 (2016), 855–75; B. S. Chimni, 'From Resettlement to Involuntary Repatriation: Towards a Critical History of Durable Solutions to Refugee Problems', *Refugee Survey Quarterly*, 23 (2004), 55–73.

[4] See, e.g., S. Olsaretti and R. Arneson (eds.), *Preferences and Well-Being* (Cambridge: Cambridge University Press, 2006).

[5] See, e.g., J. Carens, *The Ethics of Immigration* (New York: Oxford University Press, 2013); M. J. Gibney, *The Ethics and Politics of Asylum: Liberal Democracy and the Response to Refugees* (Cambridge: Cambridge University Press, 2004); and S. Fine and L. Ypi (eds.), *Migration in Political Theory: The Ethics of Movement and Membership* (Oxford: Oxford University Press, 2016).

[6] See, e.g., S. Parekh, *Refugees and the Ethics of Forced Displacement* (New York: Routledge, 2017).

Voluntary repatriation is one of three avenues promoted in the context of the international refugee regime to resolve displacement, alongside local integration in host states and resettlement to third countries – a trio of options optimistically referred to as 'durable solutions' for refugees. In theory, securing durable solutions is the ultimate goal of refugee protection, although there is a striking lack of clarity in policy and practice surrounding the conditions under which a refugee situation can reasonably be considered resolved.[7] The term 'durable solution' is not elaborated in the 1951 refugee convention or in the UNHCR statute, although the statute does instruct UNHCR to advance 'permanent solutions for the problem of refugees by assisting Governments ... to facilitate the voluntary repatriation of such refugees, or their assimilation within new national communities'. Normatively, the resolution of refugee situations requires the restoration of full, effective and equal citizenship rights for refugees – or, for those who have never enjoyed such rights, the acceptance of the refugee as an equal, rights-bearing citizen in her state of origin, or in a host country or resettlement state.[8] This position jibes with human rights principles, insofar as an effective nationality is a basic human right, and the meaningful exercise of human rights – as Arendt insists – generally remains tied to the recognition of individuals as citizens by states that are, in theory at least, the guarantors of human rights. However, it also raises complex questions when refugees have little choice but to seek out durable solutions in conflict-ridden or otherwise unstable countries, where citizenship rarely translates into robust and dependable rights protection, whether or not one has been exiled.

When the refugee convention and the UNHCR statute were negotiated in the early years of the Cold War, western powers acknowledged return as the preferred solution to refugee situations in principle, but in practice they considered it too risky and, more to the point, politically undesirable for those fleeing Communist countries. Instead, millions of these refugees were resettled in western states, and their flight and welcome in the west

---

[7] The 1951 refugee convention includes provisions on the cessation of refugee status, but most refugees are not formally recognized under this agreement, and the formal application of the cessation clauses is rare.

[8] On refugeehood as a breakdown in the relationship between states and citizens, see, e.g., A. E. Shacknove, 'Who Is a Refugee?', *Ethics*, 95 (1985), 274–84. On voluntary returns and the reconstruction of refugees' fractured citizenships, see M. Bradley, *Refugee Repatriation: Justice, Responsibility and Redress* (Cambridge: Cambridge University Press, 2013). On citizenship as a sine qua non for local integration as a solution to displacement, see L. Hovil, 'Local Integration', in E. Fiddian-Qasmiyeh et al. (eds.), *The Oxford Handbook of Refugee and Forced Migration Studies* (Oxford: Oxford University Press, 2014), pp. 488–98.

was held up as proof positive of the superiority of capitalist democracy. With the end of the Cold War, the political rationale for such large-scale resettlements evaporated. Instead, voluntary repatriation in 'conditions of safety and dignity' was resurrected as the optimal solution not only in theory but in practice, with UN High Commissioner for Refugees Sadako Ogata labelling the 1990s the 'Decade of Repatriation.' Between 1974 and 2013, more than 28 million refugees voluntarily repatriated. Although return rates have stagnated in recent years, they still far outstrip the number who are able to access resettlement (less than 1 per cent of refugees annually) or formal local integration opportunities.[9]

Given the prominence of return movements and the thorny moral questions they raise, it is striking that there is relatively little discussion of return in the political theory and philosophical literatures concerned with refugees. To the extent that return movements have been broached, the focus has typically been on issues of voluntariness and consent, the responsibilities of states of origin toward returnees, and the resolution of land disputes arising from massive, protracted displacements.[10] The normatively loaded assumption underpinning rhetoric and practice on return – that return is preferable to other options for resolving displacement – has been less commonly probed.

In what ways is the purported preferability of return manifested in the refugee regime, and to what effect? The view that (voluntary) return is the preferred solution to displacement pervades the rhetoric of UNHCR and states in the global North and South, as well as peace agreements, UN resolutions and declarations; it also permeates scholarship and the discourse and political positions of many refugee communities.[11] For example, in the New York Declaration on Refugees and Migrants, unanimously adopted by the UN General Assembly in September 2016, states commit to 'actively promote durable solutions, particularly in protracted refugee situations, with a *focus on sustainable and timely return* in safety and

---

[9] R. Hansen, 'The Comprehensive Refugee Response Framework: A Commentary', *Journal of Refugee Studies*, 31 (2018), 133.

[10] See, e.g., Bradley, *Refugee Repatriation*; Gerver, 'Refugee Repatriation and the Problem of Consent'; and J. Waldron, 'Settlement, Return and the Supersession Thesis', *Theoretical Inquiries in Law*, 5 (2004), 237–68.

[11] UNHCR has in some instances challenged the notion that there is a hierarchy among the three traditional durable solutions. See, e.g., UNHCR, *Refugee Protection and Mixed Migration: 10-Point Plan in Action* (Geneva: UNHCR, 2016), p. 186. These objections are, however, outweighed by more consistent, high-level reiterations on the part of the High Commissioner that return is the preferred solution.

dignity'.[12] The Comprehensive Refugee Response Framework that accompanies the declaration 'reaffirm[s] the *primary goal* of bringing about conditions that would help refugees return in safety and dignity to their countries', further reinforcing the assumed preferability of return.[13] While recognizing the practical impediments to return, Hansen argues that 'For refugees, repatriation is the ideal solution, as most want to return home.... Returning home signifies both a personal and a political triumph.'[14]

To be sure, states do not generally match the professed preferability of return with high levels of financial support for repatriation; typically, states expend much more money on the comparatively limited numbers of refugees who are resettled to the global North, while thousands of refugees repatriate 'spontaneously' – that is, on their own steam and on their own dime. And there are of course important exceptions to the positioning of return as the preferred solution to displacement. For instance, in the Palestinian case there is strong support for return to lost homes and lands among the refugees and Palestinians generally, but implacable resistance from the government of Israel. The return of displaced indigenous peoples to their traditional territories is often blocked by the governments of settler colonial states, notwithstanding provisions promoting such returns in standards such as the UN Declaration on the Rights of Indigenous Peoples. Generally speaking, where displacement has been long-standing, and secondary occupation of displaced persons' lands has been extensive, powerbrokers' support for return movements often wanes, even though, on some readings, the fact that displaced persons have had to wait so long to return to their homes should strengthen, rather than weaken, their claims.[15]

Such disjunctures and inconsistencies in states' support for return serve as a stark reminder that while preferring or privileging return may sometimes accord with refugees' own perspectives, and may be bolstered by important normative arguments – as discussed further below – it is usually a position motivated by states' often narrow and parochial interests. Indeed, the notion of return as the preferred solution to displacement has been vociferously critiqued as a way of foreclosing refugees' access to alternate options, making restrictions seem more justifiable or even morally laudable. 'Solutions talk', particularly the trope of return as the

---

[12] Para. 75, emphasis added.   [13] Emphasis added.
[14] Hansen, 'Comprehensive Refugee Response Framework', 133.
[15] On how the passage of time may affect displaced populations' restitution claims, see J. Waldron, 'Superseding Historic Injustice', *Ethics*, 103 (1992), 4–28; and Waldron, 'Settlement, Return and the Supersession Thesis'.

preferred solution, makes the pursuit of repatriation, local integration and resettlement seem like inherently positive undertakings. Yet the solutions framework itself can arguably legitimize keeping people in prolonged limbo as they are forced to wait for idealized solutions that, for many if not most, may never come.[16] There is also a Janus-faced dimension to how refugees' assumed preferences are valued at different stages of displacement: when refugees seek asylum in a wealthy country instead of a poorer and often unstable neighbouring state, this expression of their preferences is derided as 'asylum shopping'. In contrast, if refugees express a preference for return, their views are suddenly seen to matter, as they lend legitimacy to a 'solution' that meshes with host states' preferences, despite the risks repatriation often raises. Indeed, repatriation can expose returnees to risks from landmines and impoverishment to discrimination and retaliatory violence that outweigh those encountered in exile. Its promotion in spite of these risks often reflects not so much respect for refugees' preferences, but sedentarist assumptions about particular people belonging in particular places.[17] Propagating the idea of return as the preferred solution can also exacerbate refugees' exclusion from host societies by entrenching the perception that refugees do not integrate, and do not want to integrate, because they prefer to return – effacing the possibility of refugees contributing to different communities as dual citizens, or through the exercise of citizenship on multiple levels.[18]

2   Who Claims the Right of Return? What Is Being Claimed?

Having established this foundation for discussing return as a potentially preferred solution to displacement, in this section I identify and differentiate some of the main ways in which the right of return is interpreted and advanced by different actors, and the moral values associated with these positions. What return entails, and what it means to 'prefer' this option, can vary dramatically between actors and over time; efforts to theorize return movements and to understand the normative value of return as a

---

[16] M. Bradley, J. Milner and B. Peruniak, 'Shaping the Struggles of Their Times: Refugees, Peacebuilding and Resolving Displacement', in M. Bradley, J. Milner and B. Peruniak (eds.), *Refugees' Roles in Resolving Displacement and Building Peace: Beyond Beneficiaries* (Washington, DC: Georgetown University Press, 2019), p. 3.

[17] L. Malkki, 'National Geographic: The Rooting of Peoples and the Territorialisation of National Identity among Scholars and Refugees', *Cultural Anthropology* 7 (1992), 24–44.

[18] On multilevel citizenship, see, e.g., W. Maas (ed.), *Multilevel Citizenship* (Philadelphia: University of Pennsylvania Press, 2013).

route to resolving refugee situations need to take account of these variations in who is claiming the right of return, and how they interpret this right.

Whether return constitutes a solution to displacement, never mind a preferred solution, is significantly a matter of perspective. In suggesting that return may serve as a preferred solution, the key question is, of course: For whom? Return may seem like an ideal option from the perspective of reluctant host states and weary donors, but may be experienced by refugees themselves not so much as a solution but as a source of further problems, and even as renewed displacement. These dangers are particularly prominent when returns unfold under pressure, but even when repatriation is largely voluntary, it is still often highly disorienting and risk-ridden. That return is nonetheless still so often held up as the preferred solution for refugees is in part attributable to the fact that return is usually the only durable solution to which refugees have a clear legal right.[19] While refugees may also have moral claims to locally integrate or be resettled, these claims are not generally rooted in national and international laws. In contrast the right of return is well grounded both legally *and* morally as a claim that may be made by individuals as well as by certain groups.[20]

Most provisions of international law on the right of return pertain to its individual expression, particularly in the context of crossing international borders. For example, Article 13(2) of the Universal Declaration of Human Rights states: 'Everyone has the right to leave any country, including his own, and to return to his country,' while Article 12(4) of the International Covenant on Civil and Political Rights indicates: 'No one shall be arbitrarily deprived of the right to enter his own country.'

---

[19] It is striking, however, that return is often also positioned as the 'preferred' solution for internally displaced persons (IDPs), despite the insistence in UN-supported frameworks on internal displacement that, as citizens of the countries in which they are displaced, IDPs have the right to freely choose between returning to their communities of origin, integrating in the community in which they have sought shelter, or relocating elsewhere in their country and should be supported in pursuing the solution of their choice. The tendency to portray return as the optimal solution for IDPs as well as for refugees is a testament to the particular discursive and political power of this idea, and the drive to resolve conflict by putting people and things back where they are assumed to belong. See M. Bradley and A. Sherwood, 'Addressing and Resolving Internal Displacement: Reflections on a Soft Law "Success Story"', in T. Gammeltoft-Hansen, S. Lagoutte and J. Cerone (eds.), *Tracing the Roles of Soft Law in Human Rights* (Oxford: Oxford University Press, 2016), pp. 155–82.

[20] On moral claims to durable solutions, particularly from the perspective of reparative justice, see J. Souter, 'Durable Solutions as Reparations for the Unjust Harms of Displacement: Who Owes What to Refugees?', *Journal of Refugee Studies*, 27 (2014), 171–90. On the legal foundations of the right of return, see H. Hannum, *The Right to Leave and Return in International Law and Practice* (Dordrecht: Martinus Nijhoff, 1987).

However, the right of return, from an international legal perspective, is also an integral aspect of the individual right to freedom of movement, and the right to choose and enjoy one's place of residence.[21] As a group right, the right of return is articulated in international legal standards on the rights of indigenous peoples and is related to principles surrounding national self-determination.

Different normative questions arise depending on whether the right of return is claimed at the individual or group level, and the meaning the right carries in a particular context. Consider a refugee, Sara, from a minority ethnic group targeted in an ethnic cleansing campaign. Sara's family members were killed and she was subjected to severe torture before she escaped, and consequently requires ongoing, specialized medical assistance that she can access in the liberal democratic state in which she was granted refugee status and subsequently citizenship, but not in her country of origin. Returning to live permanently in her country of origin would be physically and psychologically detrimental to Sara, and thus clearly not a preferred option. And yet Sara herself, as a member of her persecuted ethnic group, still holds that physically returning to lost homes and lands should be an option – even a preferred option – for members of her community writ large. Sara herself exercises the right of return periodically, on a short-term basis, to participate in commemorations marking the massacre in which her family was killed. When she returns, she stays in her family home, which she reclaimed through a post-conflict property restitution process.

Sara's case draws attention to the range of ways in which the right of return can be salient. Her case underscores that the meaning refugees ascribe to the right of return, the moral values associated with it, and the consequent preferability of return as a solution to displacement can vary depending on the circumstances and the level on which the claim is being made. This suggests that it is not inconsistent to argue, for example, that return may not be preferable for particular individuals, at the same time as it may be the preferred option for some uprooted groups.

Mapping out, never mind evaluating, the diverse senses in which return may be preferred requires understanding what is actually being claimed. Too often, despite the complexity of claims involved in a case like Sara's,

---

[21] J. M. Henckaerts and L. Doswald-Beck, *Customary International Humanitarian Law* (Cambridge: Cambridge University Press, 2005); W. Kälin, *Guiding Principles on Internal Displacement: Annotations*, revised ed. (Washington, DC: American Society of International Law and Brookings Institution–University of Bern Project on Internal Displacement, 2008).

the right of return is theorized, and debated politically, in overly reductive and disjunctive ways. For example, Stilz defines return as 'a right of those who have been unjustly expelled – or their descendants – to regain permanent residency in their previous territory'.[22] She presents the right of return as a 'disjunctive right', arguing that victims of recent displacements have a right '(1) To go back if they wish; Or, (2) to waive their right of return and accept compensation/aid for building a new life somewhere else'.[23] This perspective reflects the growing influence of the 'domicile return' interpretation of the right of return. On this view, the right of return involves not only the right to reenter and recommence living in one's country of origin, but more specifically the right to reclaim lost homes and lands, and resume permanent residence there.[24] For some refugees, this may be a highly meaningful and desirable way of exercising the right of return. However, the principle should not be so narrowly conceived. Certain aspects of decision-making around return may involve disjunctive choices, but this is not necessarily the case, and many refugees have conceptualized and exercised the right of return in other ways.

Elsewhere, I have developed a typology of some of the distinct but inter-related ways in which the right of return has been interpreted and claimed by displaced persons; some of these typological categories are evident in Sara's case.[25] Briefly summarized, this typology suggests that the right of return may be understood as (1) a claim to reenter a state[26]; (2) to repossess lost homes and lands; and (3) to physically return to and resume living in communities of origin. It may also entail (4) a claim to enjoy

---

[22] A. Stilz, 'Settlement, Expulsion and Return', *Politics, Philosophy and Economics*, 16 (2017), 351–74.

[23] Ibid., 365.

[24] I draw the term 'domicile return' from Toal and Dahlman's discussion of returns to Bosnia. See G. Toal and C. Dahlman, *Bosnia Remade: Ethnic Cleansing and Its Reversal* (Oxford: Oxford University Press, 2011). On the growing influence of this view, see S. Leckie (ed.), *Housing, Land and Property Restitution Rights of Refugees and Displaced Persons: Laws, Cases, and Materials* (Cambridge: Cambridge University Press, 2007).

[25] For a discussion of this typology as it relates to IDPs, see M. Bradley, 'Durable Solutions and the Right of Return for IDPs: Evolving Interpretations', *International Journal of Refugee Law*, 30 (2018), 218–42. This section draws on 232–41 of this article.

[26] Of the different interpretations of the right of return identified in this typology, the view that the right of return entails the right to cross an international border to (re)enter one's state is perhaps the most clearly codified in international human rights law. Throughout the first decades of the post-World War II human rights and refugee regimes, almost until the end of the Cold War, the right of return was commonly understood in this manner. That is, if refugees crossed back into their state of origin, their right of return was assumed to have been upheld, and little attention was paid to where the relatively low numbers of refugees who returned in this period actually ended up. See Hannum, *The Right to Leave and Return*. This aspect of the right of return clearly pertains not only to refugees but to all those who may leave their countries, such as for work, study or tourism, and then seek to return.

freedom of movement and (5) to be recognised as a legitimate member of the political community of the state. It may further be understood as (6) a refusal to acquiesce to ethnic cleansing, (7) a claim for the redress of an injustice or harm, and (8) a religious calling, prerogative or expression of faith. These categories reflect different moral values that may potentially be realised via return, but are not mutually exclusive. In fact, they are often deeply intertwined: when refugees demand or act on their right of return, they may be advancing complex claims, including for a variety of different political, socioeconomic and remedial rights. Thus conceptualizing and exploring the norm disjunctively, and *only* in terms of domicile return, underestimates the practical and theoretical complexity of refugees' claims for the right of return, and its relationship to the resolution of displacement. The error in framing the right of return disjunctively is crystallized in considering the example of dual citizens exiled from one of the countries in which they hold citizenship. The fact that they have residency options elsewhere may reduce the urgency of their situation, but should not preclude them from returning (temporarily, periodically or in the longer term) to the country and community from which they were expelled, where they may retain significant ties on a range of levels. Such cases reflect the complexity of political identities and the possibility of identifying as a citizen across multiple constituencies; to exclude individuals with such identities from legitimately claiming the right of return risks arbitrariness and discrimination.[27]

Instead of taking a disjunctive approach focused on domicile return, the right of return may best be conceived as both a primary right with intrinsic value and a secondary right that has instrumental value in enabling access to a wider range of rights. Relatedly, the assertion of the right of return should be understood as a political process of making complex, often intertwined claims. Building on this discussion, in the following section I examine four senses in which the right of return may be of particular normative value, such that it may potentially be preferred over other approaches to resolving displacement.

3   In What Senses Might Return Be Preferable? Four Possibilities

As the preceding discussion implies, return may be understood as a principled commitment, or as a literal preference, in the sense of an option that a displaced individual or community intends to pursue, whether in

[27] See Maas, *Multilevel Citizenship*.

the long or short term, or intermittently. There may be both instrumental and intrinsic value to return as a solution to displacement; these instrumental and intrinsic values may, depending on the particularities of the case, make return preferable over and above other routes to resolving displacement.

In this section, I analyze four aspects or interpretations of the right of return and highlight their moral or normative value, particularly for refugees as individuals but also for displaced communities more broadly. I do not wish to suggest that these interpretations are salient in all cases, or that these are the most or the only pertinent reasons to support or give preference to return as a potential solution for refugees. As Straehle, for instance, discusses in Chapter 9 in this volume, enabling return may also be a way of respecting and fostering refugees' autonomy. Equally, in highlighting the potentially morally valuable aspects of return movements, I do not wish to diminish or excuse the extent to which portraying return as the 'preferred' solution to displacement is simply a self-serving move on the part of powerful states in the refugee regime to justify the containment of refugees in the global South and to evade responsibility for resettling greater numbers.[28] Beyond the risks returns may pose for individual returnees, return movements may also, as I discuss further in the conclusion, raise morally significant problems such as the destabilization of post-conflict communities or conflict over access to land and other resources. In considering whether return may, on balance, be normatively preferable, these possibilities of course need to be taken into account.

The Right of Return as a Means of Upholding Housing, Land and Property Rights

In the preceding section, I critiqued the reduction of the right of return to domicile return. While it is inappropriate to suggest that this is the only

---

[28] And yet this self-serving discourse may be understood as valuable in its own right, insofar as the notion that return is the preferred solution for refugees helps sustain the institution of asylum itself, convincing states and wary citizens who would not necessarily agree to permanent and major changes to the formal composition of the political community to open their doors on a temporary basis to massive influxes of refugees. We see this dynamic at play in Lebanon, for example. With its delicate confessional system, permanently accepting scores of Syrian refugees, most of them Sunni, would be out of the question. Based on their long and fraught experience hosting the Palestinian refugees, the Lebanese government and its citizens are well aware that returns may be a long time coming – if they come at all. And yet the principle that exercising the right of return is the preferred solution to a refugee crisis helps create political space for the otherwise unimaginable step of sheltering an estimated 1.5 million Syrian refugees in Lebanon.

way in which the right of return can be legitimately exercised, it is also important to recognize the particular value this expression of the right of return may hold. The domicile return view spans several of the typological categories noted above as it is premised on, inter alia, refugees' right to reenter their state, enjoy freedom of movement and repossess lost property. In those (admittedly rare) cases in which the domicile return interpretation is actually implemented, the return process can help to advance a broader range of related goods and rights, including property rights, tenure security, the enjoyment of home and greater socioeconomic security through the restoration of a key asset. Of course not all refugee families own land or homes. Indeed, one of the problems with reducing claims for the right of return to domicile return is that this tends to marginalize those who were landless or who rented or resided informally in their pre-displacement homes, as these refugees typically have much weaker claims (legally, but potentially also morally) to regain their prior abodes.

The domicile return interpretation has long been resonant in the Palestinian case, but efforts to end the war in Bosnia and resolve the displacement crisis that emerged from it raised the prominence of this approach to enabling 'durable solutions' for refugees.[29] The 1995 General Framework Agreement for Peace in Bosnia and Herzegovina (Dayton Agreement) was pivotal to the propagation of this interpretation of the right of return. Motivated by a desire to 'turn back the tide' on ethnic cleanings in Bosnia and to legitimate the return of refugees from unwilling host states, the agreement had unprecedently strong provisions on return and restitution, pledging that:

> All refugees and displaced persons have the right freely to return to their homes of origin. They shall have the right to have restored to them property of which they were deprived.

This interpretation of the right of return, and the connection between return and property restitution, are now encoded in dozens of peace agreements and hundreds of UN resolutions on conflicts generating large-scale displacement.

---

[29] From predominant Palestinian perspectives, this interpretation of the right of return is enshrined in UN General Assembly Resolution 194, which indicates that 'refugees wishing to return to their homelands and live at peace with their neighbours should be permitted to do so at the earliest practicable date, and that compensation should be paid for the property of those choosing not to return and for the loss of or damage to property which, under principles of international law or in equity, should be made good by the Governments or authorities responsible'. The government of Israel contends that Resolution 194 does not establish a *right* of return, but merely indicates that refugees *should* be allowed to return.

Efforts to sustainably resolve displacement often depend on the ability of the displaced to regain their homes and lands, and in this sense (among others) the popularization of the domicile return interpretation represents a significant development in efforts to protect and advance displaced persons' rights and well-being. Domicile return is intertwined with strengthened property rights both on an individual level, through housing, land and property restitution, and on the broader social level as massive property restitution processes, such as the one implemented after the Bosnian War, can be used to overhaul inoperable tenure and property ownership systems, laying the foundations for more viable post-conflict development and investment.

In theory, refugees who resettle or integrate into their countries of asylum could and arguably should be able to repossess their homes and lands even if they do not physically return to reside there. The right to restitution can be considered separately from the right of return, and a commitment to strengthening restitution rights for refugees need not *necessarily* imply the preferability of return over other approaches to resolving displacement. However, in practice, accessing formal and informal property restitution processes usually hinges on physical repatriation.[30] In cases in which there has been long-standing secondary occupation of refugees' lost homes, it would be morally difficult to justify displacing the secondary occupants if this was not to make way for refugees to physically return and resume residence in their homes, thus ending suffering and deprivations of equal or greater magnitude to those that would be created by uprooting the secondary occupants. For many returnees, reclaiming their lost homes and resuming their lives on ancestral lands alleviates suffering and deprivation precisely because their homes and lands hold deep psychological, cultural and spiritual significance, at the same time as they serve as important economic assets. This suggests that the right of return, particularly domicile return, may hold distinctive moral

---

[30] In the Bosnian case, many returnees who reclaimed their lost properties through the restitution process sold them and used the proceeds to move elsewhere in the country, particularly if this enabled them to live in a community where they would be part of the ethnic majority. Some have interpreted such moves as a failure to implement the right of return. It is certainly a practical and moral failure that some returnees who wanted to resume permanent residence in their former homes felt that they could not do so owing to concerns such as insecurity. However, refugees who repatriated, reclaimed and then sold their homes to finance the purchase of a new home in another community in the country still, in my view, exercised the right of return, albeit in a different form than domicile return. For refugees who want to return, but not necessarily to live in their former residences, restitution may increase their ability to pursue their preferred form of return.

value as a solution for refugees, opening up goods or benefits that cannot be accessed through other approaches to resolving displacement.

Affirming the Equal Rights of All Citizens

Political theorizing on displacement typically positions the refugee as a figure who has been exiled, physically but also figuratively, from her political community.[31] From this vantage, appeals for the right of return may, importantly, be understood as membership claims, and the repatriation process as an opportunity to reconstitute citizenries fractured by exile and conflict. Theoretically speaking, perhaps the greatest challenge repatriation processes raise is repositioning refugees as full citizens who can advance rights claims on equal bases with their non-displaced co-nationals.[32] If upholding the right of return is understood to entail acknowledging returnees as full and equal citizens, the right of return then becomes a springboard for other claims returnees may make as citizens.

In asserting the right of return, whether through domicile return or in other forms, refugees contest the state's prerogative to unilaterally determine who counts as a member of the national political community. All durable solutions to displacement hinge on the acceptance of refugees as full and legitimate members of the political community of a state (or several states, whether this is the refugees' state of origin, the state of asylum and/or a resettlement state) and entail some degree of contestation over the bounds of and inclusion in the political community of the state. However, the contestation of states' exclusionary power through the return process is particularly significant, as returnees engage the very states that expelled or failed to protect them in struggles for recognition as equal and valid members of the community. Returnees may thus be powerful (if often unacknowledged) protagonists in broader struggles for state reform, peace-building and post-conflict reconciliation. This dynamic was apparent, for example, in the return movements to El Salvador and Guatemala in the 1980s and 1990s, where refugees developed shared understandings of the right of return as an individual and collective right and, through asserting this right, sought to transform ideas about national belonging and

---

[31] See, e.g., H. Arendt, *The Origins of Totalitarianism*, 2nd ed. (New York: Meridian Books, 1958); M. J. Gibney, 'Refugees and Justice between States', *European Journal of Political Theory*, 14 (2015), 448–63.

[32] Bradley, *Refugee Repatriation*.

the exclusionary nature of their fractured states.[33] As a means of contesting exclusionary state power and affirming the equal rights of all citizens, return may thus be considered morally valuable or even preferable, in ways that other durable solutions to displacement are not.[34]

Return as Opposition to Ethnic Cleansing

Beyond being an opportunity to reconstitute or recast the political community of a refugee-creating state on – ideally – more inclusive and equitable foundations, return may more specifically be understood to hold value as an expression of opposition to ethnic cleansing. To see the normative significance of this perspective, consider once again the Bosnian case: after genocides and conflicts involving ethnic cleansing, such as the Bosnian War, insisting on the right to free movement, including and in particular through the permanent or temporary return of forced migrants to their communities of origin, can be a compelling form of dissent to these twisted political projects. This view was one of the motivators of the architects of the Dayton peace process, who insisted on the inclusion of robust provisions on the right of return in the treaty. As Toal and Dahlman recognize, 'None of the major powers supporting the international effort in Bosnia ever seriously thought that the demographic legacy of ethnic cleansing could be reversed. The debate was whether to accept it as an unassailable reality.'[35]

Refugees do not necessarily need to engage in domicile return for their movements to be salient in this sense. Even when refugees settle elsewhere (within their country of origin or abroad), periodic, temporary returns can be an important element of their efforts to grapple with their experiences of displacement, and express dissent in relation to the violations that fuelled it. Refugees may, as Sara's case suggests, return to visit graves or commemorate losses, and in such ways resist their individual and communal erasure from a place they have called home.[36] Absent the ability to

---

[33] M. Bradley, 'Rethinking Refugeehood: Statelessness, Repatriation, and Refugee Agency', *Review of International Studies*, 40 (2014), 101–23; M. Bradley, 'Unlocking Protracted Displacement: Central America's "Success Story" Reconsidered', *Refugee Survey Quarterly*, 30 (2011), 84–121.

[34] On returnees as leaders in peacebuilding and reconciliation, see, e.g., J. Milner, 'Refugees and the Regional Dynamics of Peacebuilding', *Refugee Survey Quarterly*, 28 (2011), 13–30.

[35] Toal and Dahlman, *Bosnia Remade*, pp. 7–8.

[36] On these forms of return in the Bosnian case, see, e.g., L. J. Nettelfield and S. E. Wagner, *Srebrenica in the Aftermath of Genocide* (Cambridge: Cambridge University Press, 2013); C. Pollack, 'Returning to a Safe Area? The Importance of Burial for Return to Srebrenica', *Journal of Refugee Studies*, 16 (2003), 186–201.

engage in such forms of return, refugees who have settled elsewhere may feel that they have not really chosen a durable solution, but have been compelled to capitulate to their expulsion. In this sense, return may be 'preferred,' not as an easy or idealized solution, but as a form of political resistance.

The Right of Return as Redress

Last, and again relatedly, the right of return may also have particular moral value as a form of redress – including, but not exclusively, through the restitution of lost homes and lands. Beyond the physical loss of homes and lands, the injustices associated with displacement may also include the destruction of communities, disruption of individual and shared life plans, non-recognition as a legitimate member of the political community, denial of basic rights and suffering experienced in often harsh conditions in exile. In light of these injustices, various international standards explicitly acknowledge that enabling the right of return may constitute a meaningful form of redress in its own right.[37]

Suggesting that return may serve as a form of redress is not to conflate it with quixotic attempts to restore the status quo ante. It is both impossible and undesirable to attempt to recreate the conditions that existed prior to refugees' displacement – not least because these were the conditions that left refugees vulnerable to expulsion in the first place. Such an approach also risks effacing the harms experienced during long years of displacement, as if putting refugees 'back where they belong' balances out injustices and suffering experienced in exile. That said, for some displaced persons return may have a significant remedial dimension that is usually not part of other durable solutions to displacement, such as resettlement or local integration. This is in part because, as discussed above, return typically requires the active support and acceptance of the state of origin – the actor usually responsible for refugees' uprooting.[38] By supporting or enabling refugees' return, states may express responsibility and begin the

---

[37] See, for example, the 2005 UN Basic Principles and Guidelines on the Right to a Remedy and Reparation for Victims of Gross Violations of International Human Rights Law and Serious Violations of International Humanitarian Law.

[38] In some contexts, other durable solutions may also have remedial value. For instance, many Iraqis and Afghans who worked as translators and in other capacities for US forces have subsequently been persecuted and had to flee as refugees. Some current and former US officials have promoted resettling them to the United States as an expression of remedial responsibility for their situation. See Souter, 'Durable Solutions', on this dynamic.

long process of accounting for the harms they perpetuated by displacing their citizens.[39] This idea is front and centre in the peace process currently unfolding in Colombia, where the government is attempting to use a range of remedies, including individual and communal returns, to redress displaced victims of the country's long-standing armed conflict.[40]

4 Conclusion: Preserving the Possibility of Return

Return is too often promoted as a foil for xenophobic and restrictionist sentiments, and comes with significant risks for returnees themselves. This has fostered a certain scepticism among many scholars and advocates concerned with refugee protection that returns can be justifiable, never mind normatively preferable. The previous discussion suggests that if returns are undertaken voluntarily, in conditions of safety and dignity, and with due respect for the rights of all involved (all admittedly big 'ifs' in most countries to which refugees return in large numbers), returns can advance rights and contribute to the achievement of moral goods in ways that the other traditional durable solutions to displacement do not.

I have argued that the moral challenges and problems that may be evoked in return processes may be exacerbated if the right of return is interpreted in overly narrow or disjunctive ways. Attentiveness to the diverse range of ways in which refugees themselves interpret and claim the right of return, and the values they associate with it, brings into focus possibilities and opportunities for compromise that may be overlooked if the right of return is narrowly equated with domicile return. Resettlement and local integration may also foster the achievement of moral goods that returns do not, such as greater diversity and inclusivity in host societies. Depending on how different actors value these potential contributions, and weigh them against each other, return may be considered the preferred solution – but this will always be a context-specific judgement, in which there may be divergences between the moral preferability of return for individuals and for displaced groups.

Context-specific judgements on the moral preferability of return must also take into account returnees' own intentions and political commitments, and the potential consequences of return for other citizens. My

---

[39] Bradley, *Refugee Repatriation*.
[40] See J. Lemaitre and K. Sandvik, 'From IDPs to Victims in Colombia: Reflections on Durable Solutions in the Post-Conflict Setting', in M. Bradley, J. Milner and B. Peruniak (eds.), *Refugees' Roles in Resolving Displacement and Building Peace: Beyond Beneficiaries* (Washington, DC: Georgetown University Press, 2019), pp. 187–210.

focus here has been on the vast majority of returnees who seek to repatriate peacefully. However, in some cases, would-be returnees are 'refugee warriors' uninterested in peaceful coexistence alongside their former neighbours. For instance, exiled Hutu militias controlling refugee camps in Zaire in the aftermath of the 1994 Rwandan genocide sought to return through violent means, as a step toward retaking power and completing the extermination of the Tutsi. Clearly, return on such terms is the precise opposite of morally preferable. Even in less extreme cases, in which returnees' intentions are peaceful, repatriation after protracted displacement may be destabilizing, and spark conflict over access to land, housing and other resources. This is particularly likely when there has been long-standing secondary occupation of refugees' lost property.[41] Generally speaking, the risks associated with such conflict and destabilization must be recognized and mitigated, rather than used as a reason to indefinitely delay voluntary exercise of the right of return.

Notwithstanding the contributions return can make to advancing rights and related moral values, and the senses in which it may therefore be preferable, it would be a mistake to foreclose, on this basis, individual refugees' access to other options. Most of the senses in which return may be normatively preferable pertain to more abstract, macro levels of analysis that may be disjointed from the rights, needs, vulnerabilities and aspirations of individual refugees. In some cases, refugee communities, states, donors and humanitarian agencies may conclude that return is, on the whole, preferable, and should be supported through the allocation of political capital and significant financial resources.[42] But as Sara's case underscores, such macro-level assessments should not eclipse the possibility that for particular individuals, certain forms of return, such as domicile return, are incompatible with respect for basic rights, physical security and dignity and are thus not only unpreferable but morally unacceptable.

If return is not tenable for particular refugees, they should be supported in accessing other durable solutions or continued asylum (with the right to work and as much autonomy in directing their own lives as possible).

---

[41] Secondary occupants may themselves have been displaced, and may have strong claims, on various grounds, to continue residing in homes and on lands that they now consider to be their own. A full discussion of this problem is not possible here. However, it should be noted that if, as Waldron has argued, the intention behind the occupation of refugees' lost homes was to preclude their return, then the long duration of secondary occupancy would not morally legitimize a claim to retain the property. See Waldron, 'Settlement, Return and the Supersession Thesis'.

[42] On the complexities of shared agency in the context of decision-making processes around attempts to resolve displacement, see B. Peruniak, 'Displacement Resolution and Massively Shared Agency', in Bradley et al. (eds.), *Refugees' Roles in Resolving Displacement and Building Peace*, pp. 55–74.

And yet even if refugees resettle or locally integrate, they retain legitimate claims to exercise the right of return, in the form(s) most relevant to them. If refugees prefer to return but cannot, then in a fundamental sense their displacement has not really been resolved – even if they do not require humanitarian assistance and have another passport. In this sense the *possibility* of return (although not necessarily domicile return) is a requisite to the resolution of refugee crises, even if it is not the active preference of all refugees, given the diverse circumstances facing them.

To what extent are different actors in the refugee regime, particularly states, international organizations and donors, obliged to try to make return a viable option? What forms of return must they enable? While it is not possible to do justice to these complex questions here, we may begin to consider them from the perspective of arguments concerned with the autonomy of migrants and refugees. In such debates, Miller has argued that autonomy requires having an adequate range of choices to choose from, not that all choices are equally available to everyone.[43] Oberman has relatedly argued that 'autonomy is infringed if and when we are coercively prevented from choosing certain options' that should otherwise be open to us.[44] With these views in mind, it is clear that the nature of the obligation that different actors are under to support returns will vary depending on the actor's moral identity, their relationship to the refugees concerned, and the constraints they are under. For example, in situations of constrained resources, it will be desirable for UNHCR, as a humanitarian agency mandated to aid refugees, to focus their efforts primarily on protecting, assisting and enabling durable solutions for refugees in particularly precarious circumstances. For states of origin, however, the obligation is different: given that would-be returnees usually remain their citizens, they must, at a minimum, remove arbitrary barriers to their return, such as laws and policies that prohibit those who fled from returning.

[43] D. Miller, 'Why Immigration Controls Are Not Coercive: A Reply to Arash Abizadeh', *Political Theory*, 38 (2010), 111–20.

[44] K. Oberman, 'Immigration as a Human Right', in Fine and Ypi (eds.), *Migration in Political Theory*, pp. 32–56.

CHAPTER 9

Refugees and the Right to Return

Christine Straehle[1]

1 Introduction

The moral challenge of asylum and refuge arises from the internationally accepted principle of *non-refoulement* laid out in Article 33 of the Geneva Convention. The moral logic of *non-refoulement* is the implicit acknowledgement of the need for help: 'Whenever a state acknowledges that it would be wrong to send someone back to her home country, it is implicitly recognizing that person as a refugee ..., that is, as someone whose situation generates a strong moral claim to admission in a state in which she is not a citizen.'[2] Signatory states of the Geneva Convention are prohibited from immediately refusing asylum claims of those who request refuge. Instead, states are mandated to evaluate refugees' demands for asylum fairly by assessing the human right violations the migrant has suffered in the past, and the likelihood of suffering grave human rights violations in the future if she were sent back into her country of origin.

Yet it is not clear *what else* the moral promise of asylum contains *besides* the strong claim to protection. As Paul Collier and Alexander Betts have argued,

> The imagined needs of refugees have been reduced to two basics – food and shelter – and it has become assumed that the most viable way to provide such rights is through camps. It was not meant to be this way. Refugee-intake strategies were originally intended to promote access to autonomy, with particular focus on the right to work and freedom of movement.[3]

[1] Earlier versions of this chapter have been presented at the Amsterdam Graduate Fall School on Migration in October 2017 and at the Centre for Ethics, Université de Montréal in February 2018. I would like to thank the audiences of both these events for their comments, in particular Robin Celikates, Peter Dietsch and Christine Tappolet. Thanks are also due to David Owen and especially David Miller for comments and suggestions.
[2] J. Carens, *The Ethics of Immigration* (New York: Oxford University Press, 2013), p. 205.
[3] A. Betts and P. Collier, *Refuge: Transforming a Broken Refugee System* (London: Allen Lane, 2017), p. 156.

The call for more extensive duties beyond provision of food and shelter has recently gained some argumentative clout in the literature on justice in migration.[4] Asylum-granting states are then taken to be called on to provide refugees with a new home and the protection of human rights, but also, over time, social, political and civic rights that characterize membership in the asylum-granting state.[5] Only through such an extensive set of rights can refugees have access to the means of autonomy and agency, so the argument goes.

My aim in this chapter is to develop an account of asylum based on the liberal value of individual autonomy. The normative claim that asylum should include access to the means of autonomy expands on the generally accepted promise of asylum as a promise to protect human rights such as the right to be protected against persecution and the right to bodily integrity. As I construe it, to be able to be autonomous, individuals also need to be able to be part of a community that resides on a specific territory. And while I accept that for some refugees, the relevant community may be or may become that of the asylum-granting state, for others the relevant community may be that of the country of origin. Hence, I want to propose that a political philosophy of refuge concerned with the conditions of individual autonomy should include a right to return as part of the rights that asylum secures.

In international law, the right to return is mentioned in Art 13 of the Universal Declaration of Human Rights, which states that

(1) Everyone has the right to freedom of movement and residence within the borders of each State.
(2) Everyone has the right to leave any country, including his own, and to return to his country.

In particular, section 2 of Article 13 suggests that there may be not only a right of exit, but also the protection of the freedom to *return* to one's country of origin. I take this as my point of departure to argue that the moral logic of asylum implies not only that asylum-granting states have moral duties to allow entry and grant admission onto their territory, but

---

[4] For an overview of recent literature, see C. Straehle, 'Justice in Migration', *Canadian Journal of Philosophy*, 48 (2018), 245–65.

[5] M. E. Price, *Rethinking Asylum: History, Purpose, and Limits* (Cambridge: Cambridge University Press, 2010); D. Owen, 'In Loco Civitatis: On the Normative Basis of the Institution of Refugeehood and Responsibilities for Refugees', in S. Fine and L. Ypi (eds.), *Migration in Political Theory: The Ethics of Movement and Membership* (Oxford: Oxford University Press, 2016), pp. 269–90.

that asylum-granting states also have a moral duty to enable the *right of return* for refugees.[6]

My argument proceeds in two steps. First, I will explore the normative basis of a possible right to return, discussing the premise of individual autonomy as it applies to refugees. I suggest that we can justify the right to return based on the idea that return to the home country, the relationships it allows for and the cultural, social and community context it provides and promotes are necessary to have access to the conditions of individual autonomy.

Second, I will discuss the feasibility of a right of return, and its possible content, proposing that it is in principle feasible for asylum-granting states to enable a right to return. I suggest that one way asylum-granting states can satisfy the emergent duties is by rethinking asylum policies, for example, by promoting professional development for refugees and by collaborating with the state of origin and international partners to make safe return possible. In my view, it is not plausible to suggest that asylum-granting states are responsible for providing returnees with the best possible options in their country of origin, such as a functioning liberal democracy or a well-established welfare state; instead, asylum-granting states ought to provide conditions that make return feasible, such as providing for opportunities to maintain professional qualifications, or acquiring them while in the asylum-grating state, and assuring bodily safety in the country of origin on return. One example of how to do so is the regulation of asylum policy. Some policies may go counter to the idea of returning home, such as those that tie asylum status to measures of integration into the host state. Having argued that a right to return is normatively justified and feasible, I conclude that a right of return should be considered one of the rights that the promise of asylum ought to help realize.

2 Individual Autonomy as the Normative Basis for the Right to Return

As we have seen, Collier and Betts appeal to the idea of individual autonomy for refugees when thinking about concrete obligations. Similarly, James Hathaway argues that the refugee regime

---

[6] The idea here is that agent A can act in ways that enable agent B to enjoy B's rights. In this vein, I construe the task for asylum-granting states as providing the necessary conditions to enable refugees to realize the right to return.

was *actually* established to guarantee refugees lives in dignity until and unless either the cause of their flight is firmly eradicated or *the refugee himself or herself* chooses to pursue some alternative solution to their disenfranchisement.... Refugee protection is ... fundamentally oriented to creating conditions of independence and dignity, which enable *refugees themselves* to decide how they wish to cope with predicaments. It is about ensuring autonomy.[7]

Most states would probably agree with the first part of Hathaway's claim; however, even the best intentioned may wonder what 'ensuring autonomy' for refugees may imply.

Individual Autonomy as a Basic Interest

Autonomy as a philosophical concept to analyse duties of asylum can be separated into value conditions and content conditions. To determine the necessary *content* of the concept, I follow Joseph Raz's account of individual autonomy.[8] According to Raz, autonomy most basically implies that individuals should be 'part authors of their own lives'.[9] This is to say that persons should have some jurisdiction over the shape their lives take. To be able to exercise such authorship, specific conditions need to be in place: autonomy depends on having access to a range of options, among which to choose the course we want to give our lives, to be reasonably free from coercion when choosing among viable options, and to be reasonably able to implement these choices.

The *value* of autonomy is based on the contribution autonomy makes to individual well-being. According to Raz, being able to be autonomous is necessary for leading good lives. Thus, individuals have a basic interest in leading autonomous lives.[10] Liberal-democratic states have the responsibility to protect the basic interests of their citizens. If autonomy is accepted to contribute to well-being, because of the link between autonomy and the basic interest in leading good lives,[11] then liberal-democratic states are taken to have duties of autonomy for those in their care.

Asylum-granting states accept duties of asylum to protect the basic interests of those whose states no longer protect them. These are the basic interests of having access to shelter and food, but also the basic interest of being free from persecution. If we agree that refuge is meant to protect

---

[7] J. C. Hathaway, 'Refugee Solutions, or Solutions to Refugeehood?', *Refuge* (2007), available at https://refuge.journals.yorku.ca/index.php/refuge/article/viewFile/21378/20048. Emphasis added.
[8] J. Raz, *The Morality of Freedom* (Oxford: Oxford University Press, 1986).
[9] Ibid., pp. 370–73.   [10] Ibid., p. 416.   [11] Ibid., p. 418.

individual basic interests, then it should also be plausible to say that the first-order interest of having access to the means of autonomy as an important component of a good life may equally demand state protection.

Of course, a first objection to my proposal could be that liberal-democratic states owe duties of autonomy to their own citizens within the liberal state, but not to asylum claimants or accepted refugees. In the first instance, we could say that autonomy is an important liberal good, and that it serves the functions just described within liberal-democratic states. However, prima facie it may seem less clear why asylum-granting states should be bound by duties of autonomy toward those who originate from home countries that are not liberal democracies, and who may wish to return there. Put differently, it may not be clear what value autonomy may play in the lives of those coming from non-liberal countries and hoping to return to such countries.

In the context of a *liberal* political philosophy of refuge, however, it seems implausible to suggest that liberal states apply different measures and values to the design of their asylum policies than indeed the liberal ones they espouse for their citizens. Liberal governments adopt and implement liberal values because liberals believe that these values are justifiable ones. Moreover, at least for some refugees it may have been the very fact that their home countries did not protect individual liberties, such as freedom of expression or freedom of religion, that made it necessary for them to flee. It would thus add insult to injury to neglect the liberal value of autonomy when deliberating about what refugees are owed at least once they are in liberal-democratic countries.

In a second instance, however, critics could argue that there is an important distinction to be drawn between citizens qua members of the state, and thus in its care, and refugees who do not have the same status. In this view, states owe treatment to their citizens that they do not owe to outsiders.[12] The distinction can be justified by pointing out that citizens share in a coercive institutional context that distributes benefits within the state, whereas those outside the context of citizenship do not experience this specific kind of coercion.[13] The concern for individual autonomy within the liberal state would then serve as a counterbalance to the coercive institutional framework of the state. As I will explain later, though, it is

---

[12] D. Miller, *Strangers in Our Midst: The Political Philosophy of Immigration* (Cambridge, MA: Harvard University Press, 2016), ch. 2.

[13] M. Blake, 'Distributive Justice, State Coercion, and Autonomy', *Philosophy and Public Affairs*, 30 (2001), 257–96.

part of the promise of asylum that asylum claimants gain status as temporary or permanent members of the asylum-granting state. If granted temporary or permanent status, then even those who seek return over time first seek membership in at least a part of the institutional system of the asylum-granting state. Most refugees hope to work in their country of asylum, and in many asylum-granting states, participation in the labour market is encouraged as a tool of integration. If they do work, refugees participate in the institutions of redistribution, such as taxation of their wages. More generally, refugees have to submit to the institutions that regulate civic and social life in the asylum-granting state, such as observing the laws of the land and obeying the police. It seems plausible to say that it is participation in these institutional practices that warrants that they be treated on par with citizens in the relevant respects, that is, in the concern that the liberal state accords to their basic interest in leading autonomous lives.

Autonomy and Community Membership

So far, I have described only the value and content conditions of autonomy as an analytical concept for a political philosophy of refuge. I now want to turn to some of the ways in which the concept of autonomy has been applied in political philosophy to show how concern for individual autonomy can justify a duty to enable the right of return. In this vein, a look at the recent literature discussing the moral status of territorial occupancy and, more relevant to my purposes here, the harm that is inflicted on those who are driven from their homeland is helpful.

A moral right to residency has been defined as in part 'a right of nondispossession, a right to remain, at liberty, in one's own home and community and not to be removed from the place of one's projects, aims, and relationships'.[14] According to at least one account, territorial occupancy is important since it allows individuals access to important means to develop their lives according to their own plans.[15] More specifically, territorial occupancy is fundamental 'for an individual's personal autonomy – his ability to form and pursue a conception of the good',[16] making

[14] M. Moore, *A Political Theory of Territory* (Oxford: Oxford University Press, 2015), p. 36.
[15] A. Stilz, 'Occupancy Rights and the Wrong of Removal', *Philosophy and Public Affairs*, 41 (2013), 337–38.
[16] A. Stilz, 'Nations, States and Territory', *Ethics*, 121 (2011), 583.

it impossible 'to move me without damage to nearly all of my life plans'.[17] Call this the *right to territorial occupancy* argument.

One of the wrongs that removal causes is the severing of important relationships. 'If we are to have any control over our lives, we have to have control over the most fundamental elements in the background conditions of our existence, and among these is the ability to stay in our communities.'[18] For many, the most relevant community may be the political one. Put differently, individuals may care about being on the territory of origin because they want to participate in the political process of their home country.[19] And indeed, political philosophers have proposed political and social self-determination as yet another important background condition for individual autonomy. Much of the literature on democratic self-determination, for instance, is based on the idea that individuals should be able to lead autonomous lives not only in the moral realm but also in the political realm.[20] Individuals should then have political rights to determine the laws of the community but also be able to associate with those with whom they wish to associate in the political realm.[21] Call this the *right to membership* argument.

Earlier, I showed that the UNDHR protects the individual right to exit one's country of origin – as I have said, together with the promise of protection against persecution and abuse, the right to exit is taken by many as the rationale underlying the principle of asylum. At this point in the discussion, we could thus make an argument from analogy: while the right

---

[17] Ibid., 584.   [18] Moore, *A Political Theory of Territory*, p. 38.

[19] To be sure, the political process in the country of origin may not be democratic, and a critic could raise the objection that the political participation argument plausibly applies only in a democracy. I do not see why this should be so: one can hope to participate in the political process through different means than standard democratic procedures, such as mobilizing against unjust regimes, joining an underground radio station or publishing critical accounts of the government. To illustrate, former dissident Vaclav Havel was highly influential in bringing down the communist regime of then Czechoslovakia through his writings while in jail. Similarly, many political dissidents in former East Germany refused moving to West Germany, something regularly offered to them by the socialist regime, since they saw their political role within the GDR.

[20] The link between individual autonomy and political self-determination can be summarized succinctly: '(1) people's membership of encompassing groups is an important aspect of their personality, and their well-being depends on giving it full expression; (2) expression of membership essentially includes manifestation of membership in the open, public life of the community; (3) this requires expressing one's membership in political activities within the community. The political is an essential arena of community life, and consequently of individual well-being.' A. Margalit and J. Raz, 'National Self-Determination', *The Journal of Philosophy*, 87 (1990), 451.

[21] In making the link between self-determination and freedom of association, I follow C. H. Wellman, *A Theory of Secession: The Case for Political Self-Determination* (Cambridge: Cambridge University Press, 2005), especially ch. 3.

to exit one's territory would provide the necessary conditions to have our interests protected against possible rights abuses by the original state government, the right to return could be understood as a right protecting the basic interest to associate with others for the purposes of political self-determination. The right to return would thus help create the physical conditions of being present on the territory to associate with those who have remained there.[22]

However, the right to associate importantly includes the right to *refuse* to associate.[23] Thus, a critic of the right to membership argument could hold that if those who remained in the country of origin now refuse to associate with exiles, then the argument from freedom of association cannot bolster a right to return as part of the right to asylum.

To illustrate this very concrete concern, take the example of Hutu refugees who left Rwanda after the civil war but who now hope to return. As Megan Bradley discusses in Chapter 8 in this volume, the local Tutsis who suffered at Hutu hands in the civil war in 1994 are certain to resent the Hutus' return, maybe even suspecting them of less than peaceful intentions. If France as a state granting asylum to Hutu refugees were now to actively seek to provide for conditions for their return, it might easily be perceived as unsavoury meddling. It seems nevertheless implausible to suggest that France would be justified if it was summarily preventing Hutu refugees from return. Unless individual Hutus had been convicted of concrete genocide-related crimes in the context of an international tribunal, preventing individuals from return would violate their rights. Put differently, especially if return is meant to foster political self-determination of individuals as members of political groups, it would be implausible to suggest that asylum-granting states pose as arbiter of the interests and choices of conflicting groups. If political self-determination is indeed a necessary part of individual autonomy, as I suggested above, and if return to the territory is a way of realizing political self-determination,

---

[22] In my view, this is not to say that freedom of association could ground a right to join *any* polity one wishes to. As I explained earlier, return to the territory is meaningful because it helps reestablish the communal relationships, including political relationships that support individual autonomy. It would be implausible to substantiate a right to join new political communities based on the assumption that such relationships can be found anywhere. Thus, to suggest that the arguments from freedom of association motivate a putative right to joining any polity would be too voluntaristic an interpretation.

[23] In the migration literature, Wellman has proposed this argument in defence of restrictive immigration regimes. C. H. Wellman, 'Immigration and Freedom of Association', *Ethics*, 119 (2008), 109–41. For an important critique of Wellman, see J. Brezger and A. Cassee, 'Debate: Immigrants and Newcomers by Birth – Do Statist Arguments Imply a Right to Exclude Both?', *Journal of Political Philosophy*, 24 (2016), 367–78.

then simply barring the possibility of return is tantamount to barring access to one component of individual autonomy.

To be sure, concerns over individual autonomy do not translate into absolute rights and prescriptions; I believe, though, that withholding access to possible grounds of autonomy demands a weighty justification. The situation may thus be one in which we have to weigh, on the one hand, the interest in political self-determination and, on the other hand, concerns over social stability. A third element to take into consideration is the hopeful returnees' earlier association with the community. We may wonder if freedom of association can be invoked to refuse association with former members. If we assume that Hutu Rwandans still have Rwandan citizenship, then presumably Tutsi Rwandans would have to strip them of this link before being justified in refusing association.

Returning to the obligations of the asylum-granting state, though, and considering circumstances of latent civil unrest, the question remains if it would be irresponsible on the part of France, say, to adopt a proactive policy to enable Hutu refugees to return if it led to reigniting civil war. One way to address the worry would be to say that France would have to assure that return not lead to civic instability, by providing further resources for the country of origin to establish safeguards, such as providing support for the local police and establishing support for civil society organizations. However, such measures would go well beyond the scope of the right of return as I imagine it here, as I explain later. In this instance, I believe that asylum-granting states are in a true dilemma, to which we can add historical considerations of colonialism and its effect.[24] The dilemma may be that asylum-granting states that want to provide individual refugees with the means to return are faced with the detrimental effects return of a group may have on the state of origin.[25]

Assessing the link between autonomy and community membership from yet a different perspective, however, critics of a right to return could furthermore object that membership in the asylum-granting state is sufficient as a basis for individual autonomy. Asylum-granting states would then only have to provide for rights of membership there – but not to provide for the possibility to rekindle membership in the state of origin.

---

[24] James Souter has suggested asylum as a reparation policy for colonial wrongs: J. Souter, 'Towards a Theory of Asylum as Reparation for Past Injustice', *Political Studies*, 62 (2014), 326–42.

[25] To put this differently, rather than understanding asylum in this instance within what Michael Blake describes in his chapter as 'the palliative model' that focuses on the individual refugee and her needs, asylum policy may need to be understood as tragic, which is to say that we 'find ourselves in circumstances in which no choice is open to us that does not entail serious wrong-doing'.

A first response to this point could appeal to the distinction between sufficient and specific options that are necessary to be able to lead autonomous lives. One could say that the question is whether autonomy demands only *sufficient* options among which members can choose, or whether they must have *specific* options. In the context of the membership argument I employ here, we could ask if providing for autonomy-enabling options demands membership in any liberal-democratic state, or if it demands membership in a specific polity, namely, the one refugees are forced to leave behind. If the needs of autonomy can be satisfied with access to a sufficient range of options, then we can assume that the option of becoming a member of the asylum-granting state is sufficient to satisfy the content condition of autonomy. The necessary option can then be provided in the asylum-granting state; asylum-granting states would thus have satisfied their duties of autonomy by simply promoting the full set of membership rights for refugees on their territory.

If, however, autonomy demands the option of a specific membership such as can be found only in the country of origin, then I believe that the bundle of rights that asylum-granting states ought to enable and protect needs to include the right of return. In support of this second view, some have argued that some options are irreplaceable, such as the option to have access to the means to practice one's religion, or to be able to marry the person one has fallen in love with.[26] Recall here my earlier discussion of the right to territory. If it is indeed the case that territorial occupancy matters because it allows individuals to plan their own lives by providing for relationships and the social and political community that are important to life-plans, then access to a different or new territory may not be sufficient to replace what has been lost. In this view, it is not autonomy-enabling to know that the community where I happen to find asylum is autonomy-enabling for others. Instead, what may matter from a perspective of autonomy is that options that I believe will allow me to be the author of my own life are not accessible. In other words, options that enable autonomy cannot always be generic – even if sufficient generic options are available, I may not be able to design the course of my own life.

The distinction between generic and specific options may not convince, however. In my view, though, there is a second and important dimension

[26] P. Cole, 'Taking Moral Equality Seriously: Egalitarianism and Immigration Controls', *Journal of International Political Theory*, 8 (2012), 121–34; A. Stilz, 'Is There an Unqualified Right to Leave?', in S. Fine and L. Ypi (eds.), *Migration in Political Theory: The Ethics of Movement and Membership* (Oxford: Oxford University Press, 2016), pp. 57–79.

to deciding whether options are autonomy-enabling. I believe that it is not the nature and range of options that define agential capacity, but whether or not I am *prevented* from accessing an option.[27] As I said earlier, options can serve autonomy only if individuals are not coerced into choosing them or, I would argue, coerced into abandoning them. Based on Raz's original account of autonomy, the need to be free from coercion when choosing among options is an integral part of having access to the conditions of autonomy. I suggest that autonomy is infringed if and when we are coercively *prevented* from choosing certain options.

To put this back into the context of the right to return: if we believe that refugees are coercively prevented from regaining membership in their country of origin – which follows from accepting severe human rights violations and threat of loss of life as a form of coercion – then we can see the force of the coercion argument for the justification of a right to return. What matters for the normative claim for the right to return as part of the promise of asylum is not that asylum-granting states provide for member-ship in their midst. Instead, what matters is that refugees are coercively prevented from membership in their country of origin, from living and engaging in political self-determination with compatriots.

To summarize the steps of the discussion so far: I have sketched the debate between those who argue that generic options are enough to support individual autonomy and those who insist that specific options are needed. I then suggested that the most relevant point is not the nature of the options, but the fact that individuals are coercively prevented from accessing some of them. Coercion is the cause for flight, and to remedy the original coercion, I suggest that asylum-granting states should accept the right to return as part of the promise of asylum. Thus, the fact that asylum-granting states may be able to offer as good if not a better set of options does not alleviate the moral wrong that the original coercion inflicts. Instead, it is the original moral wrong of having suffered coercion that a right to return aims to remedy. If this is accepted, then the fact that coercion from the state of origin has now ceased, which is to say that the original cause of coercion is over, does not nullify the moral obligation to remedy the original harm. Rather, the relevant criterion for accepting obligations to enable the right to return is the original coercion. The fact that coercion no longer is an issue in the country of origin should then

---

[27] K. Oberman, 'Immigration as a Human Right', in Fine and Ypi (eds.), *Migration in Political Theory*, pp. 32–56.

simply be viewed as making it possible for the asylum-granting state to realize the right to return.

Note, though, that one could again object that the *nature* of the coercion presumably should matter in our analysis: it may make a difference to our assessment if an individual is prevented from being a member of her original community by her original state, or if her former compatriots have formed a different community, in which hopeful returnees are not welcome, as the example of Hutu returnees illustrated. Finally, a different case yet again may be non-state violence: How should we assess the claim for return from those who were intimidated by, for example, drug lords, that is, non-state actors? I would argue that asylum-granting states have the strongest obligation to help those who wish to return after having been persecuted by their own home state; they do not have an obligation to enter into the politics of the state of origin to help eradicate drug gang violence, for example, even though they may wish to grant asylum to those who suffered such violence.

My last point may raise a further question, however, namely, that of the nature of responsibility to address the original coercion. Why should we assume that it is the responsibility of the asylum-granting state to remedy the harm of coercion, rather than that of the offending state of origin? In response, I propose a two-fold distinction: while we can agree that the first addressee of the responsibility is the state that coerced in the first place, I suggest that remedial responsibility to address the moral wrong of coercion also belongs to the asylum-granting state. In fact, the idea of remedial responsibility is precisely the basis for accepting duties of asylum: asylum-granting states are stepping in to remedy human rights abuses in the state of origin. This does not alleviate the latter's causal and outcome responsibility for the abuse, or its remedial responsibility to rectify the wrong. Yet it also does not imply that remedial responsibility is *exclusive* to the state of origin.[28]

3 Two Puzzles about the Right to Return: Content and Feasibility

The previous section has established the normative basis for a right to return. I have argued for a right to return that is motivated by a concern to

---

[28] To clarify, causal responsibility helps determine what happened and why, whereas outcome responsibility identifies a particular agent responsible for a particular outcome. Remedial responsibility in turn is simply 'the responsibility we may have to come to the aid of those who need help'. D. Miller, *National Responsibility and Global Justice* (Oxford: Oxford University Press, 2007), p. 81.

enable the good of membership as a background condition of individual autonomy. I now want to say more about the precise content of such a right, and also address the issue of feasibility: Can asylum-granting states actually enable refugees to access their community of origin so as to provide the conditions of individual autonomy? I deal with these issues in turn

Content

In her discussion of the right of return, Megan Bradley argues that just return implies putting

> returnees back on equal footing with their non-displaced co-nationals by restoring or creating a new relationship of rights and duties between the state and its returning citizens.... The conditions of just return match the essential rights a legitimate state must ensure for its citizens: equal, effective protection for their security and basic human rights, including accountability for any abuses of these rights.[29]

I share Bradley's intuition about what grounds the right of return – as discussed earlier, the right of return should be considered as necessary to reconstitute and realize the good of membership in the state of origin. Yet how should we imagine the content of the right of return? Take the case of Syrian refugees currently in Germany. Assume that Germany accepts their right to return and its duty to enable Syrian refugees to realize the right. This may imply Germany allowing refugees to exercise their professions as far as possible to prevent deskilling while in asylum, or, in the case of young refugees, Germany providing them the training necessary to acquire and pursue professional qualifications that will make it possible for them to return to their countries of origin and pursue a life there. It may also require that asylum-granting states not impose conditions of asylum that would run counter to the possibility of exercising the right of return, such as demanding that refugees relinquish their original citizenship to prove their willingness to integrate into the asylum-granting state, or to qualify for asylum benefits.

To illustrate with a concrete example: some German politicians have argued that refugees should be cut off from asylum benefits if they refuse to take German language lessons. Prima facie, learning the language of the asylum-granting state is an important tool for refugees to integrate in their

---

[29] M. Bradley, *Refugee Repatriation: Justice, Responsibility and Redress* (Cambridge: Cambridge University Press, 2013), pp. 44–45.

new home. However, if refugees hope to return to the country of origin, asylum-granting states ought to balance the demand for language acquisition with the state's obligations to enable the right of return. German governments may then conclude that it is their duty to offer professional training in English as a more widely spoken language that would benefit refugees more on the road to return, and would possibly allow them to advance further in their profession, or to learn a new one more quickly. So if the right to return is accepted as part of the promise of asylum, asylum-granting states would have the responsibility to equip refugees for the possibility to return over time. Asylum-granting states ought to adopt policies pertaining to asylum that take into consideration what happens after the end of asylum. This does not imply that refugees should not receive assistance in integrating into the asylum-granting state if they do not wish to return home. We can imagine a time window during which refugees, once accepted as such in the asylum-granting state, have the option to decide whether in principle they wish to return home, circumstances permitting, or remain in the asylum-granting state. In this vein, it would be justifiable to ask refugees early on about their intentions to return, and to suggest a choice between different services to help support these choices, such as which language to learn.

Note that this first set of responsibilities can be satisfied within the territory of the state of asylum. Yet the putative right of return also raises the question of possible obligations *outside* the territory of the asylum-granting state. We can imagine, for instance, that asylum-granting states ought to facilitate multilateral collaborations to establish peace agreements with the warring factions in Syria to create conditions for return by putting an end to the original cause for exit, such as war or genocide.[30] Such conditions may include setting up secure corridors to provide for safe passage, or deploying forces to protect specific territories for returnees. However, recall that earlier, I cautioned against asylum-granting states entering into domestic politics, such as France playing the arbiter between warring factions of Hutu and Tutsis in Rwanda. There seems to be a contradiction in my account, or so critics could say. In response, however, I think that we can make a distinction between providing for the physical safety of returnees and realizing successful return. I believe it fair to say that realizing the former is a reasonable claim within the context of the right, but not the latter. However, even in this less demanding version, the right of return raises two objections.

---

[30] This is in line with Bradley's conditions of just return. See Chapter 8 in this volume.

The first objection pertains to the question of fairness: assuming that Germany were to accept the right to return as part of the promise of asylum, why should it fall on its shoulders to enable such a right, rather than on those of the international community at large? Put otherwise, why should the obligations of enabling return be tied to the admitting state? If we understand the Geneva Convention more literally, we could say that a state that admits a specific set of refugees is doing so as a representative of the international community of states. Yet if we accept this, then it does not obviously follow that the same state is the agent with primary responsibility for enabling return. Instead, we could imagine a system that distinguishes between states taking in specific asylum-seekers and states that fund protection of specific asylum-seekers. Why then could the same not apply to the distinction between states taking in refugees and states enabling return?[31]

I agree that an international system of sharing the responsibility for asylum-seekers and protecting their rights is desirable in principle. My proposal here is based on the standard attribution of responsibility that the international community has so far established, which is that nation-states grant asylum and the status of refugee as a way to underline their responsibility for an individual. This is not to say that a better system of distributing responsibilities for asylum-seekers among asylum-granting states should not be sought, or that the international community should not design specific procedures to help asylum-granting states to enable the right to return.[32]

The second objection raises the question of motivation: if it is indeed the case that asylum-granting states have duties to enable the right of return, some may worry that this would act as a deterrent for states to accept asylum-seekers in the first place. A critic could point out that this would increase the burden on such states, which may make fewer states willing to provide for asylum, or which may drive them to limit the number of refugees they accept. In other words, the risk of framing the right of return as part of the promise of asylum is to overburden those states that accept duties of asylum. This is the case especially if enabling the right of return were to demand that asylum-granting states get involved in the country of origin, possibly by sorting out a messy situation there when establishing safe passage.

To put it pithily, the worry is one about 'rights versus numbers': if asylum-seekers may have claims against the asylum-granting state in the

---

[31] Thanks to David Owen for raising this question.   [32] Betts and Collier, *Refuge*, ch. 8.

context of the right to return, this may affect the number of refugees asylum-granting states may be willing to accept.[33] Does an expansion of rights for asylum-seekers spell the end of asylum as we know it? I believe that this addresses the question of what is owed to asylum-seekers from the wrong angle: at least on the level of principle, we cannot determine what is morally owed based on what we believe is possible in the context of limited resources. This is particularly the case if we take human rights to target the protection of basic interests, as I have assumed. Human rights then represent the minimum of what we owe to individuals, and need to be prioritized when thinking about justice obligations even if this implies that some measures of social justice in the asylum-granting state may have to be redesigned.[34] But I acknowledge that in a second step, defenders of a right to return as part of the promise of asylum will have to weigh the demands on individual states against other human rights obligations, such as obligations to those who are not able to leave and become refugees, and possible repercussions of granting asylum to the country of origin, as I have explained.

Feasibility

So far, I have assumed that enabling the right to return involves taking action outside the territory of the asylum-granting state. Yet can we assume asylum-granting states are in a position to enable rights outside their own borders? This is an important question since it would be implausible to ascribe duties to asylum-granting states that cannot be satisfied. This is the *feasibility constraint* on a right of return.

The feasibility constraint arises because a right to return may include demands on the asylum-granting state that can only be realized outside its own territory. In the first instance, one could thus be sceptical of my proposal for how the right to return should be understood by pointing out that providing for membership in asylum-granting states is much less demanding than enabling access to membership in the state of origin. It might simply be easier for asylum-granting states to satisfy duties of asylum locally, including access to membership, rather than enable return. As I explained early on, those escaping human rights abuses are looking for

---

[33] A similar concern has been raised in the context of other forms of migration, such as temporary foreign workers. M. Ruhs and P. Martin, 'Numbers vs. Rights: Trade-Offs and Guest Worker Programs', *International Migration Review*, 42 (2008), 249–65.

[34] C. Straehle, 'Falling into the Justice Gap? Between Duties of Social and Global Justice', *Critical Review of International Social and Political Philosophy*, 19 (2016), 645–61.

another state to assume (temporarily or permanently) the duty to protect their human rights and to protect their basic interests, such as that of leading good lives. Asylum-granting states are, in other words, called on to grant refugees 'status', to provide 'surrogate' membership and not only to provide temporary protection. Membership is important because it confers status as an equal; it confers the possibility to access the conditions of autonomy within the country of asylum.[35] Yet in most cases, providing for the conditions of membership is a task more easily accomplished on the territory of the state than elsewhere. States can most readily grant and enact membership in their own territory.[36] To *enact* membership implies providing full access to the set of rights that citizens usually enjoy, such as political voting rights, social association and labour rights, and civic freedoms of speech and religion. From an efficiency perspective, realizing the right to membership and the right to territorial occupancy might thus primarily be the responsibility of the state of asylum on its own territory.

My argument for the feasibility of the right to return as part of the promise of asylum is one of analogy. In recent debates, some commentators have argued that developed, rich, asylum-granting states are overburdened, and that we should therefore entertain the normative possibility that states may satisfy their moral duties toward refugees for food and shelter *outside* their territory.[37] Similarly, international refugee advocates argue that the idea of refugee protection, and what it demands, needs to be expanded in the current refuge regime.[38] The link between territory and protection needs to be severed to allow for a fairer distribution of responsibilities between wealthy, developed countries who want to do their fair share and those countries neighbouring the prime source countries for current refugee flows.[39]

In this vein, there is increasing discussion in international refuge law on the comparison between protection for refugees and the internationally sanctioned extra-territorial interventions in the context of the Responsi-

---

[35] Price, *Rethinking Asylum*, p. 168.

[36] Exceptions are children of citizens living elsewhere, who inherit membership through jus sanguinis legislation that transfers citizenship to the children of citizens.

[37] Betts and Collier, *Refuge*; Miller, *Strangers in Our Midst*; C. H. Wellman, 'Freedom of Movement and the Rights to Enter and Exit', in Fine and Ypi (eds.), *Migration in Political Theory*, pp. 80–104.

[38] J. C. Hathaway and R. A. Neve, 'Making International Refugee Law Relevant Again: A Proposal for Collectivized and Solution-Oriented Protection', *Harvard Human Rights Journal*, 10 (1997), 115–211.

[39] The main source countries in 2015 were Syria, Afghanistan or Somalia, while the main host countries were Turkey, Pakistan Lebanon, Iran and Ethiopia.

bility to Protect (R2P).[40] R2P authorizes states to intervene in the territory of other states to assure protection of human rights there. This is to say that states are given permission to override territorial sovereignty claims by those national governments that can no longer or are no longer willing to protect the human rights of their citizens in cases that are internationally considered genocide, war crimes, crimes against humanity or ethnic cleansing.[41]

Now, I do not want to abuse the analogy between R2P and enabling a right to return. All I want to highlight is that if we take the rationale for R2P seriously, which suggests that it is plausible for states to intervene on the territory of other states to protect human rights there, the feasibility of a right to return that necessitates intervention on the part of the asylum-granting state outside its territory seems clear. If we can separate protection of refugee claims from the territory of the asylum-granting state, as many commentators suggest we ought to do to distribute responsibility fairly among all states willing to satisfy duties of asylum, then the possibility of enabling the right to return outside a state's territory should equally be contemplated. Both imply that the link between satisfying duties of asylum and the territory of the duty-bound state should be severed. This does not deny that it may be more efficient and indeed easier to provide for membership on the territory of the asylum-granting state. But it does support my thesis that the moral claim for access to membership can ground a right to return, and a duty to enable the right to return.

4 Conclusion

Asylum has come to be understood in a very specific vein, which is to provide for food and safety somewhere outside a state in turmoil. This was not always the case, and while providing for immediate protection is one important part of the promise of asylum, understanding asylum in this way neglects other basic interests individuals have. One such basic interest is that of leading autonomous lives. My aim in this chapter was to develop an

---

[40] S. H. Rimmer, 'Refugees, Internally Displaced Persons and the "Responsibility to Protect"', *UNHCR New Issues in Refugee Research*, Research Paper No. 185 (2010), available at www .unhcr.org; C. Straehle, 'Thinking about Protecting the Vulnerable When Thinking about Immigration: Is There a Responsibility to Protect in Immigration Regimes?', *Journal of International Political Theory*, 8 (2012), 159–71.

[41] United Nations, *Implementing the Responsibility to Protect: Report of the Secretary-General* (New York: United Nations, 2009). Note that according to then UN Secretary General Ban Ki-Moon, R2P should be understood as a more general call to protect human dignity and human rights.

account of a political philosophy of refuge that takes seriously the liberal value of individual autonomy. Individual autonomy as I have construed it here demands access to a range of options from which to choose when designing how to lead our lives. Importantly, it demands the possibility of membership in a community to foster social and political relationships. Relying on recent work on the moral value of territorial occupancy, I have argued that at least some relationships that promote political self-determination are territorially bound. To access these, individuals need to be able to occupy or return to a territory. Thus, I have argued that the right to return enables access to the good of membership as a background condition for individual autonomy. This provides the normative justification for a right to return as part of the promise of asylum.

In a second step, I have allowed, however, that the right to return is plausible only if it is feasible to satisfy the duties that it imposes on the asylum-granting state. Thus, in the last part of my argument, I have analysed the content and feasibility of a duty to enable the right to return. States, when designing asylum policies, including policies distributing access to social goods within the asylum-granting states, should reflect the desire of some refugees to return. Asylum-granting states can intervene in states of origin to enable the right to return, by providing for safe passages and engaging in multilateral coordination of return. In conclusion, then, I suggest that based on the normative concern for individual autonomy, and the fact that enabling the right to return is feasible, refugees should have access to the right of return as one of the rights that are protected under the moral logic of asylum.

CHAPTER 10

Refugees, Rescue, and Choice

Luara Ferracioli[1]

Do refugees have a right to choose where in the world to settle? Philosophers working on the ethics of asylum have recently grappled with this question. Some have argued that the legal and institutional recognition of a right on the part of refugees to choose their preferred state of settlement would make it harder for the international community to distribute the refugee burden among member states, thereby making it harder for them to assist as many refugees as possible.[2] Even Joseph Carens, the most prominent defender of open borders, argues that under non-ideal conditions, refugees have a moral right to live somewhere safe, but lack 'a moral entitlement to choose where that will be'.[3]

Other philosophers are not convinced. Matthew Gibney holds that refugees have a right to choose their state of new residence because they have a right not only to access human rights protection, but also to 'rebuild a meaningful social world'.[4] The idea here is that if refugees can choose where to settle, they can, *prior to immigration*, take into account the projects and relationships that matter to them, and so build a new life in a state where they believe there is a particularly high chance that settlement will be successful. A similar concern has been raised by Christine Straehle, who argues that persons have an interest in imagining a future in a given place, and that this particular interest on the part of refugees can be realized only if they are able to choose a recipient state

---

[1] Special thanks to Stephanie Collins, Ryan Cox, David Miller and Christine Straehle for helpful comments on previous versions of this chapter. Work on this chapter was supported by the Netherlands Organization for Scientific Research (VENI grant: 275-20-148).
[2] See J. Carens, *The Ethics of Immigration* (New York: Oxford University Press, 2013); L. Ferracioli, 'The Appeal and Danger of a New Refugee Convention', *Social Theory and Practice*, 40 (2014), 123–44.
[3] Carens, *The Ethics of Immigration*, p. 216.
[4] M. J. Gibney, 'The Ethics of Refugees', *Philosophy Compass*, 13 (2018).

where they can actually imagine themselves pursuing the future they care about.[5]

The considerations on both sides of this debate are sound. On the one hand, we have good moral reasons to establish and maintain a refugee protection regime that does justice to recipient states and to refugees taken as a group.[67] On the other hand, we have good moral reasons to treat individual refugees respectfully, and to take their interests into account when determining how to match each one of them with a particular recipient state.

As it will become clear later in the discussion, it is not clear that refugees are always in a position to know where in the world they are most likely to flourish. This is because there is a great deal of uncertainty attached to each migration project. Moreover, even if refugees know where they are most likely to flourish, it is not obvious that an alleged interest on their part to settle where is *best* (rather than merely good) for them is sufficiently strong so as to defeat the interest that recipient states have in distributing the refugee settlement burden among themselves equitably. However, in this chapter, I hope to focus on a different, yet connected, question: Should refugees choose where to settle *within* a state? This question is not only philosophically interesting, but also politically relevant given that recipient states such as Canada, Australia, Norway, and Sweden have all adopted policies to increase the regional settlement of immigrants and refugees.[8] The interest of this chapter is thus on the question of whether a refugee can partly determine the *content* of the asylum duty owed to her by determining its location, irrespective of whether she can also determine which state should bear the duty in question. In what follows, I will give a qualified negative answer to the question of content, by arguing that refugees are not owed the opportunity to determine the content of a duty owed to them so long as they do not find themselves bearing too high a cost as a result.

---

[5] C. Straehle, 'Refuge, Claim and Place', unpublished manuscript.

[6] M. J. Gibney, 'Refugees and Justice between States', *European Journal of Political Theory*, 14 (2015), 448–63; D. Miller, *Strangers in Our Midst: The Political Philosophy of Immigration* (Cambridge, MA: Harvard University Press, 2016).

[7] If the international community increases their refugee intake, and if all refugees are similarly positioned when it comes to settling in a particular state, then this benefits refugees as a group. A regime where fewer refugees are settled, and only a lucky subset of them choose their state of settlement, is a regime that fares worse in terms of how refugees are treated as a group – even if it is true that some are better off as a result.

[8] See K. Golebiowska, M. Valenta, and T. Carter, 'International Immigration Trends and Data', in D. Carson et al. (eds.), *Demography at the Edge: Remote Human Populations in Developed Nation* (Surrey: Ashgate, 2011), pp. 53–84.

The discussion will proceed as follows. In Section 1, I make some important preliminary points. In Sections 2 and 3, I discuss the best arguments in favour of the position that refugees should choose the precise location where an asylum duty ought to be discharged. I show that these arguments do not settle the question of whether refugees have a moral entitlement to choose where to settle *within* a state. In Section 4, I argue that refugees do not have a moral entitlement to choose the location of their settlement so long as the costs to them of not being settled elsewhere are moderate. In Section 5, I finish the discussion by focusing on the question of implementation.

1 On the Definition, Grounds, and Content of Duties of Asylum

Before I proceed let me make some important preliminary points. First, in this discussion I conceive of a refugee as someone who cannot access her most basic human rights without migration.[9] I have, therefore, a broader understanding of the refugee in mind than the one specified by the 1951 Refugee Convention, but do not rely on that understanding for my argument.

Second, in this chapter, I focus on a specific duty owed to refugees: the duty to allow refugees to enter the territory of a recipient state and settle there as new residents. Note that I am agnostic on whether duties of asylum themselves entail permanent or temporary residency, so long as temporary residency is compatible with some other duty of permanent inclusion for those refugees who cannot safely return home after some substantial period of temporary residence abroad. For the remainder of this discussion, I will refer to the duty to accept refugees (at least temporarily) as a duty of asylum. There are of course other duties owed to refugees by states, but they are not relevant for our purposes.[10]

Third, I assume that for the overwhelming majority of cases involving asylum, the duty owed to refugees is grounded on the capacity of states, qua duty-bearers, to assist at moderate costs to themselves.[11] Here I focus

---

[9] M. J. Gibney, *The Ethics and Politics of Asylum: Liberal Democracy and the Response to Refugees* (Cambridge: Cambridge University Press, 2014); Carens, *The Ethics of Immigration*; Miller, *Strangers in Our Midst*.

[10] These would be negative duties not to act in ways that create refugee flows, and positive duties to support the UNHCR.

[11] P. Singer, 'Famine, Affluence and Morality', *Philosophy and Public Affairs*, 1 (1972), 229–43; P. Singer, *The Life You Can Save* (New York: Random House, 2009); P. Unger, *Living High and Letting Die: Our Illusion of Innocence* (Oxford: Oxford University Press, 1996).

on a moderate cost threshold because of the importance of upholding a moral system that carves out enough space for agents (which includes states) to pursue their own plans and projects.[12] I do not mean to deny, however, that at times, there is a clear and morally significant causal connection between the predicament of refugees and the past actions of a recipient state, which gives rise to a contribution-based duty of asylum.[13] I take it though that when a duty of asylum is grounded on the fact of past contribution to harm, states are obliged to bear higher than moderate costs to assist the refugees in question, and to *minimize* the assistance costs that arise as a result. This means that states are much more constrained in how they can go about assisting refugees when they themselves have contributed to their predicament. However, given that the overwhelming majority of refugees are owed assistance by states as a result of the latter's capacity to assist rather than any prior wrongdoing on their part, and because it is much less clear that states must minimize costs to refugees when they have not contributed to their predicament, it pays to focus on assistance-based duties in this chapter.

Fourth, it is important to make explicit in the discussion that the costs of settlement include welfare costs (e.g., additional infrastructure, settlement services, accommodation, employment opportunities, welfare provision) and integration costs (e.g., language support, multicultural policies, civic education). It is therefore a mistake to think that refugee settlement requires only that states open their borders to refugees. Now, it is true that some refugees become net benefits to the community because they bring with them skills and ideas that significantly contribute to the economy of a recipient state. Yet despite the fact that important benefits can flow, at times, from the settlement of particular refugees in a state, we cannot actually factor in such benefits at the time in which a state is asked to bear an asylum duty. And the reason why benefits cannot offset the costs of resettlement comes down to the fact that there is never a guarantee that any refugee will in fact provide a significant benefit to the recipient state due to potential changes in their circumstances. Refugees can, after all, get sick, choose not to employ their skills, change their career prospects, and

---

[12] C. Barry and G. Øverland, 'How Much for the Child?', *Ethical Theory and Moral Practice*, 16 (2013), 189–204; J. Fishkin, *The Limits of Obligation* (New Haven, CT: Yale University Press, 1982).

[13] J. Souter, 'Towards a Theory of Asylum as Reparation for Past Injustice', *Political Studies*, 62 (2014), 326–42.

so on.[14] I will therefore focus on the *costs* of settlement despite the fact that benefits also arise in many cases.[15]

Finally, given the nature of the costs attached to a duty of asylum, I will assume that governments can minimize such costs if they are able to settle refugees in a location where the overall costs of settlement are lower than other parts of the state. For instance, some parts of a recipient state have greater work opportunities than others, and services such as housing and transport are much more expensive in more popular parts of the territory, such as big cities. A refugee who gets settled in a place with low housing costs, good job opportunities, and low service costs will impose lower overall costs on a state qua duty-bearer than a refugee who gets settled in a place with high housing costs, high unemployment rates, and high services costs, all else being equal. Similarly, some parts of a recipient state are in a better position to integrate refugees than others. A refugee who gets settled in a place where there is a great deal of community support for migration will impose lower overall costs on a recipient state than a refugee who gets settled in a place where refugees and immigrants form social ghettos with low language proficiency and high rates of criminal behaviour, all else being equal. (It is certainly true that concerns around integration on the part of refugees are often ill-founded and politically motivated, but poor integration would count as a cost if what is meant by poor integration is high welfare dependency and high criminal behaviour on the part of refugees, and low trust in government and low support for immigration on the part of citizens.)

In light of the fact that settlement costs are location-sensitive, and that states can minimize such costs if they are permitted to settle refugees in a location where the overall costs of settlement are lower than other parts of the state, the question for our purposes is whether it is morally permissible for states to allocate refugees to a particular location due to the lower costs involved, thereby depriving refugees of a choice with regard to where to rebuild their social world and pursue their preferred future.

---

[14] This does not mean that states are not permitted to take such potential benefits on board when selecting refugees (see Chapter 5 in this volume), but simply that potential benefits cannot be factored in when it comes to assessing *the costs* involved in discharging an asylum duty.

[15] I do not mean to suggest that likelihood of benefits cannot be factored in when it comes to assessing the costs of many of our moral obligations. Indeed, when we have adequate knowledge of the likelihood of an event taking place, we can factor in benefits when assessing the overall cost of our duty. The problem is that in the context of asylum, we are very rarely in a position to know the likelihood of future actions on the part of refugees.

2 Refugees and Choice

In the previous section, I alluded to the fact that there are two connected questions about how much choice refugees should have about their settlement experience. The first question is whether refugees can choose their preferred duty-bearer, which makes it quite hard for recipient states to redistribute the refugee burden equitably by, for instance, implementing a refugee resettlement arrangement at the global level.[16] The second question is whether refugees can determine the precise location of their settlement by choosing where to live within a given state. Each question can be answered differently since it is in principle possible for the refugee protection regime to be set up in such a way that refugees cannot choose their state of settlement, but can choose where in the state to live. Similarly, it is in principle possible for the regime to be set up in a way such that refugees can choose their preferred state of settlement, but not the specific location within the state. And of course, it is also possible that morality requires that refugees have either full or no choice about location, be it in terms of which state to settle in or in terms of location within the state.

Before I explain why morality does not require that refugees are able to choose their preferred location within a state, it pays to investigate the strength of the arguments that have been put forward by Gibney and Straehle in favour of refugees having this choice. Although these arguments have been developed in the context of discussions about whether refugees can choose their preferred state of settlement, I hope to show in this section that they apply equally to the question of whether refugees can choose their preferred location within a state.

Let us start with Gibney's argument, which defends the claim that refugees should be placed in a position where they can adequately rebuild their social world by choosing the state where they believe they can better move on with their lives. As I have already suggested, the argument is highly pertinent to the question of location within a state, for it makes no sense to let refugees choose a state on the basis of a property P that the refugee sees as important for rebuilding her social world, but then expect her to live in a part of the state where P is absent. For instance, it makes

---

[16] Here I do not rule out the possibility that an equitable burden-sharing scheme among the international community could be partly achieved by transfer payments, with unpopular states subsidising popular states. There are, however, reasons for scepticism since it is not clear that the costs attached to population growth can be adequately compensated for with financial transfers.

little sense to let Venezuelan refugees choose to live in the United States so they can join a vibrant Latino community, but actually require them to live in Alaska, rather than California or Florida. Similarity, it makes little sense to let an Afghani refugee move to Australia so she can continue to run a camel riding business, but then force her to settle in the beachside suburbs of Sydney. In other words, if the reason why a refugee should have the ultimate say with regard to her state of settlement is that she knows best the essential components of a flourishing life for herself and her family, then she should be allowed to settle in the part of the country where such flourishing is more likely to take place.[17]

To be sure, someone taking Gibney's line on the importance of rebuilding one's social world might deny the connection between choice of state and choice of location within a state by holding that recipient states are typically fairly homogenous. The problem with this response is that there can be a great deal of diversity within states, even in territorially small places such as Switzerland and Belgium. A refugee wanting to live in Switzerland due to its progressive credentials will not be impressed by life in Appenzell, a place where women gained the right to vote on local issues only in 1991. Similarly, a French-speaking refugee wanting to live in Belgium due to the cultural connections with her state of origin will not be impressed by Dutch-speaking Bruges, despite it being a beautiful place.

Admittedly, refugees are sometimes interested in enjoying an aspect of life in a recipient state that is in fact prevalent in all parts of the territory. For instance, a refugee might want to settle in Portugal because she speaks Portuguese, or Italy because she is a Catholic. Although this shows that there are properties of a state, such as language and religion, that can be found anywhere in its territory, it looks like these are precisely the kinds of properties that also obtain in other parts of the world. A refugee who believes that the ability to speak Spanish with fellow residents is essential for her to rebuild her social world does not have a moral claim to settle *in Spain*, for there are other states where fellow residents would speak Spanish. A Gibney-like argument that would defend the refugee's right

---

[17] Of course, this line of argument needs to say something about which relationships and projects are taken to be central to a life well lived. Accounts that allow projects and relationships that are merely subjectively attractive to the agent (but not taken to be objectively good by society at large) are less likely to succeed in showing that recipient states have a duty to take such projects and relationship on board, whereas accounts that expect projects and relationships to be both subjectively *and objectively* attractive (i.e., considered valuable by the duty-bearer as well) are more promising. See, for instance, S. Wolf, *Meaning in Life and Why It Matters* (Princeton, NJ: Princeton University Press, 2010). Note though that such 'hybrid' accounts can accept that even worthwhile projects cannot impose high costs on recipient states.

to choose her state of asylum, but not her place of residence within it, is therefore liable to backfire. By appealing to cultural features that are prevalent throughout the state's territory in order to deny the choice of location, one may also weaken the case for allowing the refugee to choose the specific country in which she is granted asylum.[18]

An alternative way to try to resist the connection between choice of state and choice of location is to hold that refugees need not reside in the place where their social world takes place, but only be able to visit regularly. This would explain why a Venezuelan refugee needs only to be able to choose the United States as a place of residence, but not California or Florida. The suggestion here would be that once refugees settle in (say) Alaska, they can always choose to visit friends and family, or engage in cultural activities in other parts of the territory. The problem with this strategy should be obvious. If sporadic visits suffice for rebuilding a social world, then this fact also puts pressure on Gibney's argument for choice of state. After all, if refugees need only visit the place that matters for their pursuit of the good, then so long as they are regularly provided with tourist visas by the relevant state, they need not be settled there either temporarily or permanently.

Notice that the same results arise if we think that Straehle's account gives us the best explanation as to why refugees should choose their state of settlement. Straehle, recall, argues that refugees should settle in a state where they can actually imagine themselves pursuing the future they care about. But if Straehle's argument is sound, then why stop with choice of state? A French-speaking refugee might easily imagine a future in Geneva or Brussels but not in other parts of Switzerland or Belgium. A refugee who loves surfing might easily imagine a future in Sydney but not in the Australian outback. And of course, a refugee who is a devout Catholic might be able to imagine herself practicing her religion anywhere in Italy, but if that is indeed the case, she should also be able to imagine herself practicing her religion in other Catholic states across the globe.

So far I have been assuming that Gibney and Straehle's arguments for choice of state on the part of refugees are sound, and then showing that

---

[18] There could be properties of a state that can be found anywhere in a recipient state, but not elsewhere in the world. It is hard to imagine a case where this is true and yet the interest on the part of the refugee in enjoying a property P will be well founded, for if P is enjoyed only in a recipient state, then how has the refugee formed the right sort of attachment to P that gives her a compelling interest in continue to enjoy it? There might be some rare cases where the property in question obtains in the refugee's state of origin and in her preferred state of settlement only. I take such cases to be too rare to invalidate the argument that choice of location typically follows from choice of state if one accepts the sorts of arguments put forward by Gibney and Straehle.

they also support choice of location within a state. But as it happens, I am not convinced that these arguments are in fact sound. The reason I am sceptical is that refugees are not always right about how the essential conditions for their flourishing manifest in any given state. A doctor might think that the United States will provide her with the state-of-art hospitals that will make her excel in her professional domain, but it might be that it is Britain or Canada that has the best opportunities in place for doctors who have been trained abroad. Similarly, a refugee might only be able to picture herself easily in Greece given her Greek ancestry, but it is actually a multicultural society with a Greek immigrant community that would be most receptive and inclusive of her.

There is obviously a different argument in the vicinity here, which is not about likelihood of success for each act of migration, but rather about the value of choice with regard to one's place of residence. The idea here is that whenever a refugee values a property P that can be found in a state, she has an autonomy-based right to pursue P in the actual part of the territory where P is present and irrespective of whether she is right about how P contributes to her well-being and irrespective of whether P can be found in other parts of the world.[19] The problem, though, is that if refugees have this autonomy-based interest in choosing both state and location within state, then why don't the rest of us have it as well? An autonomy-based interest in choosing one's place in the world leads us directly to a world of open borders, which is hardly a problem for those who deny that states have a *prima facie* right to exclude prospective immigrants, but certainly is for philosophers trying to show that *only* refugees have a moral entitlement to choose their preferred state of settlement.

I mentioned before that even if it is true that refugees have an interest in choosing their state of residence, it is still not clear that such an interest is sufficiently strong to defeat an interest that recipient states have in distributing the refugee burden equitably among themselves. After all, not only do recipient states have an interest in avoiding free-riding on the part of other states, or in avoiding being unfairly burdened by the refugee protection regime, but there are also good reasons to think that if the refugee burden could be distributed evenly among the international community, citizens of recipient states would see the refugee protection regime as

---

[19] J. Carens, 'Aliens and Citizens: The Case for Open Borders', *Review of Politics*, 49 (1987), 251–73; Carens, *The Ethics of Immigration*; P. Cole, *Philosophies of Exclusion: Liberal Political Theory and Immigration* (Edinburgh: Edinburgh University Press, 2000); K. Oberman, 'Can Brain Drain Justify Immigration Restrictions?', *Ethics*, 123 (2013), 427–55.

complying with important norms of procedural and distributive fairness.[20] Such a change in how the refugee protection regime is perceived could potentially make citizens in recipient states much more receptive to a higher refugee intake than they are now, which would be an important step toward creating a just regime for both refugees and host societies.[21] Proponents of choice must therefore show that the interests of refugees in choosing their state of settlement (and by implication location) trump all these other interests at stake.

3   Refugees and Social Equality

If an appeal to the value of choice does not settle the question of whether refugees can choose where in the state to settle, is there a different argument that can do the work? The most promising case in favour of allowing refugees to partly determine the content of an asylum duty owed to them is the argument found in the work of so-called relational or democratic egalitarians.[22] Such arguments for choice of location would run roughly as follows: refugees might not have a right to choose which state to settle in as a result of the human rights violations they have suffered in the hands of their government, but once they settle in a particular state, they must be treated by the government of that state in the same way as the government treats all other members of society. And because citizens and other migrants can in fact choose where to live in a state, it is only fair that refugees can make that choice as well. In other words, denying refugees the right to choose their preferred location inevitably places them in a position of 'second-class citizenship' and violates the justice requirement that citizens are able to relate to one another as equals.

This sort of argument is certainly conclusive when it comes to refugees who have already been granted citizenship in a state. After all, citizens who were once refugees will in fact count as second-class citizens if they are denied an important right of citizenship: the right to choose where in a country to settle. The trouble is that refugees are typically not in fact citizens for the first years of settlement, and as a result, they lack other rights of citizenship such as standing for office and voting. Indeed, prior to

---

[20] Ferracioli, 'The Appeal and Danger of New Refugee Convention'.
[21] Ibid. See also Carens, *The Ethics of Immigration*.
[22] M. Walzer, *Spheres of Justice: A Defense of Pluralism and Justice* (New York: Basic Books, 1983); E. Anderson, 'What Is the Point of Equality?', *Ethics*, 109 (1999), 287–337; N. Kolodny, 'Rule over None II: Social Equality and the Justification of Democracy', *Philosophy and Public Affairs*, 42 (2014), 287–336.

becoming citizens, refugees are in a similar position to other groups of immigrants, who also lack many of the entitlements typically attached to citizenship. International students, for instance, sometimes lack the entitlement to work full-time or to work altogether. Temporary labour migrants are sometimes allowed to work only in a specific industry or for a specific employer. This means that other immigrants also lack important entitlements that are enjoyed by the citizens of a state: the entitlement to work, to freely choose one's occupation, and to determine one's overall working hours.

Apart from depriving immigrants of important moral rights, some visa arrangements significantly constrain one's freedom in important personal matters. Immigrants on spouse visas, for instance, are not as free as everyone else when it comes to ending a romantic relationship and starting a new one. Someone on a family reunification visa is not as free as everyone else when it comes to severing family ties. And so on, and so forth.

In fact, not only are immigrants more constrained than citizens when it comes to pursuing important projects and relationships, but their residence in the state is often conditional on the pursuit of a project or relationship that is typically territorially located. There is therefore a sense in which many immigrants are also somewhat constrained in their ability to choose *where* in a state to settle.

In response to this line of argument, one could argue that all these migration arrangements are illegitimate and migrants and refugees should access all the rights of citizenship from the moment they arrive in a state. Strong cosmopolitans might be tempted toward this position, but there is compelling empirical evidence showing that awarding immigrants fewer rights leads to a higher number of immigrants being admitted, while extending these rights leads to a lower immigration intake.[23] The result here is that a constrained package of rights for immigrants might be necessary if we want migration to be available for more than a tiny majority of the world population. And of course, citizens in most societies have no appetite for completely open borders, which means that there is a trade-off in practice between the overall number of immigrants and the set of rights afforded to them by any given recipient state.

---

[23] M. Ruhs and P. Martin, 'Numbers vs. Rights: Trade-Offs and Guest Worker Programs', *International Migration Review*, 42 (2008), 249–65. Note that the trade-off between numbers and rights is explained by the fact that the more expansive the rights, the more costly for employers and host societies to include immigrants.

But quite apart from the feasibility considerations just mentioned, there are also good *moral* reasons for thinking that shared citizenship itself gives rise to special moral obligations that are absent in other contexts.[24] This picture of co-citizenship as giving rise to special rights and obligations allows for there to be a transition phase from residency without citizenship on the part of immigrants (which includes refugees) to residency with citizenship on the part of *former* immigrants, where the demands of relational egalitarianism apply less strongly to immigrants than to citizens. Note that the proponents of this position can easily recognize that the enjoyment of many core rights is non-negotiable and unrelated to one's citizenship status. Moreover, they can recognize that such a transition phase cannot last too long, and that after some years, all immigrants acquire a right to become citizens of their state of ongoing residence.

To be sure, a proponent of the claim that refugees must be able to choose their preferred location within a state need not disagree that the demands of relational egalitarianism apply less strongly to immigrants than to citizens. The disagreement might be about what counts as a core right, since many would hold that to deny refugees a right to settle in their preferred location within a state is to violate their right to freedom of movement. In fact, proposals for regional settlement in Canada have been controversial precisely because the Canadian Charter of Rights and Freedoms acknowledges the mobility rights of both citizens and permanent immigrants.[25]

I certainly agree that refugees and migrants should have their right to freedom of movement respected while they reside in a state, and that states are not allowed to prevent them from visiting any part of the territory that is open to the public. However, I am not convinced that the choice of where *to settle* in a state counts as the exercise of a right to freedom of movement. There are a couple of reasons for my scepticism.

First, if it is indeed true that my right to freedom of movement *is* violated because I cannot afford to live in Manhattan, then we make a mockery of the idea of a right to freedom of movement. This is not to deny that there is an important difference between the government preventing me from settling in Manhattan and my finances taking that choice off the table. I take it, though, that the difference is not explained in terms of how

---

[24] D. Miller, 'Reasonable Partiality towards Compatriots', *Ethical Theory and Moral Practice*, 8 (2005), 63–81; S. Scheffler, *Boundaries and Allegiances: Problems of Justice and Responsibility in Liberal Thought* (New York: Oxford University Press, 2001).

[25] Golebiowska, Valenta, and Carter, 'International Immigration Trends and Data', p. 62.

much freedom I have to move around the borough. If I cannot afford to live in Manhattan because I autonomously chose to become a struggling musician, or if the government prevents me from living there due to the high environmental costs of overpopulation, then it seems to me that, in both cases, the inability to live in Manhattan does not amount to any form of rights violation.

Second, and most importantly, no one thinks that citizens have their right to freedom of movement violated when they are prevented from taking up residence in national parks, beach foreshores, and other parts of the territory that are protected from human settlement. And even when it comes to already populated areas of a state, we can easily imagine cases where liberal democracies must impose a ban on future settlement without expelling those who already reside there. For instance, a historic part of a city might need low density to survive, which would require states to prevent new residents from settling there. I take it that successful criticisms of this response would need to appeal to considerations other than the value of the right to freedom of movement.

To summarize: there appears to be a strong relational egalitarian argument for choice of location on the part of refugees. However, such argument succeeds only if it is true that relational egalitarianism does not allow for a distinction to be made between immigrants and citizens. Given that some philosophers believe that co-citizenship gives rise to special rights and obligations, and given that there are feasibility concerns around the erasure of the distinction between citizens and immigrants, I take it that we are better off looking for answers to the question of choice in location elsewhere. In what follows, I will argue that when it comes to assistance-based duties of assistance (or rescue), victims themselves are obliged to take on some of the costs of their assistance if that decreases the costs for the duty-bearer. If I am right about this obligation on the part of victims, then we are in a good position to explain why refugees do not have a moral entitlement to choose the location of their settlement, even if we were to allow that they have a right to choose which state should open their borders to them.

4 Duties of Victims and Lack of Choice

In this section, I argue that when it comes to clear cases of assistance-based duties where neither the victim nor the duty-bearer are responsible for the predicament in question, duty-bearers have a duty to assist up to the point at which costs become higher than moderate, but they are not obliged to bear all the costs below this threshold if some costs can be shifted to the victim herself. To see the point, consider the following cases:

> Bob's neighbour: Bob is sitting in his veranda writing some music. Unbeknownst to his neighbour Peter (also a musician), Bob can hear him discussing his medical prognosis with his doctor on the phone. Peter has less than a week to undergo life-saving treatment but he cannot afford the $20,000 involved. Both men live in a society without universal health coverage, and Peter has now exhausted all means available to him. In fact, Peter can only survive if he miraculously comes across $20,000 in the next twenty-four hours. Despite being a struggling musician, Bob has managed to save $20,000 over the years to buy his dream piano, a Fazioli. Bob has two ways of helping here. The first option is that Bob gives the $20,000 to Peter instead of buying a piano. The second option is that Bob offers to buy Peter's piano (which is not nearly as good as a Fazioli, but still good enough to play), so that Bob still acquires a piano at the end, while Peter bears the cost of no longer owning a piano.[26]
>
> Accident: A retired man has an accident due to an unexpected storm while going for a walk in his neighbourhood, and ends up needing a wheelchair. His local neighbours find out about what has happened and put money together to buy him a wheelchair (the equivalent of a month of work for each of them). As it happens, the retired man has a lot of savings and can cover half of the cost of the wheelchair, and so does not need all the money that has been raised. Once the neighbours learn about this fact, they choose not to give him all the money they have raised.

Now, I take it that in both cases above, the costs involved in assisting the victims are in fact moderate. Having to give up on one's dream of buying a Fazioli counts as a moderate cost in light of what is at stake, which is life-saving treatment for a sick man. Similarly, a month's worth of work for helping a person to be mobile after an accident also seem a moderate cost to bear in light of the importance of mobility for a minimally decent life.

Despite the fact that both cases above require only moderate sacrifices on the part of the duty-bearers, it seems completely permissible for Bob to ask Peter to sacrifice his piano so that Bob doesn't end up being prevented from fulfilling his lifelong dream of owning a piano himself. And of course, it is certainly permissible for the neighbours in the accident case to withhold some of the money they have raised on finding out that the victim has enough savings to cover half of the cost of the wheelchair.

---

[26] This case is a modified version of Bob's internet banking by Barry and Øverland, 'How Much for the Child?'.

So, what explains these intuitions? As far as I can see, when the victim herself is capable of playing a role in her assistance, she ought to bear some of the costs herself. Now, the question of how exactly such costs must be distributed between victim and duty-bearer is extremely interesting and deserving of a whole separate discussion.[27] What we can say with confidence here is that victims can in fact be asked to bear up to moderate costs in order to minimize the costs for the duty-bearers. One reason for this might be that there is a requirement of respect for agency that we do not impose costs on others for our own sake when we can bear those costs ourselves. A morality that allowed victims to escape any costs simply because they are victims would fail to take the agency of both victims and duty-bearers sufficiently seriously.

There is another explanation available here, however, which is about the value of sharing unlucky burdens around. Such an explanation would appeal to the value of equality rather than the value of autonomy. How should we evaluate this explanation? One point to make here is that the value of equality makes sense only if both parties are indeed roughly equal in power and/or standing, for we do not typically think that a wealthy investor should share the cost of a shelter with a homeless man if what we ultimately care about is creating a more equal world. One might therefore think that such argument would not apply to asylum cases because states are vastly more powerful than refugees and have a lot more resources than they have.[28]

Although it is true that there is a power imbalance between one state and one refugee, we must not forget that states are a collective agent, and that we can cogently understand the duty of states towards refugees as a duty of one collective towards another (i.e., refugees taken as a group). Whereas we might think that the power imbalance between a state and a refugee is too great for equality considerations to apply, it is much less obvious that the power imbalance between a state and all of the refugees they take in is so great for considerations of equality not to matter. And obviously, if states have a refugee intake that is currently much lower than what morality requires, then one might argue that they are allowed to shift the costs to refugees only once they reach a moderate cost threshold by taking in a greater number of refugees. Everything I say here is compatible with this position.

---

[27] For a connected discussion on the permissibility of imposing harms on victims in order to rescue them, see S. Collins, 'When Does "Can" Imply "Ought"?', *International Journal of Philosophical Studies*, 26 (2018), 354–75.

[28] I thank Stephanie Collins for suggesting this potential explanation and objection to me.

It is important to emphasize that nothing that I have said so far denies that victims need our help, and that their predicament can impose up to moderate costs on us. The point is simply that victimhood does not entail immunity to sacrifice. The interests of both victims and duty-bearers matter equally despite the fact that they are not both victims. Also, it is important to emphasize that morality would not allow duty-bearers to impose higher than moderate costs on victims in order to minimize the costs that they themselves must bear. For instance, I take it that it would be impermissible for Bob to make Peter give him all his possessions, including a good piano, in return for the $20,000.

If I am right that duty-bearers can impose only up to moderate costs on victims in order to minimize the costs they themselves must bear, we are now in a position to answer the most important question for our purposes in this chapter: When refugees are denied the opportunity to settle in their preferred part of a state, are they being asked to bear more than moderate costs as a result?

I take it that whether or not the costs associated with a lack of choice in location are indeed moderate depends on the details of the case. In particular, it depends on where exactly in a state refugees are being asked to settle so that states bear lower costs when discharging their asylum duty. If these areas are places where people can lead decent lives, but not as good lives as they could elsewhere, then the costs are moderate. Many people, including many philosophers, do not find jobs in their preferred location, but that does not mean that they cannot lead decent lives. If refugees are settled in places where jobs, schools, and medical and psychological facilities are available, and where their basic rights are not under threat due to systemic violence, then it does not seem that they are being asked to bear costs that are higher than moderate in the process of their settlement.

If, however, essential services are not available and/or violence is widespread, then the costs involved are in fact too high. For countries where violence and poverty are clearly distributed across geographic lines (think of the United States or Brazil), it is unfair to expect refugees to settle in a very poor and unsafe area, when there are decent locations elsewhere for them to live. But if the choice is indeed between a good enough location and a more desirable one, then the cost of requiring refugees to settle in a place that is good enough does not seem too high once we realize that the recipient state is discharging an assistance-based duty *to the benefit of the refugee* which allows that state to pass on some of the costs to the refugee herself.

5 Implementation

At this stage in the discussion, a reader might agree with me that it is in fact fair to expect refugees to bear some of the costs of settlement by expecting them to settle where it is less costly for the state, but simultaneously disagree that it is in fact feasible for states to determine the exact location of settlement within their territory.

In light of such concerns, I will conclude the discussion by indicating three strategies that states might permissibly employ in order to direct refugees to a specific location. These strategies range from incentives to coercive measures, and so differ in their ability to guarantee that refugees will in fact settle where the state wants them to.

The first strategy is to accelerate the acquisition of citizenship for refugees who settle in the state's preferred location (in case they are settled permanently) or attach additional points to refugees hoping to apply for permanent residence after some years of temporary residence qua refugees (in case they are settled temporarily).[29] In the latter case, residing in the state's preferred location might not guarantee permanent inclusion, but it might make it more likely, for instance, by allowing location to replace other factors that increase one's likelihood of being settled permanently within a state: age, family ties, and professional skills.

A second strategy is to give refugees a financial incentive to settle in the state's preferred location. This can be done with the use of tax incentives or cash payments.[30] Now, of course, incentives cannot be too generous since they would in effect cancel out the revenue saved by insisting that refugees settle in the state's preferred location. Nevertheless, there would still be scope for tax incentives or cash benefits that would make both refugees and states better off financially than they would have been if refugees had simply settled in their preferred location within the state.

A final strategy is to make entry in the state conditional on refugees settling in a specific part of the territory. This can be achieved by threatening refugees with fines or deportation in case of non-compliance.[31] Although this strategy would be much more coercive than the first two (and so less desirable as a result), it is not clear that it is impermissible for states to act in this way if it is true that the allocated location is one where

---

[29] A version of this strategy has been employed in Australia. See Golebiowska, Valenta, and Carter, 'International Immigration Trends and Data', p. 62.

[30] This strategy has been employed in Norway. See ibid., p. 63.

[31] Note that deportation will be impermissible if no decent state accepts to include the refugee in question.

refugees will have all of their human rights adequately promoted and protected. After all, we have just established that it is permissible for duty-bearers to demand that victims bear some costs if the costs are below a moderate threshold, and that is what states would be doing if they made entry conditional on settlement in a specific location.

6   Conclusion

In this chapter I have asked the following question: Do refugees have a right to partly determine the content of an asylum duty owed to them by determining where in a state to settle? Although there are certainly good reasons in favour of the position that refugees must be allowed to choose the location of their settlement, I have argued that the answer to this question depends on how we understand the relationship between victim and duty-bearer in cases of assistance more generally. If I am right in suggesting that duty-bearers need not shoulder all the costs of the duty in cases where the victims themselves can shoulder some of the costs, then it follows that refugees may permissibly be asked to bear some of the costs of their settlement by being settled where it is less costly for recipient states.

CHAPTER 11

Philosophical Foundations for Complementary Protection

Matthew Lister[1]

A significant percentage of the people outside their country of citizenship or residence who are unable to meet their basic needs on their own, and need international protection, do not fall under the definition set out in the UN Refugee Convention. This has led many – both academic commentators and activists – to call for a new, expanded refugee definition, preferably backed up by a new, binding, international convention. In earlier work, I have resisted this call, arguing that there is good reason to pick out a sub-set of those in need of international aid – a set that largely, if not completely, corresponds to those picked out by the Refugee Convention – for special benefit and protection. However, even if Convention refugees are in some ways special, we are left with the question of what, if anything, is owed to those in need of aid who are not Convention refugees. In this chapter, I set out philosophical foundations for so-called complementary protection.

Following Jane McAdam, I take 'complementary protection' to be protection 'to persons falling outside the formal legal definition of "refugee"', where this protection is seen as *complementary* to those assumed under the 1951 Refugee Convention (as supplemented by its 1967 Protocol)'.[2] I will argue that while states which are able to provide such protection at reasonable cost have an obligation to do so, the different sorts of threats faced by those in need of complementary protection will typically justify providing a different sort and a different degree of protection than that provided to Convention refugees, at least in usual cases. I will explain why and how complementary protection may differ from

[1] Thanks to Luara Feraccioli, Michael Sevel, Kevin Walton, Patrick Emerton, David Tan, Jayani Nadarajalingam, Suzy Killmister, Maria O'Sullivan, and, especially, Christine Straehle and David Miller for helpful comments on earlier versions of this chapter.
[2] J. McAdam, *Complementary Protection in International Refugee Law* (Cambridge: Cambridge University Press, 2007), pp. 2–3.

refugee protection,[3] and the limiting cases when the protection offered must converge.

1 What Is Complementary Protection, and Why Is It Needed?

As used in this chapter, 'complementary protection' is international protection provided by a state to a non-citizen who is outside her or his country of citizenship or habitual residence[4] who is not covered by the UN Refugee Convention.[5] This protection therefore potentially covers people fleeing from natural disasters[6] and environmental degradation (such as drought); many people fleeing from international or civil wars; people fleeing from generalized violence, perhaps, but not necessarily relating to societal breakdown; and some people fleeing crime. Importantly, complementary protection is appropriate in these cases when the need to flee is not caused by persecution on the basis of a protected ground recognized under the Refugee Convention (race, religion, nationality, membership in a particular social group, or political opinion). Any of the above situations is one where persecution on the basis of a protected ground is possible, and if it exists, then we have a straightforward case for refugee protection.

Many people in situations like the above will not, however, be fleeing persecution on the basis of a protected ground. This can be because the danger is from a natural process such as a hurricane or volcano, or because the danger is directed at everyone in an area merely because they are in the area, and not because the person in question has a protected trait. Finally, the danger might be directed at the person in question individually, such as

---

[3] In this chapter I will typically use the term 'refugee' to mean people falling under the UN Refugee Convention definition of a refugee unless otherwise noted. I do this not to attempt to solve normative questions by definition, but for the sake of terminological ease and consistency.

[4] After this point, I will use 'county of citizenship' to mean 'country of citizenship or habitual residence'.

[5] I will not here give any significant space to protection provided under the Convention Against Torture (CAT). This is not because the CAT is unimportant – it often is in practice, because of its unconditional prohibition on non-refoulement, allowing at least minimal protection for people who would otherwise be excluded under the Refugee Convention or complementary protection on various exclusion grounds, and is important theoretically in setting an absolute limit on state discretion on immigration controls. However, as most who qualify for protection under the CAT would also qualify for protection either under the Refugee Convention or under complementary protection if no exclusion ground applies, I will largely leave this issue aside.

[6] I have argued that people fleeing certain natural disasters – ones reasonably expected to be long-term or open-ended, where internal relocation is not a viable option – should be given the same treatment as Convention refugees, given that they meet what I take to be the logic of the Refugee Convention. See M. Lister, 'Climate Change Refugees', *Critical Review of International Social and Political Philosophy*, 17 (2014), 618–34. I maintain this position, but will here consider primarily natural or environmental disasters of a more limited sort.

when criminals or gangs in a weak or failed state target business owners or more prosperous members, but not because the person in question has a protected trait.

The common element for complementary protection, then, is being in need of international protection, while being outside one's country of citizenship, where the danger that necessitated the flight is not connected with persecution on the basis of a protected ground. The lack of persecution is primarily what distinguishes these cases from cases of refugee protection. Before going on to explain the importance of this difference, I will explain why we should think of complementary protection, as discussed in this chapter, as applying only to people outside their country of citizenship, and not to all people in need of aid, regardless of their location. The answer to this question is related to the type of aid provided by complementary protection. As will be discussed in more detail later, the basic remedy provided by complementary protection is the ability to enter into and remain in a safe country for a set period of time. (How the period of time changes – and may, at the limit, become indefinite or permanent – in different circumstances is a topic for later in the chapter.)

Aid given to people in need while they remain inside their country is not, therefore, complementary protection in the sense discussed here. Because providing aid to people in situations of the sort noted above while they remain inside their country has different predictable costs, it has a different normative structure. In some cases, aid in place may be cheaper, at least in the long run, than providing complementary protection. This is arguably so in the case of natural disasters that are serious in the short term but that do not present ongoing threats.[7] Such situations do present significant difficulties in determining which states should bear the cost of providing aid, a problem eliminated, or at least ameliorated in the first instance, when people in need of aid present themselves at the frontier. In other scenarios, providing aid in place may be of such difficulty or cost that it is unclear that requiring it can justified. Intervention into many civil or international wars will often fit this description, especially when we note that intervention is far from certain to improve the situation, as the ongoing conflict in Syria shows.

Aid given to people who either are already in a safe country or arrive at a frontier is different. It is easy to assign first responsibility (even if effective burden-sharing remains a goal for the future), and the amount of risk one

---

[7] When we consider that most people do not typically wish to leave their homes, the desirability of providing aid in place when possible increases.

must undertake to provide the aid is comparatively small. The level of aid that must be provided will clearly depend on the resources of the host country in question (it would not make sense to expect or require Uganda to provide the level of aid that Germany can), and there may be upper limits to the amount of aid that can be required (to rule out the largely theoretical spectre of a society being 'swamped'), but because the sort of aid required by complementary protection is well suited to the situations where it is applied, it makes sense to apply it in those situations.

2 How Does (or Should) Complementary Protection Differ from Refugee Protection?

Having described the basic nature of complementary protection above, we may now ask how it differs (or should differ) from protection for Convention refugees. That there should be any difference is a contested issue. Jane McAdam, the leading expert on complementary protection, has argued that 'a legal status equivalent to that accorded by the Refugee Convention ought to apply to all persons protected by the extended principle of *non-refoulement*' and that 'there is no legal justification for differentiating between the status of Convention refugees and the status of beneficiaries of complementary protection'.[8] I will argue that there is good moral reason to distinguish between refugees, narrowly understood, and those owed complementary protection. This moral difference is in turn able to ground a justification for different legal treatment as well.

Differential treatment for those granted complementary protection and those granted refugee protection would potentially be justified if there were normally or usually predictable differences between the groups. My account of what is special about refugees provides a basis for such a difference. As I have elsewhere noted, in the case of people who are persecuted on the basis of a protected ground, we have good reason to think, first, that the danger that the people face is not likely to be short term; second, that there is usually no way to end the danger to them other than by giving them a new permanent residence; and, finally, that alternatives to providing a new permanent residence are unlikely to be morally acceptable or cost–benefit justified.[9]

---

[8] McAdam, *Complementary Protection*, p. 1.
[9] On Convention refugees, see M. Lister, 'Who Are Refugees?', *Law and Philosophy*, 32 (2013), 645–71. On people fleeing certain long-lasting natural events, not currently covered by the Refugee Convention, see Lister, 'Climate Change Refugees'.

The case is different for those covered by complementary protection, as set out in this chapter. In these cases, we can typically expect that the danger faced by those protected in this way will not be of indefinite duration but of a significantly shorter period. We may also hope that the danger faced can be addressed by means of aid or intervention at acceptable moral and monetary costs by other states, facilitating a return home by those so protected. Because the rights those in need can claim are related in a close way to the nature of the danger they face, there is therefore good reason to provide a different set of rights to those granted complementary protection rather than refugee protection.

Some examples can help make the case clearer. Because I have elsewhere set out the argument that, in the case of those eligible for refugee protection under the Refugee Convention,[10] we cannot reasonably expect the danger faced to be short term (in the relevant sense), and so must provide a 'durable solution' – that is, a new state in which permanent residence and eventually full membership is available – I will not rehash those arguments here. I will argue that, in the case of people who do not fit under the Refugee Convention (or certain extensions that I have argued for), we can usually, or typically, expect that temporary protection will suffice. If this is so, and if what we owe people in need is connected with how we are best able to help them, then there is some justification for treating complementary protection as distinct from refugee protection, at least insofar as this difference of need persists, a point to which I will return.

This is not the only possible justification for treating complementary protection as distinct from refugee protection. Matthew Price, for example, has argued that asylum – refugee protection as applied to Convention refugees – is and should be normatively different from other sorts of aid to people in need in that it essentially involves a political rebuke to governments who engage in persecution.[11] Furthermore, cases of government action that justify asylum, on Price's account, signify a breaking of the normative bond between the state and the person persecuted.[12] These two factors are missing in cases where complementary protection is needed. In these cases, we are often dealing with states that are unable to provide the protection needed, either in the short term or for a somewhat longer period. A state is not properly rebuked, Price argues, for being *unable* to

---

[10] See Lister, 'Who Are Refugees?' and 'Climate Change Refugees'.

[11] See M. E. Price, *Rethinking Asylum: History, Purpose, and Limits* (Cambridge: Cambridge University Press, 2009), p. 14. Price's 'political rebuke' account is unorthodox in rejecting the so-called nexus requirement for asylum, but this need not concern us here.

[12] Ibid., p. 167.

protect its citizens. And, in these cases, the bond between the state and the citizen is not fundamentally ruptured in the way it is when the state persecutes its own citizens. When these factors are considered together, Price argues, we see that what is owed to people who qualify for complementary protection is temporary assistance, not the granting of a new nationality.

Jane McAdam, on the other hand, has insisted that 'there is no legal justification for distinguishing between the status of Convention refugees and beneficiaries of complementary protection'.[13] Given this, McAdam argues, we should see the Refugee Convention not as picking out a special group of people in need of aid in a special way (as both Price and I have argued from different grounds), but as a *lex specialis*, which sets standards as a sort of example that ought to apply equally to all people in need of aid, regardless of the source of their need.[14] If McAdam's claim is merely that there is no legal requirement found in international law that would compel treating Convention refugees and those who receive complementary protection differently, then she is arguably correct.[15] But, insofar as her claim is that there is no good reason for different treatment, I will attempt to show it is mistaken. Furthermore, the moral differences, when joined with certain pragmatic considerations, provide good reason for not establishing a legal regime providing the same protections to those found to be Convention refugees and those in need of complementary protection, at least not in the first instance. (Limits to this claim will be discussed later.)

3 Distinguishing Complementary Protection from Refugee Convention: Arguments from Political Morality

Recall that on my account of refugees, those in need of refugee protection are picked out by the particular nature of their need – it is such that we can reasonably expect the need to be long-lasting, or at least of indefinite duration, and there is no good way to meet the need at acceptable cost and risk except by providing a new nationality to the people in need. I have argued that those covered by the Refugee Convention are paradigm

---

[13] McAdam, *Complementary Protection*, p. 11.   [14] Ibid., p. 17.

[15] McAdam recognizes that states do not in fact typically give the same protection to Convention refugees as to others in need of aid, and that this difference is enshrined in many legal schemes providing some sort of complementary protection. McAdam, *Complementary Protection*, p. 41. Given the role that state practice plays in determining international law, this is arguably relevant for the legal issue, placing tension on McAdam's strong claims about the law. However, on its own this is of only modest importance to the moral and political question addressed in this chapter.

examples of such people, although at least some people displaced by environmental harms also clearly fit. On other accounts of refugee protection, such as Price's 'political rebuke' account, or Max Cherem's account[16] focusing more specifically on persecution, people covered by the Refugee Convention are also picked out as especially in need of the sort of 'durable solution' provided for in refugee protection, particularly in countries such as the United States, Canada, and, in certain cases, Australia.[17]

Some examples can help illustrate why the case of those in need of complementary protection can typically be expected to be different from Convention refugee protection. I will offer several scenarios. Consider first people who must flee from one country to another because of a natural disaster which effects one part of their country, leaving other parts safe, but which makes it impossible or highly dangerous, in the short term, for the people fleeing either to remain in their home country or to flee to another part of their country. We might imagine people in a mountainous border region impacted by heavy rains leading to flooding, landslides, and impassable roads to safe regions in their own country, but having safe passage to a neighbouring country. In such a case, principles of complementary protection would call for admitting the people in need; providing them with short-term lodging, food, and other basic supplies; and helping them return either to their home region or to other safe regions in their home country when the immediate danger has passed. In a case like this, it is clear that there is no need to provide the sort of long-term protection and access to new membership called for by Convention refugee protection.

Other types of natural or environmental danger may be more widespread, impacting all or most of a state (the recent earthquakes in Haiti or Honduras after Hurricane Mitch might be good examples). Here the whole territory of the state is rendered unsafe, at least for a period, and people need longer protection, at least until aid can be provided incountry. Because the whole territory is impacted in cases like this, it is

---

[16] M. Cherem, 'Refugee Rights: Against Expanding the Definition of a "Refugee" and Unilateral Protection Elsewhere', *Journal of Political Philosophy*, 24 (2016), 183–205.

[17] The United States provides permanent resident status to refugees or asylees who have been in the United States for one year and who remain refugees (8 USC. § 1159(b)). Most people deemed 'protected persons' in Canada (a category in some ways broader than the Convention refugee definition) may apply for permanent resident status as soon as they are so designated. See www .canada.ca/en/immigration-refugees-citizenship/services/application/application-forms-guides/ guide-5205-applying-permanent-residence-within-canada-protected-persons-convention-refugees .html#5205E2. In Australia, those who meet the refugee definition are eligible for 'permanent' visas at the time of the decision. For discussion, see J. Vrachnas et al., *Migration and Refugee Law: Principles and Practice in Australia*, 3rd ed. (Cambridge: Cambridge University Press, 2012), pp. 182–86.

less plausible to facilitate return to a safe part of the country. However, even in severe cases, such as that with Hurricane Mitch in Honduras, with the implementation of direct aid to the countries, they may become safe enough within a predictable time frame so as to justify making complementary protection presumptively temporary.[18] In many cases like this, if people are required to return, even if aid is provided, they will return to a country facing significant difficulty and probably lower standards of living. However, as what is owed to those seeking complementary protection is not any particular standard of living, but only a reasonably safe place to live, then the presumptive ability of the state in question to return to minimally acceptable standards, at least with outside aid, in foreseeable periods of time, again helps show why complementary protection may be presumptively temporary, as opposed to Convention refugee protection.

Next consider countries faced with war, either international war or civil war. In such cases, people may be cut off from safe parts of the state, if they exist, necessitating flight into a neighbouring state. Or the whole state may be unsafe, making anyone who flees a potential beneficiary of complementary protection. The ongoing struggle in Syria is a clear example, but fighting in the Balkans, in the Caucuses, in Central Africa, and other countries provide all-too-numerous examples. In the case of any war, it is hard to know how long it will last, and so of course it would be foolish to assume that only relatively short-term protection would be needed. However, it is not unusual for wars to last a relatively short time.[19] This again gives some good reason for the presumptive protection provided by complementary protection to be limited in duration, unlike Convention refugee protection.

Finally, consider people who flee from generalized societal breakdown or widespread criminal activity that is beyond the power of the government to control. Somalia, Libya, and several Central American states might here provide us with examples. These cases are perhaps the hardest to fit into my model, as we have limited experience with reviving failed states or bringing such widespread criminality under control. Perhaps these cases might fit with the more extreme cases of environmental or natural

---

[18] In fact, in the case of Honduras and Hurricane Mitch, Temporary Protected Status ('TPS') in the United States persisted for more than twenty years, to the current time, leading to significant controversy over its pending removal by the Trump administration. The situation in Honduras has been complicated by the rise of powerful criminal gangs, making this no longer a pure case. To my mind, the repeated extensions of TPS for Hondurans was likely itself a mistaken policy, but one that, when put in place, gave rise to new obligations, as discussed later.

[19] The wars in the Balkans, for example, lasted from ten days to a bit less than four years.

disasters I have claimed should be seen as fitting into the logic of the Refugee Convention. Even here, however, we might rather take a more conservative approach, hoping to use outside aid to restore the countries to sufficient stability (as doing so is somewhat less likely to be unduly costly than is intervention into a functioning society), and hold that presumptively temporary protection of the sort provided by complementary protection should be the first step.

At this point it is important to note two complications to my account so far, and show how they do not invalidate the general approach. First, we should note that, in each of the sorts of cases I have discussed above, it is possible that at least some of the people involved – perhaps a significant percentage of them – will in fact qualify as Convention refugees. This is because none of these scenarios, as described, is incompatible with people suffering, or having a well-founded fear of suffering, persecution on the basis of a protected ground. To take what is perhaps the easiest example, some people who have to flee from a civil war may have to flee not merely because they are civilians in the way of combatants, but because they are members of a disfavoured ethnic or religious group which would be singled out for maltreatment amounting to persecution by an approaching army. Environmental harms may also give rise to Convention refugees. If a disfavoured ethnic group lives in a remote area of the country, and is intentionally cut off from aid needed in response to the harm caused by natural disasters and prevented from safely relocating within the remaining unaffected areas within the country because of their ethnicity, then they are plausibly Convention refugees. In cases like this, we should provide Convention refugee status to anyone who warrants it, even if they could also be covered by complementary protection. As I will discuss in relation to mass flight/influxes later, we may have good pragmatic reasons for first applying complementary protection to everyone in question and only later screening people to see if they might qualify for Convention refugee protection, but these pragmatic reasons do not negate the obligation to provide Convention protection to those who warrant it. Therefore, the fact that some people who qualify for complementary protection on my account would also qualify for Convention refugee protection is no inherent problem.[20]

---

[20] We might worry that states, eager to avoid the greater duties that come with Convention refugee protection, will simply grant complementary protection to all people seeking aid and not proceed to see if any need or warrant Convention refugee protection. McAdam has noted reason to worry about such practices in relation to the EU Qualification Directive, a form of complementary protection. See McAdam, *Complementary Protection*, p. 51. This is a real worry, but as the most

The second potential complication to my account arises from the fact that, while I have said that those in need of Convention refugee protection 'typically' or 'usually' will need protection for an indefinitely long period of time, warranting granting them access to full membership and eventually citizenship, and that those in need of complementary protection 'typically' or 'most often' need only temporary protection, implying that they do not, at least at first, need access to full membership and citizenship, there will be many exceptions to this claim.[21] This is to say, some people who qualify under current law as Convention refugees would, in fact, be able to safely return to their homes within a tolerably short period of time, and some who qualify for complementary protection will not be able to safely return for significant enough periods of time that it will seem unreasonable to not grant them full membership. Does this tell against having policies of the form I have suggested?

I will address later how what is owed to those granted complementary protection should change over time, as periods of need grow, but the more basic point should be addressed first. Once we see that we are here trying to craft just policies, not engage in conceptual analysis or metaphysics, and see that policies are, by their nature, general, this difficulty loses much of its force. Policies must be crafted, at least in the first instance, for typical or usual cases. The existence of cases that do not fit well into the policy, by itself, does not undermine the basic correctness of the policy.[22] What matters for crafting a policy is that it get the core cases correct without too many anomalies, and that there is a way to deal with anomalous cases. We find this both in the case of Convention refugees (where the 'cessation' clause allows for the ending of protection when the threat to the refugee is in fact short lived) and, at least potentially, in complementary protection, where threats that turn out to be long term can, and should, give rise to more permanent protection. Therefore, the fact that there are exceptions to the general claims about the type of protection needed under Convention refugee protection and complementary protection is not, on its own, a

---

likely alternative is not providing protection at all to those who qualify for complementary protection, I think it is a risk that must be taken.

[21] This is noted in McAdam, *Complementary Protection*, p. 92.

[22] On this point, often missed by philosophers, see M. Dempsey and M. Lister, 'Applied Legal and Political Philosophy', in K. Lippert-Rasmussen, K. Brownlee and D. Coady (eds.), *A Companion to Applied Philosophy* (Oxford: Wiley Blackwell, 2017), pp. 315–19. In particular, the tendency of philosophers to treat what are best seen as anomalies as (philosophical) counter-examples is shown to be mistaken when we are considering policies, all of which are, of necessity, both over- and under-inclusive.

problem for the account presented here, given that each approach gets the core or most typical cases correct.

4   Distinguishing Complementary Protection from Refugee Convention: Pragmatic and Political Arguments

There are also strong arguments for distinguishing complementary protection from Refugee Convention protection that are political or pragmatic in nature. If the great weight of the moral arguments told in favour of providing the same protection for all in need, these arguments would, perhaps, not be persuasive on their own, but, given that there are good moral reasons for the distinction, these more practical arguments can provide further weight. One reason sometimes given for having only one form of protection for those in need of international aid is the idea that this will ensure that a high level of protection is given to all who need it. The worry here seems to be that, if more than one level of protection is possible, states will tend to 'level down', providing only the lower level.[23] While this is a legitimate worry, I think that it gets the nature of the risk wrong. Insofar as we retain Convention refugee protection as a distinct standard, we maintain that there is a higher standard that must morally and be met by parties to the Refugee Convention. If we move to create a new standard, one which encompasses both standard Refugee Convention protection and complementary protection, we are more likely to get the sort of levelling down feared than if we have two distinct standards, as there is no reason to think that the higher standard of Convention refugee protection would be applied to everyone in need of aid, and good reason to doubt this.

Similar arguments tell against the idea that we should attempt to craft a single, unified account of protection, one which covers all cases but perhaps provides protection on a sliding scale of need.[24] Doing so would risk the possibility of lowering the level of protection to Convention refugees at least as much as raising the level owed to others in need of aid. While it is clear that the current Refugee Convention is far from perfect,[25] it does provide the basis for strong protection to many in need of

---

[23] This worry is discussed by both Price and McAdam. See Price, *Rethinking Asylum*, p. 166, and McAdam, *Complementary Protection*, p. 51.

[24] For helpful discussion about the wisdom of attempting to institute a new refugee convention, see L. Ferracioli, 'The Appeal and Danger of a New Refugee Convention', *Social Theory and Practice*, 40 (2014), 123–44.

[25] See, e.g., the extension argued for in Lister, 'Climate Change Refugees'.

aid. Reopening it for negotiation would risk this. On the other hand, addressing complementary protection on its own would rather provide another layer of protection to the total tool-kit, one which would supplement the Refugee Convention, the Convention Against Torture, and other regional and more basic human rights commitments.

5   Functional Aspects of Complementary Protection

In this section I will provide detail on the workings of complementary protection as justified above. I will look at the relationship between complementary protection and mass flight or influx, at how 'individualized' the harm feared must be, and at how complementary protection should be able to serve as both a shield from removal and a key for entry.

Complementary Protection and Mass Flight/Influx

Complementary protection is often associated with protection for people in the case of mass flight from danger or influx into a country. Given the examples listed above of paradigm cases where complementary protection is appropriate, this is no surprise. Natural or environmental disasters, civil war, and international war all often give rise to large-scale movements of people. Furthermore, we may think that large-scale movements of people call for and justify more streamlined procedures of the sort often associated with complementary protection. I contend, however, that the connection between complementary protection and mass flight is only superficial and pragmatic, not deep or fundamental. There are two reasons for this. First, as noted briefly before, it is not unusual for people involved in a mass flight or influx to be properly eligible for Convention refugee protection, at least when they are carefully evaluated. Revising the Refugee Convention to cover certain long-term environmental harms will make this even clearer. This shows that there is no necessary connection between mass flight/influx and complementary protection.

   Mass flight or influx, however, does tend to present difficulties for traditional Convention refugee protection procedures, insofar as those are highly individualized and semi-juridical in nature. These procedures are arguably appropriate when time and resources allow for them, given the weighty nature of the protection that is, or ought to be, associated with Convention refugee protection – membership in a new state. However, when large numbers of people arrive in a short time, such procedures are often highly unwieldy and cannot be properly applied – certainly not at acceptable costs. This suggests that there will often be grounds for providing a less individualized and less generous protection in the short term for those involved in mass flight or influx. This sort of immediate protection, provided to everyone who fits certain general characteristics, for a set period of time, can be seen as an application of complementary protection, even it is not the only form.

How Individualized Should Complementary Protection Decision Be?

This raises our next question – how individualized should complementary protection adjudication be? In the case of Convention refugee protection, decisions to grant protection are typically highly individualized, in that they involve particular applications, close inspection of claims, and a need to show that the applicant meets the relevant requirements of the Refugee Convention. These decisions are often undertaken in a judicial or semi-judicial forum, and can require gathering substantial amounts of evidence. It is at least arguable that the very weighty remedy of granting access to new membership justifies this relatively onerous process. There is reason to doubt, however, that such process is justified in the case of complementary protection.

Persecution on the basis of a protected ground – a core aspect of traditional Convention refugee protection – involves an intentional targeting, at least to a degree, of particular individuals.[26] It is at least not implausible that targets of persecution could and should be able to show that persecution is taking place on the basis of the protected ground, that they have a well-founded fear of the persecution, and that they have the trait in question, at least to the standard of proof properly required for refugee determination. As seen from our examples earlier, this sort of targeting is at least not required, and will often be uncommon, in situations justifying complementary protection. Environmental disasters do not care whom they harm, and even armies in wars often are not directly targeting civilians. Even if armies do target civilians, this is usually because of their location more than specific traits. While some dangers which may give rise to a claim for complementary protection, such as danger from criminals whom the government cannot control, may involve a degree of

---

[26] The targeting may be focused on the trait – the protected ground – rather than the specific individual who has it more personally, but it is still a distinct, important feature of the person who is targeted.

targeting, we can see here that this is not a necessary feature in the same way that it is with Convention refugee protection.

Given the above factors, it is implausible to require the same sorts of individualized evidence and semi-juridical proceedings for complementary protection, even apart from the lesser degree of protection offered at first. It should usually suffice to show that the applicant has general features that make or would make him or her susceptible to the harm feared. For example, if the protection offered is due to a state-wide natural disaster affecting a whole country, what would need to be shown is that the person in question is a citizen of the country in question, and perhaps that he or she did not have the right to be in any other safe state. While these procedures would make dealing with mass flight or influx easier, they are also appropriate for other situations, such as when people already in a safe state are able to apply for leave to not return to a state where they would face appropriate danger. In the somewhat more rare case where complementary protection is applied to people who face some degree of targeting, but the situation does not fit within the Refugee Convention model (such as certain cases of fearing crime), more specific evidentiary showings may be appropriately required, but this follows easily from the fact that there will not be general criteria to appeal to. In the most common cases, however, both the nature of the threats that justify complementary protection and the lesser degree of aid initially offered suggest that less individualized and less juridical procedures are appropriate for determining when protection is due.

Should Complementary Protection Be a Shield (from Removal) or a Key (to Enter)?

One major difference between different currently existing forms of complementary protection is whether they provide a means for people outside a state to enter it to seek protection, or merely provide a shield from removal to people already in a state to a third state where danger would be likely. The EU's Qualification Directive is an example of a form of complementary protection that provides a key to entry.[27] A person who warrants 'subsidiary protection' (the technical term for the type of complementary protection provided under the Qualification Directive) may appear at a border and invoke the law so as to not be turned away. On

---

[27] Council Directive 2004/83/EC of 29 April 2004. For discussion of the Qualification Directive, see McAdam, *Complementary Protection*, pp. 53–110.

the other hand, TPS in the United States functions only as a shield from removal for those already in the United States when the protection is granted,[28] and provides no right to enter the United States for those not already in the country at the time the protection is ordered. TPS in the United States provides protection to a broader range of individuals than does the Qualification Directive, but limits this to those currently present, so as to avoid serving as a draw for those not already in the country. The question for this section is whether restricting complementary protection to serving only as a shield from removal for those already in a country, but not as a key to enter, is justified by the logic of complementary protection.

While the worry in the United States about its TPS program becoming an attractor for unwanted migration has some pragmatic force, limiting complementary protection to only those currently inside a safe country when the danger strikes would go against the normative logic of the idea. As has been noted above, one justification for states to provide protection inside themselves, whether Convention refugee protection or complementary protection, is that this can usually be done without grave risk to the state taking in those in need. Furthermore, insofar as the protection is supplied primarily to those who journey to the state – as opposed to the state going out on its own to provide the aid – the costs of providing the aid may be reduced. The later discussion of the normative foundations for providing complementary protection will further make clear that reducing it to only a shield against deportation, and not allowing it to be a key to enter, is normatively insufficient. Therefore, unlike the current US TPS program, complementary protection should provide a means for those in need of aid to enter a safe country. Of course, considerations of burden sharing may imply that the state of first entry need not be the state where even the sort of temporary protection appropriate for complementary protection must take place. But, except in the most extreme cases of emergency, decisions about which state should host those in need of complementary protection will need to be made after an initial grant of entry.

6 Degrees of Protection, and Changing Protection over Time

Recall that the point of complementary protection is to provide needed protection to people fleeing dangers other than those that would give rise to Convention refugee protection, and who cannot receive protection in

---

[28] 8 USC. §1254a(c)1(A)(i)–(ii).

their home states. Once we recall the wide variety of dangers that might necessitate complementary protection, it becomes clear that not all dangers require the same sort or degree of protection. (This is one more contrast with Convention refugee protection since, as I have elsewhere noted,[29] one of the defining features of Convention refugees is that, whatever the particular danger they face, they can typically be helped effectively only by being provided with a new state in which to have full membership.) Different sorts of protection may be appropriate, then, in responding to different sorts of threats.

When a threat is either plausibly expected to be short lived or where movement to a safe part of the home state is reasonably possible, then basic humanitarian aid will likely be all that is required. This would consist in providing shelter, food, immediate medical treatment, clothing, and similar things, but need not consist in more. Such basic levels of aid would be most plausible for people fleeing natural disasters (or, possibly, some very limited military engagements) which affect only a particular portion of a country or which could be addressed within a matter of weeks or, at most, months. Other threats, however, will predictably last longer. This might be because of a more significant natural disaster or environmental harm, or more widespread and significant fighting in a country. In cases like this, more aid will be needed, such as more secure housing and at least limited forms of social integration, such as access to education for children, more significant forms of health care (including at least ongoing maintenance care), and, if the period of protection extends beyond a few months, at least some degree of access to the labour market, including aid in finding work. When the need for aid stretches beyond a few months, but is still such that return seems plausible in a reasonably short period of time (such as a few years, at most), then full employment rights and normal education for children should be made available, as well as access to at least most forms of health care.[30] Importantly, while these degrees of protection are presented as successive, there is no necessity that they (or other

---

[29] Lister, 'Who Are Refugees?'. Price reaches a similar conclusion on the basis of his 'membership principle' and the associated 'political rebuke' theory of asylum. See Price, *Rethinking Asylum*, pp. 167–69. I explain why my more pragmatic protection-based approach is preferable to Price's in M. Lister, 'The Place of Persecution and Non-state Actors in Refugee Protection', in A. Sager (ed.), *The Ethics and Politics of Immigration: Core Issues and Emerging Trends* (London: Rowman and Littlefield, 2016), pp. 47–51.

[30] It may be reasonable to place restrictions on access to healthcare, so as to keep the cost of helping those in need down. Truly elective procedures may be excluded, and less expensive options taken, such as providing eyeglasses rather than laser eye surgery. Pressing further into these details would require more details of healthcare policy than I am able to provide.

intermediate steps) be followed in order. While basic humanitarian aid will often be the starting place in the case of mass flight or influx, once the nature of a situation is well grasped, it may make sense to simply apply the most plausible degree of protection for that situation, rather than marching through intermediate steps.

Unfortunately, it is not unusual for situations that could have required temporary protection to linger on for indefinitely long periods of time, either because the underlying problem has not or could not effectively be solved[31] or because further developments complicate the original problem, making return unsafe and implausible.[32] Many current systems of complementary protection do not have ways to deal with such situations.[33] For example, TPS, in the United States, explicitly prohibits those holding the status from gaining permanent resident status under most circumstances.[34] There is good reason to reject such schemes and to insist on eventual access to full membership for those granted complementary protection for significantly extended periods. Two considerations are useful to look at here.

First, recall that the most important justification for granting Convention refugees full membership in a safe society was the reasonable expectation that they could not return to their home state within an acceptably short period of time.[35] If that justifies granting new membership to Convention refugees, then it would seem to also justify granting full membership to those given complementary protection in situations where we have compelling reason to believe that they will not go home in an acceptable period of time. Having lived a number of years in the host society provides this knowledge. Second, there are more general reasons to

---

[31] A well-known natural disaster case is that of Montserrat, rendered largely uninhabitable by volcanic activity. When it became clear that the threat was unlikely to be temporary, the second Bush administration, rather than follow the path suggested here, simply revoked the TPS for citizens of Montserrat in the United States. While it is perhaps yet too early to say, we may worry that the civil war in Syria will continue for such a time and degree that an indefinite need for protection is plausible.

[32] As noted above, the situation of people from Honduras with TPS in the United States after hurricane Mitch is perhaps like this, with a mixture of general economic problems and serious violence from dangerous criminal gangs contributing to this population having TPS in the United States for more than twenty years.

[33] We may also ask what sorts of institutional structures are most likely to be able to implement an adequate system of administration and review here. I cannot hope to answer these difficult, largely practical, questions in this chapter, but see no intrinsic reason to think that well-crafted state-based institutions would be less likely to work than would international institutions, especially given the difficulties of agreeing on international rules and institutions with real bite.

[34] 8 USC. §§1254a(f); 8 USC. §1229b(b)(1).   [35] Lister, 'Who Are Refugees?'.

think that anyone who lives in a society for a significant period of time should have access to full membership. This is most clearly the case for migrants who are voluntarily admitted, but the reasoning can be extended beyond these cases.[36] Therefore, if those granted complementary protection remain in the host country for extended periods of time, they ought to be granted access to full membership.[37] While there may be some worry that such a requirement will encourage host states to end protection when it is still needed – we ought not take this lightly – we may also hope that this requirement will encourage states to help make home countries safe, by providing aid, development assistance, or security, thereby allowing those given complementary protection to return home safely in a relatively short period of time. Because the justification for different treatment for those owed complementary protection and Convention refugee protection is a difference in need, in cases where this difference in need can no longer be made out, the grounds for different types of protections lapse. When the normative difference between people owed complementary protection and those who warrant Convention refuge protection has lapsed, it is therefore appropriate to provide the same level of protection – access to full membership – to each. This will be a limiting case for complementary protection, as in many – probably most – cases, shorter term protection will suffice, while indefinite protection is the paradigm case for those owed Convention refugee protection.

7   Why Provide Complementary Protection?

The last two (related) questions are, in some ways, the most fundamental – why should states grant complementary protection to those who need it, and why think they will or would do this? The two questions are related. If there is good reason to think that most states will not do what they ought to, then the obligations of other states may change in light of collective action problems and free-riding. So, if we want to argue that states should provide the protection described here, we need to show that it is at least not largely implausible that they would do it. While these questions are in some ways more fundamental than those above, the way that the normative question interacts with the practical one makes it necessary to first

---

[36] M. Lister, 'Citizenship, in the Immigration Context', *Maryland Law Review*, 70 (2010), 218–29; J. Carens, *Immigrants and the Right to Stay* (Cambridge, MA: MIT Press, 2010).

[37] For helpful discussion of how the passage of time can change moral and legal rights and obligations, see E. Cohen, *The Political Value of Time: Citizenship, Duration, and Democratic Justice* (Cambridge: Cambridge University Press, 2018).

describe in some detail what complementary protection would consist in before showing if it is feasible and required.

The normative requirement to provide complementary protection has two grounds. The first stems from a general duty of states to provide aid to those in need. Several different grounds for such a duty have been proposed, including a 'Natural Duty of Justice', as argued for by Allen Buchanan, which grounds 'a limited moral obligation to help ensure that all persons have access to institutions that protect their basic rights',[38] and a duty of humanitarianism, argued for by Matthew Gibney,[39] among other approaches. These duties may be thought to be owed to other states, as the agents of their citizens, in the first instance, but in cases where a state cannot or will not provide protection, shifting the obligation to individuals in need is the required step. The second ground relates to the necessary conditions for granting states a right to control their own borders. We may hold that if states have a right to control their own borders, this is conditional on such a right not putting others in unacceptable conditions. The duty to accept refugees, I have argued, is one plausible constraint on this right. I have attempted to show, in this chapter, that providing complementary protection is a reasonable further requirement.

Finally, is it reasonable to expect states to be willing to provide this protection, given that it potentially creates a duty to provide aid to many millions of people? I claim that it is reasonable, for two reasons. First, as McAdam notes, many states already accept some degree of obligation to provide complementary protection.[40] Given this, the duty set out here does not create a fully new right, but rather formalizes and clarifies duties already widely accepted. Second, the duty to provide complementary protection set out here could form the basis of a new multilateral agreement, similar in some ways to the Refugee Convention, which would help establish international norms and prevent collective action problems and free-riding. While an agreement cannot do this on its own, it may be an essential step toward this end.

---

[38] See A. Buchanan, *Justice, Legitimacy, and Self-Determination: Moral Foundations for International Law* (Oxford: Oxford University Press, 2004), p. 27. For helpful discussion of how such a natural duty of justice relates to questions of protecting human rights, see J. Mandle, *Global Justice* (Cambridge: Polity Press, 2006), pp. 46–48.

[39] M. J. Gibney, *The Ethics and Politics of Asylum: Liberal Democracy and the Response to Refugees* (Cambridge: Cambridge University Press, 2004), pp. 230–33.

[40] McAdam, *Complementary Protection*, p. 42.

Of course, even if everything I have argued for in this chapter is accepted, many questions about complementary protection, both practical and theoretical, remain. I hope, however, to have shown the basic normative commitments that follow from a duty to provide complementary protection, how and why this type of protection differs from Convention refugee protection, and gone some way toward explaining why states might take on this burden. If this is so, then the case for complementary protection is now more clearly made.

CHAPTER 12

The Ethics of Sanctuary Policies in Liberal Democratic States

Patti Tamara Lenard[1]

States offer refuge in multiple ways, one of which is in the form of 'sanctuary'. As the term is used colloquially, 'sanctuary' refers to a set of policies or actions that offer a range of forms of protection to people whose immigration status is precarious in some way. In particular, sanctuary is a type of refuge offered not to refugees, who are typically legally present in a state, but rather to those who may have fallen afoul of a state's immigration rules. These individuals can include temporary labour migrants, whose short-term work visas have expired, refugee claimants, failed asylum-seekers and others who may be under deportation orders, members of mixed-status families (in particular where undocumented parents have citizen children), as well as stateless individuals. Usually, sanctuary is provided to individuals by sub-state authorities, to protect individuals who – absent sanctuary – would struggle to access a variety of services legally or safely, some of which may be essential to protecting their human rights. Many policies are justified as sanctuary policies, and it is my goal in this chapter to argue that the vast majority of them can be defended in current democratic states.

I begin by identifying and disaggregating the various policies adopted in the name of sanctuary along with their justifications. I then offer an

[1] I owe thanks to Carolyn Frank for the research on which this analysis is based. Ms. Frank compiled documents from more than thirty jurisdictions in Canada, the United States and the United Kingdom, including jurisdictions that adopted and rejected sanctuary status. I also owe thanks to Serena Parekh for inviting me to present a version of this chapter at a small workshop on sanctuary at Northeastern University (and to the thoughtful engagement of all the participants), and especially to Shelley Wilcox for tremendously valuable written comments on the draft I presented there; to the friendly audiences at the Queen's University Philosophy Colloquium, and especially to Sue Donaldson, Christine Sypnowich, and Stephen Larin for written comments; to Wayne Norman for inviting me to present this work at the Kenan Centre for Ethics, at Duke University; to the critical and perceptive audience of the Moral Philosophy Seminar at the Australian National University; and to the editors of this volume for helpful written comments.

account of minimal immigration justice – I take this term to include justice across all migration streams, including refugee admissions – which informs my analysis of sanctuary policies. The central objection that people offer to sanctuary policies is that they interfere with a state's ability to control entry to and exit from a territory, that is, with a state's sovereign right to control its borders. I shall suggest that sanctuary policies are indeed problematic when they impede the ability of a state to control admission to its territories, but my analysis suggests that relatively few of the policies justified in terms of offering sanctuary are directly, or even indirectly, related to the state's ability to do so. To make this case, I distinguish between immigration admission and immigration enforcement, that is, between admitting migrants at the border and enforcing immigration policies on a particular territory. I offer this distinction to point out that sanctuary policies are in general focused on challenging the enforcement of immigration in specific local jurisdictions. More particularly, I show that conflicts about sanctuary policies generally hinge on which jurisdiction rightfully has democratic authority in specific policy domains, especially with respect to collaborating with immigration enforcement (and so these conflicts arise most acutely in federal and quasi-federal states). If, I argue, the legitimacy of divided power – a governmental structure where distinct jurisdictions have authority over specific and delimited policy domains – is taken seriously, there will often be reasons to defer to sub-state jurisdictions in matters relating to immigration enforcement, thus leaving considerable justifiable space for sanctuary policies. And so, I conclude, sanctuary policies are nearly always justified in democratic polities.

1 Sanctuary Policies: Some Disaggregation

Three broad categories of policies are adopted in an effort to provide sanctuary: (1) don't ask, don't tell policies, which permit residents in a particular jurisdiction to access services, such as health care or the police, without providing proof of immigration status; (2) non-cooperation policies, which assert an unwillingness of local service providers, including but not limited to local police forces, to cooperate with national immigration forces in various ways; and (3) physical sanctuary actions, which provide a temporary, safe home for individuals at risk of deportation, most often (at least historically) in churches.

Don't Ask, Don't Tell Policies

'Don't ask, don't tell' policies ask service providers to provide services to residents of a jurisdiction independent of their immigration status.[2] There are two common justifications for these policies.

One justification focuses on the importance of protecting the human or civil rights of all residents of a jurisdiction. The Seattle Ordinance outlines its objective to 'protect the civil liberties and civil rights of all residents', for example, and the failed movement to declare Howard County, Maryland, a sanctuary city was defended by citing the long tradition of the county in 'upholding the human rights' of all residents.[3] This justification notices that many locally provided services are in the business of protecting the human rights of residents. For example, emergency health care at least is treated as a basic human right, and often hospitals and other urgent care providers deliver services locally. Therefore, protecting the basic human right to emergency health care for all residents can be accomplished only by assuring residents that this care will be offered to them without their being required to show proof of immigration status. The justification relies on an assumption about the likely behaviour of individuals who are, or are not, assured that their legal status will, or will not, be questioned. Where residents are assured that they will not be required to provide proof of immigration status, they will choose to access services available to residents of that jurisdiction.

Perhaps the most common domain in which this justification is offered focuses on access to primary education for children. Of course, primary education is generally agreed to be among the basic human rights possessed by children, and in many jurisdictions, primary education is delivered locally. In order to protect this right for children in a given jurisdiction, say defenders of 'don't ask, don't tell' policies, it is essential that education providers not require proof of legal immigration status. The provision of primary education to children, however, has extra importance because in many jurisdictions there are large numbers of mixed-status families, that is, families where parents do not possess legal status, but where their children do, for example, because they were born on the territory and are therefore

[2] Joseph Carens offers a general case for this kind of policy, in terms of building a 'firewall' between essential service providers and federal immigration authorities. See J. Carens, 'The Rights of Irregular Migrants', *Ethics and International Affairs*, 22 (2008), 163–88.

[3] S. Tavernise, 'Sanctuary Bills in Maryland Faced a Surprise Foe: Legal Immigrants', *New York Times*, 8 May 2017, available at www.nytimes.com/2017/05/08/us/legal-immigrants-who-oppose-illegal-immigration.html.

citizens. In these cases, the decision to not require proof of immigration status as a condition of enrolling children in school protects the right of citizen children to access this education, that is, to permit them to access education without instilling fear in their parents of deportation or family break-up.[4]

A second justification for 'don't ask, don't tell' policies is grounded in communities' commitment to equality of all residents with respect to their ability to access public services in general. This justification typically highlights that communities are diverse along racial and ethnic lines, and often also along immigration status lines, and simply states that catering to the needs of the *community* requires treating all residents equally in terms of access to service provisions, whatever the services. To cite just one example, Vancouver's 'Access to City Services' policy emphasizes the importance of permitting all residents to access all available municipal services, not simply those that are required from a commitment to human rights protection, so that their equality *as residents* can be secured.[5] A variation of this justification emphasizes the importance of inclusivity, rather than simply equality of access. Chicago's 'Welcoming City Ordinance' begins by noting that 'Chicago is a city of immigrants and strives to make an immigrant friendly and safe environment.' New York City's recent amendments to its initial 'City Policy Concerning Aliens' emphasize that 'immigrants have deep roots in the community and should be protected, welcomed, and supported'. Sanctuary proclamations often state that residents who are undocumented are essential contributors to the city, as well, and so emphasize that these individuals are entitled to services provided to everyone. Correspondingly, they continue, asking residents to provide proof of their immigration status in order to access services amounts to a form of discrimination, which undermines the inclusivity of the jurisdiction in question. In some cases, sanctuary city policies include a commitment to combat discrimination, including specific steps that can be taken to do so.[6]

---

[4] M. Flegenheimer, 'New York City Proposal Would Limit Detention of Migrants', *New York Times*, 2 October 2014, available at www.nytimes.com/2014/10/03/nyregion/city-would-stop-honoring-many-immigrant-detainment-orders.html.

[5] City of Vancouver, *Access to City Services without Fear for Residents with Uncertain or No Immigration Status* (2016), available at council.vancouver.ca/20160406/documents/pspc3.pdf.

[6] See B. Shingler, 'Montreal Becomes "Sanctuary City" after Unanimous Vote', *CBC News Online*, 20 February 2017, available at www.cbc.ca/news/canada/montreal/montreal-sanctuary-city-1.3990835; Ville de Montréal, *Déclaration de Montréal contre la discrimination raciale* (1989), available at http://ocpm.qc.ca/sites/ocpm.qc.ca/files/pdf/PD02/3e.pdf; Ville de Montréal, *Déclaration de Montréal pour la diversité culturelle et l'inclusion* (2004), available at http://ville

Non-cooperation Policies

At least in contemporary US discourse, 'non-cooperation' policies are the best-known of sanctuary policies; these are policies that adopt a jurisdiction-wide refusal by local service providers to cooperate with federal immigration enforcement agencies. This refusal can manifest in a range of ways, for example, when local service providers refuse to convey known information about a client's immigration status to federal authorities, when they issue an ordinance to prevent local police from detaining individuals based on suspicions that they may be present unlawfully in the country, when they refuse to respond to requests by federal immigration authorities to inform them when they come into contact with a person of interest to them or even when they refuse to follow a command issued by such authorities, for example, by refusing to detain someone who is suspected of violating federal immigration law.[7]

There are several justifications offered for policies of non-cooperation. Especially in the United States, one reason is self-interested; this work, of alerting and detaining individuals at the behest of federal immigration authorities, is costly, and local jurisdictions sometimes refuse to do so on the grounds that they are not guaranteed financial compensation for the costs they incur. For example, Boulder, Colorado's 2017 'Sanctuary City Ordinance' notes that no municipal funds will be used to support federal immigration investigations.[8] New York City's 'City and Country of Refuge Ordinance' also explicitly states that city resources should be directed at local law enforcement rather than federal immigration enforcement.

A second justification focuses on other costs of such cooperation to the wider community. In particular, some jurisdictions defend their policies of non-cooperation by arguing that *cooperation* might undermine a community's capacity to protect the security and safety of their residents in general. This fear may generally dissuade residents of precarious status

---

.montreal.qc.ca/pls/portal/docs/page/charte_mtl_fr/media/documents/d%c9claration%20diversit%c9%20et%20inclusion%20(2004).pdf.

[7] Variations of these policies feature in many policies captured as 'sanctuary city' policies, including, just to name some examples, City of Chicago, *Welcoming City Ordinance* (2012), available at www.cityofchicago.org/content/dam/city/depts/mayor/Office%20of%20New%20Americans/PDFs/WelcomeCityOrdinance.pdf; A. Burness, 'Defying Trump, Boulder Declares Itself a Sanctuary City', *Daily Camera*, 3 January 2017.

[8] Burness, 'Defying Trump'. The unanimous adoption of this ordinance was largely symbolic, and effected no policy change, since Boulder had already operationalized a variety of non-cooperation and don't ask, don't tell policies, in support of its undocumented population.

from accessing services, but in the case of 'non-cooperation' policies, jurisdictions are often expressing their particular worry about accessing *police* services. A jurisdiction is safer if its residents trust the police force that operates within it, from the perspectives of victims and wrong-doers, and also from the perspective of the community as a whole. On the contrary, in jurisdictions where residents *fear* police officers *because* they are worried about deportation or the break-up of their families, the ability of the police force to do their work is impeded in significant ways; residents may refuse to cooperate with police, for example, by refusing to report crime. New York City's 'City Policy Concerning Aliens' notes, for example, that the safety of the entire community will be enhanced if all city residents are able to cooperate with local law enforcement without fearing that they will be detained or that federal immigration authorities will be alerted to their presence.[9] San Francisco's 'City and Country of Refuge Ordinance' notes explicitly that efforts must be made to 'encourage trust and cooperation between residents and city officials, especially police'.[10] Similarly, the Executive Order that established Philadelphia as a sanctuary city noted the importance of protecting trust relations between immigrants and local law enforcement.[11]

Physical Sanctuary

A final set of actions captured by the term 'sanctuary' are those that provide actual physical sanctuary for specific individuals, usually those who face imminent deportation. Historically, in Canada and the United States, and across many European countries,[12] this form of sanctuary is provided in or by churches, whose members believe that their religious commitment demands that they offer sanctuary to those who are most in need. In many countries, church property is treated as morally off-limits by state authorities, and so seeking haven in a church can provide some protection from deportation, at least to the extent that authorities respect the jurisdiction of church authorities over their houses of worship.

---

[9] City of New York, *City Policy Concerning Aliens* (1989), available at www.nycourts.gov/library/queens/PDF_files/Orders/ord124.pdf. The clause referred to here was added in 2014.

[10] City of San Francisco, *City and Country of Refuge Ordinance* (1989), available at https://sfgov.org/oceia/sites/default/files/Documents/SF%20Admin%20Code%2012H-12I.pdf.

[11] City of Philadelphia, *City of Philadelphia Action Guide: Immigration Policies* (2018), available at www.phila.gov/2018-01-08-immigration-policies/.

[12] For example, the contributions to R. Lippert and S. Rehaag (eds.), *Sanctuary Practices in International Perspectives: Migration, Citizenship and Social Movements* (New York: Routledge, 2012).

An alternative way in which physical sanctuary is provided to individuals threatened with deportation is by non-governmental organizations, sometimes in collaboration with religious organizations, who shuttle (sometimes legally and sometimes unlawfully) individuals across borders – for example, from the United States to Canada – in an effort to secure better chances at attaining asylum.

These physical sanctuary actions have two general defenses. One defence, used to justify the sheltering of individuals, as well as the shuttling of individuals across borders, emphasizes the injustice of particular immigration laws. Correspondingly, says this defence, offering physical sanctuary to individuals who are threatened with deportation as a result of the application of unjust laws is morally *justified*.[13] It is, in effect, a form of civil disobedience, in which individuals acting from a commitment to moral principle act in ways to undermine (and ideally overturn) unjust laws.[14]

A second justification for these actions focuses on the injustice in the *enforcement* of immigration laws in a particular case, rather than the laws themselves. They aim to shield an individual, usually one believed to have been treated unfairly in some way by the regular asylum process. Correspondingly, usually those offering sanctuary aim at ensuring fair access to due process laws to those they are sheltering, for example, by extending time limits given to asylum claimants to get their application for asylum in order, or by ensuring that new and pertinent information can be presented to adjudication boards rather than ignored. The justification is made in terms of fair access to due process for all residents, including asylum-seekers or other non-status migrants, rather than in terms of the injustice of the law itself.

In both cases, actors who engage in these actions are often also aiming to gain public support for the individuals whom they are sheltering, or are engaging in advocacy work in defence of the just treatment of migrants, by immigration policies in general. These two justifications often travel together, but it is essential to separate them at the level of moral justification, since as I will show later, we may wish to judge their legitimacy as actions differently.

---

[13] S. Wilcox, 'How Can Sanctuary Policies be Justified?', *Public Affairs Quarterly*, 33(2), pp. 89–113 (2019).

[14] H. Perla Jr. and S. B. Coutin, 'Legacies of the 1980s US–Central American Sanctuary Movement', in Lippert and Rehaag (eds.), *Sanctuary Practices*, p. 80.

2 Sanctuary Policies and Democratic Politics

Having outlined in broad brush the set of policies and actions typically captured by the term 'sanctuary', I turn now to whether they can be justified in democratic states. Here, I suggest there is no single answer to this question; the types of policies adopted in the name of sanctuary are too varied, in their intentions and in their impact, to be treated as an aggregate. As a result, the analysis will take place in several steps, intended to evaluate whether specific categories of policies and actions can be justified. Although there will be exceptions to note as I proceed, the general argument I intend to make is this: where minimal criteria of immigration justice are met, sanctuary policies which undermine the normal operation of immigration authorities are unjustified. Where they are not met, however, a relatively wide range of sanctuary policies can be justified. Much therefore hinges on what the minimal criteria of immigration justice are, whether in general we can say that they are met and whether sanctuary policies impede the normal operation of immigration authorities.

How should we think about sanctuary policies in the broader context of the literature on the political theory of immigration? The main locus of disagreement among political theorists of migration stems from the tension between the right to move, and how expansively we should understand it, and the right of states to control their borders. For those who understand the right to move expansively, states' right to control their borders is correspondingly limited; for those who understand it less expansively, states are permitted wider discretion in controlling their borders.[15] For the purposes of this chapter, I assume that there are at least some conditions under which borders between states, and the control of these borders by states, are legitimate. Correspondingly, there are cases where a potential migrant can justly be refused admission. What these precise conditions are is a source of significant disagreement among scholars, which I do not intend to engage here. However, it seems plausible to make the following claim: even though there is disagreement about when states may legitimately exclude, there are minimal conditions that immigration policies must meet in order to satisfy the standards of immigration justice. A minimally

---

[15] For some of these debates, see S. Fine and L. Ypi (eds.), *Migration in Political Theory: The Ethics of Movement and Membership* (Oxford: Oxford University Press, 2016); J. Carens, *The Ethics of Immigration* (New York: Oxford University Press, 2013); D. Miller, *Strangers in Our Midst: The Political Philosophy of Immigration* (Cambridge, MA: Harvard University Press, 2016).

just admissions policy – to territory and to membership – must reject the use of overtly discriminatory admissions criteria; it must respect international law by admitting asylum-seekers to the state's territory and giving them access to a fair hearing, and by respecting rules of *non-refoulement*; it must prioritize family reunification, understood expansively; and it must permit all long-term residents to attain legal status in some form. Any admissions policy that violates these basic criteria is, straightforwardly, unjust.

Beyond these minimal criteria, questions around about how open or closed to new migrants a state should be should take place in open and deliberative democratic forums. Of course, even where these minimal criteria are met, there will be people who believe that the immigration system remains unjust and not simply unreasonable. At least as a first pass, however, it is reasonable to defend the claim that, where there is a disagreement about the content of a fuller account of immigration justice, disagreements (and authoritative resolutions to them) should be deliberated and resolved in the normal confines of democratic institutions.

There are at least two immediate complications with this analysis, however. The first stems from the fact that, in many cases of sanctuary policies, there are sub-state jurisdictions involved, with real authority over a range of policy questions. The sub-state jurisdictions – sometimes cities, sometimes municipalities, sometimes states or provinces – are independent political entities, with specific responsibilities toward the citizens and residents of the jurisdiction over which they have authority. The scope for sanctuary policies in a democratic state of course varies according to the powers accorded to sub-state jurisdictions: in some, federal or quasi-federal, there is greater scope to shape laws, whereas in unitary states, it will be a matter of how vigorously a national law or policy is applied in practice.

How does this bear on the question of the possible justifiability of sanctuary policies? In order to assess their justifiability, it is important to notice that it is generally taken to be legitimate to have different levels of government, and in particular that many states permissibly assign different responsibilities to different levels of government as a matter of course.[16] As a general rule, the idea behind dividing the powers of government is that each level takes responsibility for certain tasks, and, as a matter of convention (and sometimes law) one level of government does not interfere with

---

[16] This is not to deny that sub-national entities often play a critical role in shaping admission priorities.

others in carrying out the tasks for which it is responsible.[17] In some cases, levels of government will request, and receive, cooperation from other levels; in others, perhaps not.

A challenge arises, as in cases of sanctuary policies, when one level of government claims that another is subverting or undermining the capacity of another to carry out its tasks. This is a challenge to be expected in cases where different levels of government are normally responsible for different tasks. As a result, one impact of accepting a federal division of power as legitimate is that citizens in a federal state are not treated identically in every jurisdiction; so long as this non-identical treatment is within certain boundaries, for example, set by a national constitution, it is regarded both as consistent with the equality demanded by democratic citizenship in that state and as an instantiation of the commitment that federal states make to giving some powers to sub-state jurisdictions to adopt policies, in at least some domains, that are consistent with their own, local, priorities.

As the cases of sanctuary policies outlined above demonstrate, differences across jurisdictions can appear both in terms of service provision (as in the don't ask, don't tell policies) and with respect to law enforcement (as in the non-cooperation policies). For example, it can be reasonable in a federal state that citizens in one jurisdiction have access to low-cost extended hospital stays (for example, after giving birth) as part of their provincial or state health coverage, whereas citizens in another do not. One might respond that this sort of differentiation, in a federal state, is acceptable with respect to service provision, but not law enforcement, where we ought to have a stricter requirement of equal treatment across an entire territory. Yet federalism's charge to respect the local priorities and circumstances of sub-state jurisdictions, and moreover to guarantee local authorities the discretion to act on these within their jurisdictions, means that it is treated as consistent with the equality demanded by citizenship in federal states that even the enforcement of some laws will be undertaken differently in different jurisdictions. The zealousness with which speeding offenses are prosecuted, or with which searches for concealed drugs or weapons are carried out, may well be distinct across sub-state jurisdictions, for example; again, so long as differences in law enforcement fall within reasonable boundaries, usually set by a national constitution, federal states are prepared to accept even differences here, as part of their obligation to

---

[17] For accounts of divided powers in federal states, and the principle of subsidiarity which I am describing here, see the essays in J. E. Fleming and J. Levy (eds.), *Federalism and Subsidiarity* (New York: New York University Press, 2014).

respect the division of power between national and sub-state jurisdictions. These differences are also understood to be consistent with the equality demanded by a commitment to democratic citizenship.

It is important to keep the normalcy, and indeed the legitimacy, of divided powers in mind when considering one of the most powerful critiques of sanctuary policies, namely, that the adoption of sanctuary policies by sub-state jurisdictions prevents national-level authorities from carrying out one of their central tasks, to protect and control borders, which is an essential aspect of protecting the safety and security of citizens and residents of a state.

A second complication in these debates, which emerges especially in states where there are multiple jurisdictions responsible for specific and distinct policy domains, is that there is often a conflation of immigration policies themselves and their enforcement.[18] Immigration policies typically focus on admission, where admission is understood to be both to territory and to membership (both temporary and permanent). Above, when I delineated the minimal criteria of immigration justice, they were plainly criteria for immigration *admission* justice. But these policies (like all policies) must also be enforced, and the enforcement of immigration policy (and any policy) is subject to a slightly different set of moral considerations. Even if one agrees that states have at least some right to control their borders, one may not believe that they can do anything they like to enforce the policies that they adopt to control admission to territory and membership. To take just one concrete example, one may believe both that, as a sovereign state, the United States has a right to control its borders and that a policy of separating parents from (especially very young) children at the border is morally objectionable. In other words, there are always minimal standards of justice that states must observe, in their enforcement policies, regardless of how permissive or exclusive their admission policies are.[19]

This distinction matters, in particular with respect to understanding the worry that sanctuary policies operate to undermine a state's capacity to

---

[18] Political theorists have recently begun to give attention to the distinct challenges raised by immigration enforcement as distinct from admissions policy. See J. J. Mendoza, 'Enforcement Matters: Reframing the Philosophical Debate over Immigration', *Journal of Speculative Philosophy*, 29 (2015), 73–90; A. Sager, 'Immigration Enforcement and Domination: An Indirect Argument for Much More Open Borders', *Political Research Quarterly*, 70 (2017), 42–54; P. T. Lenard, 'The Ethics of Deportation in Liberal Democratic States', *European Journal of Political Theory*, 14 (2015), 464–80.

[19] This is basically the argument that Joseph Carens makes with respect to the treatment of irregular migrants. See Carens, 'The Rights of Irregular Migrants'.

control immigration, for two reasons. One reason is that sanctuary policies generally target enforcement rather than admission policies, so to the extent that the objection is that sanctuary policies undermine immigration control, they do so by targeting enforcement mechanisms rather than admission mechanisms. There are of course many connections between admission and enforcement policies; effective and fair admission policies may well depend on the existence of fair and effective enforcement policies. But the point to note is that sanctuary policies often implicate enforcement, and correspondingly the complaint that they impede immigration control is rendered less plausible to the extent that we recognize that they do not aim at immigration admission policies directly. Additionally, sanctuary policies impact neither the ability of a central government to enforce their admission priorities at the border itself nor the procedures that must be followed to gain membership status. This is not to deny that sub-state jurisdictions can often influence who is admitted to a state; it is simply to observe that, as a matter of course, sub-state jurisdictions do not typically attempt to undermine the state's sovereignty over admission to a territory in the first place.

A second reason is that matters of immigration enforcement have a significant impact on sub-state jurisdictions. Sub-state jurisdictions are often responsible to deliver essential services to constituents – including education, health care, and public safety in the form of policing and fire-fighting services – and so they have a significant stake in who resides in their jurisdiction and how they are treated. As a result, it is reasonable – at least at the level of moral evaluation – to believe that these sub-state jurisdictions can and should have a say in how these services are delivered within their jurisdiction, and to whom. So, where above I noted simply that it is possible that immigration decisions can be made in two separate and distinct democratic forums, we can now see that matters are much more complicated than this. Questions of immigration admission are made in central democratic forums, where citizens of a state (via their elected representatives) deliberate the merits of possible admission policies, but questions of enforcement are more clearly subject to deliberation in multiple democratic forums, and may produce different strategies for it. This is what happens in the case of sanctuary jurisdictions, which adopt policies that appear to limit immigration enforcement policies in some key ways. The provisional justification for doing so is that these sub-state jurisdictions are the right democratic domain in which to make some forms of enforcement decisions, because the mechanisms by which immigration enforcement is pursued have the most impact on their jurisdictions, in particular on their ability to make self-determining decisions about how to deliver essential services and to whom, on their territory. To be clear: sub-state jurisdictions are not themselves charged with enforcement, but make choices about how and when to collaborate (or not) with national-level immigration enforcement units.

So far, so good. Yet sceptics of the claims advanced here will inevitably point to Arizona, to notice the dangers of acknowledging and prioritizing sub-state jurisdictional politics in immigration enforcement matters. In 2010, legislators in Arizona decided that federal immigration enforcement was lax, and moved to make it more stringent, for example, by making it illegal to not carry immigration documents on one's person, and most famously by giving the police extensive powers to detain people believed to be in the country without documentation.[20] The more general point is that, by focusing on sanctuary policies, and by provisionally defending the right of sub-state jurisdictions to make decisions that implicate immigration enforcement, it may seem that the deck is stacked in favour of people who stand to benefit from them. But I do not intend that. Rather, I mean simply to say that the greater impact of immigration enforcement on sub-state jurisdictions suggests a provisional reason to believe that their democratic adoption of sanctuary policies can be justified, where they seem to conflict with priorities and preferences, also expressed democratically, at the level of the central government. So, what do I say to the Arizona laws? In the case of Arizona, there is plenty of evidence that the kinds of policies it adopted encouraged discrimination against Hispanic citizens and residents (lawfully present as well as undocumented), and on those grounds were not morally justified. If policies like those adopted in Arizona are adopted democratically, and if they do not violate the minimal standards of immigration admission justice, and – this is crucial – they do not violate other democratic standards, they can be justified. This latter criterion in particular was not met in Arizona.

Sceptics can reasonably say at this point that although I may be right in principle to disconnect enforcement policies from admission policies, as two separate domains of immigration policy, they are in practice more connected than I am suggesting here. In particular, the central government's admission priorities do require support from sub-state jurisdictions in order to be effective. Although it may be correct to observe that in very general terms, priority should be given to sub-state jurisdictions in matters of immigration enforcement, whereas priority should be given to the

[20] R. C. Archibold, 'Arizona Enacts Stringent Law on Immigration', *New York Times*, 23 April 2010, available at www.nytimes.com/2010/04/24/us/politics/24immig.html.

central government in matters of admission, as a matter of practical politics, nevertheless, the central government has a strong interest in enforcement, as a way to offer support for admission priorities. This argument might be bolstered by the claim that there is significant value in requiring and protecting the consistent enforcement of the law; doing so respects and supports the rule of (immigration) law across a state's territory. Expressed in this way, US President Donald Trump's claim that sanctuary jurisdictions undermine federal immigration priorities may seem to make more sense: the refusal by sanctuary jurisdictions to do their part in supporting immigration enforcement, maximally, undermines the central government's ability to make and protect admission decisions.

Now that the objection to sanctuary policies in general is clear, I shall proceed by evaluating them in terms of their relationship to a central government's immigration admission authority. From the earlier discussion, to summarize, I am deploying the following assumptions through the analysis that follows. (1) Admission decisions in immigration are mostly the jurisdiction of a central government,[21] whereas enforcement is mostly carried out in sub-state jurisdictions, who have agency with respect to how enthusiastically to implement national-level enforcement policy. The use of the word 'mostly' is intended to signal that there is interaction between these, but that priority should be granted to the relevant jurisdiction in matters of conflict (where the conflict generates conflicting incompatible policies, both of which were adopted in appropriately democratic environments). (2) It is a reasonable, but not determinative, objection by central immigration authorities that some forms of refusal to collaborate in enforcing immigration law, by sub-state jurisdictions, undermine the central government's (democratically justified) ability to act in defence of admission priorities.

3   Are Sanctuary Policies Justified?

In Section 1, I outlined the set of sanctuary policies in operation presently, and identified the most common justifications offered in their defence. The purpose there was to show that the justifications for these policies are

---

[21] I say 'mostly' because there are cases where sub-state jurisdictions are invited to have an active role in determining admission, for example, in the case of the Canadian Provincial Nominee Program, which invites provinces to select among potential labour migrants according to their labour market needs. For more on this program, see D. Nakache and S. D'Aoust, 'Provincial and Territorial Nominee Programs: An Avenue for Permanent Residency for Low-Skilled Temporary Foreign Workers?', in P. T. Lenard and C. Straehle (eds.), *Legislating Inequality: Temporary Labour Migration in Canada* (Montreal: McGill-Queen's University Press, 2012), pp. 158–77.

both wide-ranging and, generally, defensible, in and of themselves. The analysis that follows thus assumes that the proposed justifications for the policies are themselves adequate to defend them, if they did not have additional impact that we must evaluate. So, the purpose in this section is to go one step further, to ask whether – although they are prima facie reasonable policies – nevertheless they should be overridden. When might it be defensible to argue that they should be overridden? I shall suggest that, if they actively undermine the capacity of central immigration authorities to carry out their duties, to protect and control borders, then we may have reason to reject them. So, although sanctuary policies may turn out to be permissible in some scenarios, it may well be that they are morally problematic in cases where the minimal criteria for immigration justice are met.[22] In particular, if sanctuary policies are explicitly justified with respect to, and direct their operations at, immigration policies and their enforcement by central authorities, then whether the minimal criteria of justice are met is relevant. If they are not met, we must ask whether sanctuary policies, in cases where they do impede the operation of these (unjust) immigration policies, are a permissible response to this injustice; in this case, we have reason to defend them for their contribution to achieving immigration justice. But, if the criteria of justice are met, then we have reason to judge them harshly, and perhaps reject policies and actions that impede the operation of immigration enforcement.

Sanctuary Policies as Acts of Resistance

Let us suppose that it is both reasonable and permissible to assume, as a starting point, a position of non-interference by one level of government in the affairs of another. If we believe, as I suggested earlier and as is generally the case, that it is legitimate to distribute responsibility among levels of government, then policies which delineate the responsibilities that one level has toward those in its jurisdiction should be treated as normatively non-problematic. There seems no cause to argue that treating these spheres as distinct and autonomous, and asking them to carry out their respective tasks, undermines the capacity of either to do its tasks, at least prima facie. As a result, the vast majority of 'don't ask, don't tell' policies will prove to be normatively justified, simply on the basis that local service providers

---

[22] On the distinction between morally permissible and morally required, see J. Carens, *Culture, Community and Citizenship: A Contextual Exploration of Justice as Evenhandedness* (Oxford: Oxford University Press, 2000).

have a job to do, and their ability to do this job may be hindered by the requirement that they collect the immigration status of those to whom they provide services.

Some non-cooperation policies require engaging more concretely with cross-jurisdictional conflicts. On the one hand, non-cooperation policies do make reference to the separation of powers between levels of government. They do so by arguing for the distinct remit of local police forces and federal immigration authorities. After all, both are charged with protecting the physical safety of citizens, and so it can seem plausible to expect, or at least hope, that they will be able to work together in pursuit of their shared objectives. And yet, some local police forces believe that the jurisdiction for which they are responsible is *better* served if in some cases they refuse to actively cooperate with federal immigration authorities, and this suggests that the remit – to provide safety and security – is not interpreted to mean the same thing to, or to impose the same set of obligations on, those charged with ensuring it.

Recall that the justification for these policies, which is utilitarian in form, proposes that where the providers of emergency services are not able to count on the cooperation of all individuals in a jurisdiction, the overall *costs* to that community rise. In other words, the justification offered is not made in terms of subverting or otherwise undermining immigration policy, but rather in terms of providing a particular *emergency* service which the jurisdiction is charged to provide; if emergency service providers are forced to cooperate with central immigration authorities, their ability to do their job is undermined. To take just one well-observed example, victims of domestic violence will be less likely to call the police if they believe that they (or their tormentor) will face deportation as a result.[23] In these kinds of cases, emergency service providers are positing that their *omitting* to carry out requests (or orders) by central immigration authorities is justified with reference to the moral requirements they have to carry out their own jobs. This justification emphasizes that the services provided are essential to protecting not only the human rights of residents, understood as individuals, but also the community as a whole, and prioritizes these essential services over cooperation with immigration authorities, on the grounds that the provision of these services would be compromised if cooperation were offered.

---

[23] L. Carasik, 'Whom Do Sanctuary Cities Protect?', *Boston Review*, 9 March 2017, available at http://bostonreview.net/law-justice/lauren-carasik-whom-do-sanctuary-cities-protect.

In their most plausible objections to sanctuary jurisdictions, critics do not dispute whether essential services should be provided to all residents. Rather, what they dispute is that these service providers can permissibly *refuse* to transmit immigration status information to the federal authorities, when it is known. Why not ask service providers to confirm immigration status, along with name and address, over the course of delivering services? Why not require that service providers, whose salaries are paid by tax dollars, forward immigration statuses to national immigration authorities? The request may be morally permissible, but so long as we acknowledge that conflict between jurisdictions here as legitimate – one that is permissible and defensible in the context of democratic politics – the requirement that one authority be coerced into cooperation is not. Non-cooperation policies adopted in the name of sanctuary are often permissible, even where minimal justice in immigration is met.

Let me consider in some more detail, though, a specific conflict that is said by critics of sanctuary policies to be produced as a result of the unwillingness of local police forces to actively collaborate with immigration enforcement authorities. The most powerful of objections launched against non-cooperation policies are those that claim that, in refusing to notify immigration authorities of someone's immigration status, or in refusing to detain them, the security of a state is threatened. These sorts of claims are sensationalized by political actors who highlight (rare) cases where non-status residents are detained by local authorities, but who are then released to commit violent crimes when they might have been detained and deported, if only the requested cooperation between levels of government had been carried out.

Leaving aside the general question of whether mere unlawful presence is criminal or administrative,[24] it is clear enough that citizens have a shared interest in detaining and convicting dangerous criminals, where 'dangerous' refers to crimes that harm property or persons. In other words, if it is the case that a commitment to non-cooperation translates into the releasing of individuals who are known to be dangerous, out of the simple conviction that everyone (even criminals) should be shielded from deportation, that is a reason to be wary of non-cooperation policies. The specific worry is that where local authorities are sympathetic to the likely impact of cooperation – the deportation of the individual held in custody or detention –they will release otherwise known dangerous offenders. And yet, as

---

[24] I do not happen to think that unlawful presence is criminal, but I do not believe that the argument I am making in the paragraphs that follow hinges on agreeing with me here.

they are written, non-cooperation policies in general exempt their non-cooperation in cases of (potential) dangerous offenders. For example, although a recent bid to make Ottawa a sanctuary city failed, it was a key piece of its proposed policy that municipal service providers should refuse cooperation with federal immigration authorities, except where doing so is required *by law*.[25] More specifically, in cases where dangerous offenders are apprehended, there are normal criminal procedures in place. As a matter of policy, they asuch procedures are followed in cases of suspected significant criminality, even where risks of deportation loom.

A more specifically stated worry is that as a result of non-cooperation policies, the full identity of individuals sought by law enforcement is somehow ignored (for fear of identifying an individual who would then be subject to deportation), and correspondingly even where dangerous offenders are apprehended by local law enforcement, their status as criminals may not be discovered. But, where law enforcement, whether local or national, apprehends a *wrong-doer*, it is legitimate and indeed expected that it will confirm his or her identity. In other words, given the normal operation of police procedure in most democratic states, the risk that an individual wanted for a dangerous crime is released into the general population, because of a commitment in a sub-state jurisdiction to non-cooperation, is very low.

What then of physical sanctuary actions? Physical sanctuary actions are justified either in terms of combatting an unjust immigration policy, by attempting to circumvent and so undermine it, or by reference to the unjust application of immigration policy and its enforcement, with the objective of securing access to due process for those who are protected by physical sanctuary spaces. These policies require more scrutiny, because they operate in ways that are *intended* to circumvent or undermine immigration policy and its enforcement, and so are importantly different from the policies considered above. Recall that these actions take two general forms, one of which attempts to protect individuals from the reaches of immigration authority, by sheltering them in physical space, often but not always a church or other religious space, and another of which attempts to transport individuals at risk of deportation to the safety of other jurisdictions, that is, across borders. Recall also that these actions can have either of two general objectives, one of which is to circumvent or undermine immigration law, and one of which is to slow it, on the grounds that it is being applied unjustly in a particular case.

---

[25] See Sanctuary City Ottawa, 2018, https://ottawasanctuarycity.ca/.

How should we respond to physical sanctuary actions where we know that the minimal criteria of immigration justice are not met? Again, notice that these policies do one of three things: provide physical sanctuary to those who are subject to unjust laws, move individuals to jurisdictions where their rights are more likely to be protected, and signal the importance of changing unjust laws so that they come closer to meeting criteria of immigration justice. Correspondingly, they are justified in terms of protecting basic human rights in general, or in specific cases, and in terms of the importance of achieving immigration justice. Their *intention* is precisely to circumvent the enforcement of what their proponents believe are unjust laws. So, whereas non-cooperation policies and don't ask, don't tell policies are evaluated largely according to whether, in pursuit of their own morally justified objectives, they simultaneously undermine the protection of a minimally just immigration system, physical sanctuary policies must be evaluated in terms of their objective to undermine the operation of an immigration system (either in general or in a particular case), which is rightly or wrongly believed to be unjust.

How should we respond to physical sanctuary actions if we believe that minimal criteria of immigration justice are met, however? In cases where we genuinely believe that immigration justice is achieved, we have reason to be sceptical of physical sanctuary actions where the objective is to undermine or circumvent immigration laws.[26] Rather, under these conditions, those who wish to object to immigration policies should and can be required to enter the democratic process in order to change the law. In many cases, those who adopt physical sanctuary actions are aiming to do just that, to engage in civil disobedience in the hopes of raising awareness of an unjust law. Having said that, however, it is important to notice that often – even in cases where minimal criteria of immigration justice are met – immigration laws may be misapplied in a particular case. So, it is worthwhile to assess instantiations of physical sanctuary actions for the possibility that the demand is to reassess a case in which injustice has been done in an otherwise just system.

I have tried to distinguish between when these actions/policies are aimed explicitly at undermining the enforcement of immigration policy and when they are aimed at protecting a specific person whom it is believed is unfairly the victim of the policy (where the policy itself is reasonably understood to be just in the abstract). It is worth noting that

---

[26] I leave aside, here, the question of the right *legal* response in these cases, however; my comment here is just meant to signal the correct moral response.

even in cases where the actions taken by those offering sanctuary are judged to be problematic in some form, there will be a great many cases where there are good reasons to protect the specific people to whom sanctuary is being offered. Notwithstanding criticism of how churches and other organizations select cases for sanctuary protection,[27] those who are offered sanctuary are often individuals who have real and strong ties to the community in which they are resident and/or are people for whom deportation would cause particular hardship. That is to say, even in cases where we have reason to criticize physical sanctuary actions as they are practiced, we may have reason to judge in favour of protecting the specific individuals who are at risk of deportation. I do not mean in this context to engage in the larger question of the appropriate treatment of irregular migrants;[28] rather, I simply mean to note that we should evaluate these kinds of sanctuary cases on a case-by-case basis, with due consideration to a range of contextual factors, rather than jumping immediately from the evaluation that a particular sanctuary action is unjust to the conclusion that the person offered sanctuary can justly be deported.

4 Conclusion

The purpose of this chapter has been to examine sanctuary policies and the justifications offered for them. I observed that sanctuary policies encompass a range of policies and actions – don't tell policies, non-cooperation policies, and physical sanctuary actions. I argued that the central justifications for these policies are distinct, and therefore whether sanctuary policies can be justified in the first place depends on which policies are at issue, in particular. Sanctuary policies, I noted in the introduction, are criticized for impeding the state's ability to control immigration, but I argued that the matter is not quite so simple. Rather, it is essential to distinguish between immigration admission, which is a central government power, and immigration enforcement, which sub-state jurisdictions have significant power to influence. In many cases, I suggested, sub-state jurisdictions bear the brunt of immigration enforcement, and therefore it is legitimate and fair that their democratic publics determine whether and how to enforce immigration, including by adopting (or not) both don't ask, don't tell policies and non-cooperation policies. In the case of physical

---

[27] In some cases, the selection of whom to offer sanctuary is itself problematic.

[28] On this question, see instead Carens, 'The Rights of Irregular Migrants'; D. Miller, 'Irregular Migrants: An Alternative Perspective', *Ethics and International Affairs*, 22 (2008), 193–97.

sanctuary actions, however, the actions taken are meant to impede or at least slow – and in some cases entirely circumvent – immigration enforcement, and often immigration admission, and must be evaluated differently. The tension between these actions and immigration enforcement policies is especially strong where the minimal immigration justice criteria are met, and we have reason to be critical of them in those cases. Even here, however, we ought to take seriously the willingness of those who offer physical sanctuary to break the law, as interlocutors who are focused on generating support for more inclusive immigration laws. In summary, then, in democratic states as we know them, sanctuary policies of most types are justified.

Bibliography

Adelman, J., 'Hirschman's Choice: Exiles and Obligations of an Anti-Fascist', *Transatlantica: American Studies Journal*, 1 (2014). Available at https://journals.openedition.org/transatlantica/6864.

Aleinikoff, T., T. Alexander, D. A. Martin, H. Motomura, M. Fullerton and J. P. Stumpf (eds.), *Immigration and Citizenship: Process and Policy*, 7th ed. (St. Paul, MN: West Academic Publishing, 2011).

Amnesty International, 'Turkey: Illegal Mass Returns of Syrian Refugees Expose Fatal Flaws in Eu-Turkey Deal' (2016), available at www.amnesty.org/en/press-releases/2016/04/turkey-illegal-mass-returns-of-syrian-refugees-expose-fatal-flaws-in-eu-turkey-deal/.

Anderson, E., 'What Is the Point of Equality?', *Ethics*, 109 (1999), 287–337.

Applbaum, A., *Ethics for Adversaries: The Morality of Roles in Public and Professional Life* (Cambridge, MA: Harvard University Press, 1999).

Arendt, H., *The Origins of Totalitarianism*, 2nd ed. (New York: Meridian Books, 1958).

Ayers, J. W., C. R. Hofstetter, K. Schnakenberg and B. Kolody, 'Is Immigration a Racial Issue? Anglo Attitudes on Immigration Policies in a Border County', *Social Science Quarterly*, 90 (2009), 593–610.

Baban, F., S. Ilcan and K. Rygiel, 'Syrian Refugees in Turkey: Pathways to Precarity, Differential Inclusion, and Negotiated Citizenship Rights', *Journal of Ethnic and Migration Studies*, 43 (2017), 41–57.

Bakewell, O., 'Encampment and Self-Settlement', in E. Fiddian-Qasmiyeh, G. Loescher, K. Long and N. Sigona (eds.), *The Oxford Handbook of Refugee and Forced Migration Studies* (Oxford: Oxford University Press, 2014), pp. 127–38.

Baldwin-Edwards, M. and D. Lutterbeck, 'Coping with the Libyan Migration Crisis', *Journal of Ethnic and Migration Studies* (2018), 1–17.

Barry, C. and G. Øverland, 'How Much for the Child?', *Ethical Theory and Moral Practice*, 16 (2013), 189–204.

Baubock, R., *Transnational Citizenship: Membership and Rights in International Migration* (Aldershot: Edward Elgar, 1994).

Beitz, C., *The Idea of Human Rights* (Oxford: Oxford University Press, 2009).

Betts, A. and P. Collier, *Refuge: Transforming a Broken Refugee System* (London: Allen Lane, 2017).

Blake, M., 'Distributive Justice, State Coercion, and Autonomy', *Philosophy and Public Affairs*, 30 (2001), 257–96.

'Equality without Documents: Political Justice and the Right to Amnesty', *Canadian Journal of Philosophy*, 40 (2010), 99–122.

Migration, Justice, and Mercy (Cambridge: Cambridge University Press, forthcoming).

Borjas, G. J., 'The Economic Benefits from Immigration', *Journal of Economic Perspectives*, 9 (1995), 3–22.

Heaven's Door: Immigration Policy and the American Economy (Princeton, NJ: Princeton University Press, 1999).

Boubtane, E., J. C. Dumont and C. Rault, 'Immigration and Economic Growth in the OECD Countries 1986–2006', *Oxford Economic Papers*, 68 (2016), 340–60.

Bradley, M., 'Unlocking Protracted Displacement: Central America's "Success Story" Reconsidered', *Refugee Survey Quarterly*, 30 (2011), 84–121.

Refugee Repatriation: Justice, Responsibility and Redress (Cambridge: Cambridge University Press, 2013).

'Rethinking Refugeehood: Statelessness, Repatriation, and Refugee Agency', *Review of International Studies*, 40 (2014), 101–23.

'Durable Solutions and the Right of Return for IDPs: Evolving Interpretations', *International Journal of Refugee Law*, 30 (2018), 218–42.

Bradley, M. and A. Sherwood (2016) 'Addressing and Resolving Internal Displacement: Reflections on a Soft Law "Success Story"', in T. Gammeltoft-Hansen, S. Lagoutte and J. Cerone (eds.), *Tracing the Roles of Soft Law in Human Rights* (Oxford: Oxford University Press, 2016), pp. 155–82.

Bradley, M., J. Milner and B. Peruniak, 'Shaping the Struggles of Their Times: Refugees, Peacebuilding and Resolving Displacement', in M. Bradley, J. Milner and B. Peruniak (eds.), *Refugees' Roles in Resolving Displacement and Building Peace: Beyond Beneficiaries* (Washington, DC: Georgetown University Press, 2019), pp. 1–20.

Brezger, J. and A. Cassee, 'Debate: Immigrants and Newcomers by Birth – Do Statist Arguments Imply a Right to Exclude Both?', *Journal of Political Philosophy*, 24 (2016), 367–78.

Broome, J., 'Fairness', *Proceedings of the Aristotelian Society*, 91 (1990–91), 87–101.

Buchanan, A., *Justice, Legitimacy, and Self-Determination: Moral Foundations for International Law* (Oxford: Oxford University Press, 2004).

Carasik, L., 'Whom Do Sanctuary Cities Protect?', *Boston Review*, 9 March 2017, available at http://bostonreview.net/law-justice/lauren-carasik-whom-do-sanctuary-cities-protect.

Carens, J., 'Aliens and Citizens: The Case for Open Borders', *Review of Politics*, 49 (1987), 251–73.

Culture, Community and Citizenship: A Contextual Exploration of Justice as Evenhandedness (Oxford: Oxford University Press, 2000).

'The Rights of Irregular Migrants', *Ethics and International Affairs*, 22 (2008), 163–88.

Immigrants and the Right to Stay (Cambridge, MA: MIT Press, 2010).

The Ethics of Immigration (New York: Oxford University Press, 2013).

Cartagena Declaration on Refugees (1984), available at www.oas.org/dil/1984_cartagena_declaration_on_refugees.pdf (accessed 19 August 2018).

Cherem, M., 'Refugee Rights: Against Expanding the Definition of a "Refugee" and Unilateral Protection Elsewhere', *Journal of Political Philosophy*, 24 (2016), 183–205.

Chimni, B. S., 'The Meaning of Words and the Role of UNHCR in Voluntary Repatriation', *International Journal of Refugee Law*, 5 (1993), 442–60.

'From Resettlement to Involuntary Repatriation: Towards a Critical History of Durable Solutions to Refugee Problems', *Refugee Survey Quarterly*, 23 (2004), 55–73.

City of Chicago, *Welcoming City Ordinance* (2012), available at www.cityofchicago.org/content/dam/city/depts/mayor/Office%20of%20New%20Americans/PDFs/WelcomeCityOrdinance.pdf.

City of New York, *City Policy Concerning Aliens* (1989), available at www.nycourts.gov/library/queens/PDF_files/Orders/ord124.pdf.

City of Philadelphia, *City of Philadelphia Action Guide: Immigration Policies* (2018), available at www.phila.gov/2018-01-08-immigration-policies/.

City of San Francisco, *City and Country of Refuge Ordinance* (1989), available at https://sfgov.org/oceia/sites/default/files/Documents/SF%20Admin%20Code%2012H-12I.pdf.

City of Vancouver, *Access to City Services without Fear for Residents with Uncertain or No Immigration Status* (2016), available at council.vancouver.ca/20160406/documents/pspc3.pdf.

Cohen, E., *The Political Value of Time: Citizenship, Duration, and Democratic Justice* (Cambridge: Cambridge University Press, 2008).

Cohen, G. A., 'The Structure of Proletarian Unfreedom', *Philosophy and Public Affairs*, 12 (1983), 3–33.

Cole, P., *Philosophies of Exclusion: Liberal Political Theory and Immigration* (Edinburgh: Edinburgh University Press, 2000).

'Taking Moral Equality Seriously: Egalitarianism and Immigration Controls', *Journal of International Political Theory*, 8 (2012), 121–34.

Collins, S., 'When Does "Can" Imply "Ought"?', *International Journal of Philosophical Studies*, 26 (2018), 354–75.

Cornelius, W. A., 'Death at the Border: Efficacy and Unintended Consequences of US Immigration Control Policy', *Population and Development Review*, 27 (2001), 661–85.

Cox, A. B. and A. O. Hosein, 'Immigration and Equality', unpublished manuscript.

Crawley, H., F. Düvell, K. Jones, S. McMahon and N. Sigona, 'Destination Europe? Understanding the Dynamics and Drivers of Mediterranean Migration in 2015', MEDMIG *Final Report* (2016), available at www.medmig.info/research-brief-destination-europe.pdf.

Cusumano, E. and J. Pattison, 'The Non-governmental Provision of Search and Rescue in the Mediterranean and the Abdication of State Responsibility', *Cambridge Review of International Affairs*, 31 (2018), 53–75.

Dempsey, M. and M. Lister, 'Applied Legal and Political Philosophy', in K. Lippert-Rasmussen, K. Brownlee and D. Coady (eds.), *A Companion to Applied Philosophy* (Oxford: Wiley Blackwell, 2017), pp. 313–27.

Dummett, M., *On Immigration and Refugees* (London: Routledge, 2001).

Durieux, J.-F., 'Three Asylum Paradigms', *International Journal on Minority and Group Rights*, 20 (2013), 147–77.

Ekins, R., 'How to Be a Free People', *American Journal of Jurisprudence*, 58 (2013), 163–82.

Ekins, R., P. Hennessey, T. Tugendhat and K. Mahmood, 'Aiding the Enemy', *Policy Exchange* (2018), available at http://policyexchange.org.uk/publica tion/aiding-the-enemy/.

Elster, J., 'Taming Chance: Randomisation in Individual and Social Decisions', *Tanner Lectures on Human Values*, 9 (1988), 107–79.

Ferracioli, L., 'The Appeal and Danger of a New Refugee Convention', *Social Theory and Practice*, 40 (2014), 123–44.

Fine, S. and L. Ypi (eds.), *Migration in Political Theory: The Ethics of Movement and Membership* (Oxford: Oxford University Press, 2016).

Finnis, J., 'Nationality, Alienage and Constitutional Principle', *Law Quarterly Review*, 123 (2007), 417–45.

'Judicial Law-Making and the "Living" Instrumentalisation of the ECHR', in N. W. Barber, R. Ekins, and P. Yowell (eds.), *Lord Sumption and the Limits of Law* (Oxford: Hart Publishing, 2016), pp. 73–120.

Fishkin, J., *The Limits of Obligation* (New Haven, CT: Yale University Press, 1982).

Fleming, J. E. and J. Levy (eds.), *Federalism and Subsidiarity* (New York: New York University Press, 2014).

Ford, R., 'Acceptable and Unacceptable Immigrants: How Opposition to Immigration in Britain Is Affected by Migrants' Region of Origin', *Journal of Ethnic and Migration Studies*, 37 (2011), 1017–37.

Fullinwider, R. K., *Conscripts and Volunteers: Military Requirements, Social Justice, and the All-Volunteer Force* (Totowa, NJ: Rowman and Allanheld, 1983).

Gammeltoft-Hansen, T. and J. Hathaway, '*Non-refoulement* in a World of Cooperative Deterrence', *Law and Economics Working Papers*, Paper 106 (2004), available at http://repository.law.umich.edu/law_econ_current/106.

Gatrell, P., *The Making of the Modern Refugee* (Oxford: Oxford University Press, 2013).

Gerver, M., 'Refugee Repatriation and the Problem of Consent', *British Journal of Political Science*, 48 (2016), 855–75.

Gibney, M. J., *The Ethics and Politics of Asylum: Liberal Democracy and the Response to Refugees* (Cambridge: Cambridge University Press, 2004).

'Refugees and Justice between States', *European Journal of Political Theory*, 14 (2015), 448–63.

'The Ethics of Refugees', *Philosophy Compass* 2018; 13:e12521. https://doi.org/10.1111/phc3.12521.

Gkliati, M., 'The Application of the EU–Turkey Agreement: A Critical Analysis of the Decisions of the Greek Appeals Committee', *European Journal of Legal Studies*, 10 (2017), 81–123.

Golebiowska, K., M. Valenta, and T. Carter, 'International Immigration Trends and Data', in D. Carson et al. (eds.), *Demography at the Edge: Remote Human Populations in Developed Nation* (Surrey: Ashgate, 2011), pp. 53–84.

Goodin, R., *Protecting the Vulnerable* (Chicago, IL: University of Chicago Press, 1985).

Goodwin-Gill, G. and J. McAdam, *The Refugee in International Law*, 3rd ed. (Oxford: Oxford University Press, 2007).

Greenhill, K. M., *Weapons of Mass Migration: Forced Displacement, Coercion, and Foreign Policy* (Ithaca, NY: Cornell University Press, 2010).

Gregory, D., 'From a View to a Kill: Drones and Late Modern War', *Theory, Culture and Society*, 28 (2011), 188–215.

Gross, M., *Bioethics and Armed Conflict: Moral Dilemmas of Medicine and War* (Cambridge, MA: MIT Press, 2016).

Grotius, H., On the Law of War and Peace, trans F. Kelsey (Washington: Carnegie Institution, 1913).

Gzesh, S., 'Central Americans and Asylum Policy in the Reagan Era', *Migration Information Source*, 1 April 2006, available at www.migrationpolicy.org/article/central-americans-and-asylum-policy-reagan-era.

Hannum, H., *The Right to Leave and Return in International Law and Practice* (Dordrecht: Martinus Nijhoff, 1987).

Hans, A. and A. Suhrke, 'Responsibility Sharing', in J. Hathaway (ed.), *Reconceiving International Refugee Law* (The Hague: Martinus Nijhoff, 1997), pp. 83–109.

Hansen, R., 'The Comprehensive Refugee Response Framework: A Commentary', *Journal of Refugee Studies*, 31 (2018), 131–51.

Hathaway, J. C. (ed.), *Reconceiving International Refugee Law* (The Hague: Martinus Nijhoff, 1997).

Hathaway, J. C., *The Rights of Refugees under International Law* (Cambridge: Cambridge University Press, 2005).

'Refugee Solutions, or Solutions to Refugeehood?', *Refuge* (2007), available at https://refuge.journals.yorku.ca/index.php/refuge/article/viewFile/21378/20048 (accessed 16 March 2018).

Hathaway, J. C. and M. Foster, *The Law of Refugee Status* (Cambridge: Cambridge University Press, 2014).

Hathaway, J. C. and R. A. Neve, 'Making International Refugee Law Relevant Again: A Proposal for Collectivized and Solution-Oriented Protection', *Harvard Human Rights Journal*, 10 (1997), 115–211.

Hathaway, O. A., 'Do Human Rights Treaties Make a Difference?', *Yale Law Journal*, 111 (2001), 1935–2042.

Heller, C. and L. Pezzani, 'Death by Rescue', *Forensic Architecture Agency* (2016).

Henckaerts, J. M. and L. Doswald-Beck, *Customary International Humanitarian Law* (Cambridge: Cambridge University Press, 2005).

Hidalgo, J., 'The Case for the International Governance of Immigration', *International Theory*, 8 (2016), 140–70.

Hosein, A. O., 'Immigration: The Argument for Legalization', *Social Theory and Practice*, 40 (2014), 609–30.

'Arguments for Regularization', in A. Sager (ed.), *The Ethics and Politics of Immigration: Core Issues and Emerging Trends* (London: Rowman and Littlefield, 2016), pp. 159–79.

The Ethics of Migration: An Introduction (London: Routledge, 2019).

Hovil, L., 'Local Integration', in E. Fiddian-Qasmiyeh et al. (eds.) *The Oxford Handbook of Refugee and Forced Migration Studies* (Oxford: Oxford University Press, 2014), pp. 488–98.

Hurley, J., E. Mentzakis, M. Giacomini, D. DeJean and M. Grignon, 'Non-market Resource Allocation and the Public's Interpretation of Need: An Empirical Investigation in the Context of Health Care', *Social Choice and Welfare*, 49 (2017), 117–43.

Johnsson, A. B., 'Duties of Refugees', *The International Journal of Refugee Law*, 3 (1991), 579–84.

Jones, W. and A. Teytelboym, 'The International Refugee Match: A System That Respects Refugees' Preferences and the Priorities of States', *Refugee Survey Quarterly*, 36 (2017), 84–109.

'Matching Systems for Refugees', *Journal on Migration and Human Security*, 5 (2017), 667–81.

Kälin, W., *Guiding Principles on Internal Displacement: Annotations*, revised ed. (Washington, DC: American Society of International Law and Brookings Institution–University of Bern Project on Internal Displacement, 2008).

Kinder, R. and C. D. Kam, *Us against Them: Ethnocentric Foundations of American Opinion* (Chicago, IL: University of Chicago Press, 2010).

Kolodny, N., 'Rule over None II: Social Equality and the Justification of Democracy', *Philosophy and Public Affairs*, 42 (2014), 287–336.

Korey, W., 'Jackson-Vanik: A "Policy of Principle"', in M. Friedman and A. D. Chernin (eds.), *A Second Exodus: The American Movement to Free Soviet Jews* (Boston, MA: Brandeis University Press, 1999), pp. 97–114.

Kritzman-Amir, T., 'Not in My Backyard: On the Morality of Responsibility Sharing in Refugee Law', *Brooklyn Journal of International Law*, 34 (2009), 355–93.

Kukathas, C., 'Are Refugees Special?', in S. Fine and L. Ypi (eds.), *Migration in Political Theory: The Ethics of Movement and Membership* (Oxford: Oxford University Press, 2016), pp. 249–68.

Lazin, F., *The Struggle for Soviet Jewry in American Politics* (Lanham, MD: Rowman and Littlefield, 2005).

League of Nations, *Convention Concerning the Status of Refugees Coming from Germany* (1938), available at www.refworld.org/docid/3dd8d12a4.html (accessed 12 August 2018).

Leckie, S. (ed.), *Housing, Land and Property Restitution Rights of Refugees and Displaced Persons: Laws, Cases, and Materials* (Cambridge: Cambridge University Press, 2007).

Lemaitre, J. and K. Sandvik, 'From IDPs to Victims in Colombia: Reflections on Durable Solutions in the Post-Conflict Setting', in M. Bradley, J. Milner and B. Peruniak (eds.), *Refugees' Roles in Resolving Displacement and Building Peace: Beyond Beneficiaries* (Washington, DC: Georgetown University Press, 2019), pp. 187–210.

Lenard, P. T., 'The Ethics of Deportation in Liberal Democratic States', *European Journal of Political Theory*, 14 (2015), 464–80.

Lever, A., 'Why Racial Profiling Is Hard to Justify: A Response to Risse and Zeckhauser', *Philosophy and Public Affairs*, 33 (2005), 94–110.

Lippert, R. and S. Rehaag (eds.), *Sanctuary Practices in International Perspectives: Migration, Citizenship and Social Movements* (New York: Routledge, 2012).

Lister, M., 'Citizenship, in the Immigration Context', *Maryland Law Review*, 70 (2010), 175–233.

'Who Are Refugees?', *Law and Philosophy*, 32 (2013), 645–71.

'Climate Change Refugees', *Critical Review of International Social and Political Philosophy*, 17 (2014), 618–34.

'The Place of Persecution and Non-state Actors in Refugee Protection', in A. Sager (ed.), *The Ethics and Politics of Immigration: Core Issues and Emerging Trends* (London: Rowman and Littlefield, 2016), pp. 45–60.

'The Rights of Families and Children at the Border', in E. Brake and L. Ferguson (eds.), *Philosophical Foundations of Children's and Family Law* (Oxford: Oxford University Press, 2018), pp. 153–70.

Loescher, G., *The UNHCR and World Politics: A Perilous Path* (Oxford: Oxford University Press, 2001).

Maas, W. (ed.), *Multilevel Citizenship* (Philadelphia, PA: University of Pennsylvania Press, 2013).

Maley, W., *What Is a Refugee?* (Melbourne: Scribe Publications, 2016).

Malkki, L., 'National Geographic: The Rooting of Peoples and the Territorialisation of National Identity among Scholars and Refugees', *Cultural Anthropology* 7 (1992), 24–44.

Malone, L. and G. Wood, 'In re Kasinga', *American Journal of International Law*, 91 (1997), 140–47.

Mandle, J., *Global Justice* (Cambridge: Polity Press, 2006).

Margalit, A. and J. Raz, 'National Self-Determination', *The Journal of Philosophy*, 87 (1990), 439–61.

McAdam, J., *Complementary Protection in International Refugee Law* (Cambridge: Cambridge University Press, 2007).

Mendoza, J. J., 'Enforcement Matters: Reframing the Philosophical Debate over Immigration', *Journal of Speculative Philosophy*, 29 (2015), 73–90.

Miller, D., 'Reasonable Partiality towards Compatriots', *Ethical Theory and Moral Practice*, 8 (2005), 63–81.

National Responsibility and Global Justice (Oxford: Oxford University Press, 2007).

'Irregular Migrants: An Alternative Perspective', *Ethics and International Affairs*, 22 (2008), 193–97.

'Why Immigration Controls Are Not Coercive: A Reply to Arash Abizadeh', *Political Theory*, 38 (2010), 111–20.

'Justice in Immigration', *European Journal of Political Theory*, 14 (2015), 391–408.

Strangers in Our Midst: The Political Philosophy of Immigration (Cambridge, MA: Harvard University Press, 2016).

'A Response to Song, Stilz and Oberman', *European Political Science*, 17 (2018), 661–66.

Milner, J., 'Refugees and the Regional Dynamics of Peacebuilding', *Refugee Survey Quarterly*, 28 (2011), 13–30.

Motomura, H., *Americans in Waiting: The Lost Story of Immigration and Citizenship in the United States* (New York: Oxford University Press, 2006).

Nagel, T., 'The Problem of Global Justice', *Philosophy and Public Affairs*, 33 (2005), 113–47.

Nakache, D. and S. D'Aoust, 'Provincial and Territorial Nominee Programs: An Avenue for Permanent Residency for Low-Skilled Temporary Foreign Workers?', in P. T. Lenard and C. Straehle (eds.), *Legislating Inequality: Temporary Labour Migration in Canada* (Montreal: McGill-Queen's University Press, 2012), pp. 158–77.

Nettelfield, L. J. and S. E. Wagner, *Srebrenica in the Aftermath of Genocide* (Cambridge: Cambridge University Press, 2013).

Nozick, R., *Anarchy, State, and Utopia* (New York: Basic Books, 1974).

Nussbaum, M., 'The Costs of Tragedy: Some Moral Limits of Cost–Benefit Analysis', *The Journal of Legal Studies*, 29 (2000), 1005–36.

Oberman, K., 'Can Brain Drain Justify Immigration Restrictions?', *Ethics*, 123 (2013), 427–55.

'Immigration as a Human Right', in S. Fine and L. Ypi (eds.), *Migration in Political Theory: The Ethics of Movement and Membership* (Oxford: Oxford University Press, 2016), pp. 32–56.

'Immigration, Citizenship, and Consent: What Is Wrong with Permanent Alienage?', *Journal of Political Philosophy*, 25 (2017), 91–107.

'Reality for Realists: Why Economic Migrants Should Not Just "Go Home and Wait for Assistance"', *European Political Science*, 17 (2018), 658–61.

Olsaretti, S., 'Freedom, Force and Choice: Against the Rights-Based Definition of Voluntariness', *Journal of Political Philosophy*, 6 (1998), 53–78.

Olsaretti, S., and R. Arneson (eds.), *Preferences and Well-Being* (Cambridge: Cambridge University Press, 2006).

Orchard, P., *A Right to Flee: Refugees, States, and the Construction of International Cooperation* (Cambridge: Cambridge University Press, 2014).

Owen, D., 'Citizenship and the Marginalities of Migrants', *Critical Review of International Social and Political Philosophy*, 16 (2013), 326–43.

'In Loco Civitatis: On the Normative Basis of the Institution of Refugeehood and Responsibilities for Refugees', in S. Fine and L. Ypi (eds.), *Migration in Political Theory: The Ethics of Movement and Membership* (Oxford: Oxford University Press, 2016), pp. 269–90.

'Refugees, Fairness and Taking Up the Slack: On Justice and the International Refugee Regime', *Moral Philosophy and Politics*, 3 (2016), 141–64.

'Refugees and Responsibilities of Justice', *Global Justice*, 11 (2018), 23–44.

Parekh, S., *Refugees and the Ethics of Forced Displacement* (New York: Routledge, 2017).

Pateman, C., *The Problem of Political Obligation: A Critical Analysis of Liberal Theory* (Chichester: Wiley and Sons, 1979).

Perla, H., Jr. and S. B. Coutin, 'Legacies of the 1980s US–Central American Sanctuary Movement', in R. Lippert and S. Rehaag (eds.), *Sanctuary Practices in International Perspectives: Migration, Citizenship and Social Movements* (New York: Routledge, 2012), pp. 73–91.

Peruniak, B., 'Displacement Resolution and Massively Shared Agency', in M. Bradley, J. Milner and B. Peruniak (eds.), *Refugees' Roles in Resolving Displacement and Building Peace: Beyond Beneficiaries* (Washington, DC: Georgetown University Press, 2019), pp. 55–74.

Pitt-Rivers, J., 'The Law of Hospitality', *HAU: Journal of Ethnographic Theory*, 2 (2012), 501–17.

Pollack, C., 'Returning to a Safe Area? The Importance of Burial for Return to Srebrenica', *Journal of Refugee Studies*, 16 (2003), 186–201.

Price, M. E., *Rethinking Asylum: History, Purpose, and Limits* (Cambridge: Cambridge University Press, 2009).

Rawls, J., *A Theory of Justice* (Cambridge, MA: Belknap Press of Harvard University Press, 1971).

Justice as Fairness: A Restatement (Cambridge, MA: Belknap Press of Harvard University Press, 2001).

Raz, J., *The Morality of Freedom* (Oxford: Oxford University Press, 1986).

Rimmer, S. H., 'Refugees, Internally Displaced Persons and the "Responsibility to Protect"', *UNHCR New Issues in Refugee Research*, Research Paper No. 185 (2010), available at www.unhcr.org.

Risse, M. and R. Zeckhauser, 'Racial Profiling', *Philosophy and Public Affairs*, 32 (2004), 131–70.

Rubio-Marin, R., *Immigration as a Democratic Challenge: Citizenship and Inclusion in Germany and the United States* (Cambridge: Cambridge University Press, 2000).

Ruhs, M. and P. Martin, 'Numbers vs. Rights: Trade-Offs and Guest Worker Programs', *International Migration Review*, 42 (2008), 249–65.

Sager, A., 'Immigration Enforcement and Domination: An Indirect Argument for Much More Open Borders', *Political Research Quarterly*, 70 (2017), 42–54.

Sangiovanni, A., 'How Practices Matter', *Journal of Political Philosophy*, 24 (2016), 3–23.

Scheffler, S., *Boundaries and Allegiances: Problems of Justice and Responsibility in Liberal Thought* (New York: Oxford University Press, 2001).

Schmidtz, D., 'Islands in a Sea of Obligation: Limits to the Duty to Rescue', *Law and Philosophy*, 19 (2000), 683–705.

Schneider, G., 'The Cooperation Duties of Asylum Seekers', available at www .ipw.uni-hannover.de/fileadmin/politische_wissenschaft/Dateien/luise_ druke/schneider_541_570.pdf.

Schuck, P., 'Refugee Burden-Sharing: A Modest Proposal', *Yale Journal of International Law*, 22 (1997), 243–97.

Shachar, A., *The Birthright Lottery: Citizenship and Global Inequality* (Cambridge, MA: Harvard University Press, 2009).

Shacknove, A. E., 'Who Is a Refugee?', *Ethics*, 95 (1985), 274–84.

Shklar, J. N., 'Obligation, Loyalty, Exile', *Political Theory*, 21 (1993), 181–97.

Sikkink, K., *The Justice Cascade* (New York: W. W. Norton, 2011).

Silverman, S. J., 'The Difference That Detention Makes: Reconceptualizing the Boundaries of the Normative Debate on Immigration Control', in A. Sager (ed.), *The Ethics and Politics of Immigration: Core Issues and Emerging Trends* (London: Rowman and Littlefield, 2016), pp. 105–24.

Simmons, A. J., *Moral Principles and Political Obligations* (Princeton, NJ: Princeton University Press, 1981).

Singer, P., 'Famine, Affluence, and Morality', *Philosophy and Public Affairs*, 1 (1972), 229–43.

The Life You Can Save (New York: Random House, 2009).

Song, S., 'The Significance of Territorial Presence and the Rights of Immigrants', in S. Fine and L. Ypi (eds.), *Migration in Political Theory: The Ethics of Movement and Membership* (Oxford: Oxford University Press, 2016), pp. 225–48.

Souter, J., 'Durable Solutions as Reparations for the Unjust Harms of Displacement: Who Owes What to Refugees?', *Journal of Refugee Studies*, 27 (2014), 171–90.

'Towards a Theory of Asylum as Reparation for Past Injustice', *Political Studies*, 62 (2014), 326–42.

Spijkerboer, T. P., 'The Human Costs of Border Control', *European Journal of Migration and Law*, 9 (2007), 127–39.

Stilz, A., 'Nations, States and Territory', *Ethics*, 121 (2011), 572–601.

'Occupancy Rights and the Wrong of Removal', *Philosophy and Public Affairs*, 41 (2013), 324–56.

'Is There an Unqualified Right to Leave?', in S. Fine and L. Ypi (eds.), *Migration in Political Theory: The Ethics of Movement and Membership* (Oxford: Oxford University Press, 2016), pp. 57–79.

'Settlement, Expulsion and Return', *Politics, Philosophy and Economics*, 16 (2017), 351–74.

'The Morally Excruciating Dilemma of Refugees', *European Political Science*, 17 (2018), 654–58.

Straehle, C., 'Thinking about Protecting the Vulnerable When Thinking about Immigration: Is There a Responsibility to Protect in Immigration Regimes?', *Journal of International Political Theory*, 8 (2012), 159–71.

'Falling into the Justice Gap? Between Duties of Social and Global Justice', *Critical Review of International Social and Political Philosophy*, 19 (2016), 645–61.

'Justice in Migration', *Canadian Journal of Philosophy*, 48 (2018), 245–65.

'Refuge, Claim and Place', unpublished manuscript.

Suhrke, A., 'Burden-sharing during Refugee Emergencies: The Logic of Collective versus National Action', *Journal of Refugee Studies*, 11 (1998), 396–415.

Toal, G. and C. Dahlman, *Bosnia Remade: Ethnic Cleansing and Its Reversal* (Oxford: Oxford University Press, 2011).

Triadafilopoulos, P., 'Dual Citizenship and Security Norms in Historical Perspective', in T. Faist and P. Kivisto (eds.), *Dual Citizenship in Global Perspective: From Unitary to Multiple Citizenship* (Basingstoke: Palgrave Macmillan, 2007), pp. 27–41.

Unger, P., *Living High and Letting Die: Our Illusion of Innocence* (Oxford: Oxford University Press, 1996).

UNHCR, *Convention and Protocol Relating to the Status of Refugees* (Geneva: UNHCR, 1996).

UNHCR Resettlement Handbook (Geneva: UNHCR, 2011).

Convention Relating to the Status of Stateless Persons (Geneva: UNHCR, 2014).

'"Detained and Dehumanised" Report on Human Rights Abuses against Migrants in Libya' (2016).

Refugee Protection and Mixed Migration: 10-Point Plan in Action (Geneva: UNHCR, 2016).

'Refugees Operational Data Portal: Mediterranean Situation' (2018), available at http://data2.unhcr.org/en/situations/mediterranean.

United Nations, *Implementing the Responsibility to Protect: Report of the Secretary-General* (New York: United Nations, 2009).

Verdirame, G. and B. Harrell-Bond, *Rights in Exile: Janus-Faced Humanitarianism* (New York: Berghahn Books, 2005).

Ville de Montréal, *Déclaration de Montréal contre la discrimination raciale* (1989), available at http://ocpm.qc.ca/sites/ocpm.qc.ca/files/pdf/PD02/3e.pdf.

Déclaration de Montréal pour la diversité culturelle et l'inclusion (2004), available at http://ville.montreal.qc.ca/pls/portal/docs/page/charte_mtl_fr/media/documents/d%c9claration%20diversit%c9%20et%20inclusion%20(2004).pdf.

Vineberg, R., 'Canada's Refugee Strategy: How It Can Be Improved', University of Calgary School of Public Policy Publications, 11 (2018), available at https://d3n8a8pro7vhmx.cloudfront.net/cdfai/pages/3533/attachments/original/1523488412/Canadas_Refugee_Strategy.pdf?1523488412.

Virgil, *Aeneid: A Prose Translation*, trans. D. West (London: Penguin Classics, 1995).

Vrachnas, J., M. Bagaric, P. Dimopoulos and A. Pathinayake, *Migration and Refugee Law: Principles and Practice in Australia*, 3rd ed. (Cambridge: Cambridge University Press, 2012).

Waldron, J., 'Superseding Historic Injustice', *Ethics*, 103 (1992), 4–28.

'Special Ties and Natural Duties', *Philosophy and Public Affairs*, 22 (1993), 3–30.

'Settlement, Return and the Supersession Thesis', *Theoretical Inquiries in Law*, 5 (2004), 237–68.

Walzer, M., *Obligations: Essays on Disobedience, War, and Citizenship* (Cambridge, MA: Harvard University Press, 1971).

'Political Action: The Problem of Dirty Hands', *Philosophy and Public Affairs*, 2 (1973), 160–80.

'The Moral Standing of States: A Response to Four Critics', *Philosophy and Public Affairs*, 9 (1980), 209–29.

Spheres of Justice: A Defense of Pluralism and Justice (New York: Basic Books, 1983).

Wellman, C. H., *A Theory of Secession: The Case for Political Self-Determination* (Cambridge: Cambridge University Press, 2005).

'Immigration and Freedom of Association', *Ethics*, 119 (2008), 109–41.

'Freedom of Movement and the Rights to Enter and Exit', in S. Fine and L. Ypi (eds.), *Migration in Political Theory: The Ethics of Movement and Membership* (Oxford: Oxford University Press, 2016), pp. 80–104.

Wilcox, S., 'In Defense of Sanctuary Cities', presented at Northeastern University (2017).

Wolf, S., *Meaning in Life and Why It Matters* (Princeton, NJ: Princeton University Press, 2010).

Index